Drupal 10 Development Cookbook

Practical recipes to harness the power of Drupal for building
digital experiences and dynamic websites

Matt Glaman

Kevin Quillen

BIRMINGHAM—MUMBAI

Drupal 10 Development Cookbook

Copyright © 2023 Packt Publishing

All rights reserved. No part of this book may be reproduced, stored in a retrieval system, or transmitted in any form or by any means, without the prior written permission of the publisher, except in the case of brief quotations embedded in critical articles or reviews.

Every effort has been made in the preparation of this book to ensure the accuracy of the information presented. However, the information contained in this book is sold without warranty, either express or implied. Neither the author, nor Packt Publishing or its dealers and distributors, will be held liable for any damages caused or alleged to have been caused directly or indirectly by this book.

Packt Publishing has endeavored to provide trademark information about all of the companies and products mentioned in this book by the appropriate use of capitals. However, Packt Publishing cannot guarantee the accuracy of this information.

Associate Group Product Manager: Alok Dhuri
Publishing Product Manager: Akshay Dani
Content Development Editor: Rosal Colaco
Technical Editor: Maran Fernandes
Copy Editor: Safis Editing
Project Coordinator: Manisha Singh
Proofreader: Safis Editing
Indexer: Manju Arasan
Production Designer: Prashant Ghare
Business Development Executive: Puneet Kaur
Developer Relations Marketing Executive: Rayyan Khan and Deepak Kumar

First published: March 2016
Second edition: September 2017
Third edition: January 2023

Production reference: 1200123

Published by Packt Publishing Ltd.
Livery Place
35 Livery Street
Birmingham
B3 2PB, UK.

ISBN 978-1-80323-496-0

www.packtpub.com

Contributors

About the authors

Matt Glaman is an open source developer who has been working with Drupal since 2013. Since then, he has contributed to Drupal core and over 60 community projects. He is also a speaker at multiple Drupal community events, including DrupalCon. Matt is currently a principal software engineer at Acquia and was previously a product lead at Centarro, helping maintain Drupal Commerce.

I would like to thank, and am grateful to, my beautiful and loving wife for putting up with the late nights split between work, spending time contributing to the Drupal community, and writing this book. I would also like to thank my children; thank you for giving up your playtime so that Daddy could write this book.

Thank you, Andy Giles, for helping get me to my first Drupal camp and kicking off my Drupal career. I would also like to thank my mentors, Bojan Živanović, David Snopek, and Ryan Szrama, as well as everyone else in the Drupal community!

Kevin Quillen has been working with Drupal since 2006. He's contributed several community modules, and built websites using Drupal for brands such as Dogfish Head Craft Brewery, the National Bureau of Economics, Harvard University, MTV, Yale University, Verizon, the Museum of Science, and countless others. You can find him engaged and helping community members on Slack, Drupal StackExchange, or sharing his thoughts on his personal blog. Kevin is also an Acquia Triple Certified Drupal Expert, an Acquia Certified Site Studio Site Builder, and an Acquia Certified Cloud Platform Pro. He is currently a principal developer and Drupal practice lead at Velir.

Thank you to years of unyielding support from family, friends, and colleagues who believe I can go the distance and continually push me to succeed. I am also eternally grateful and extremely thankful to the entire Drupal community and everyone I have met along the way as a result. Let's continue the journey!

About the reviewers

Justin Cornell is a Software Engineering Lead with 10 years of Drupal experience. He has developed and led teams through web projects ranging from brochure-style sites for local businesses to complex, high-traffic web applications for global industry leaders..

Tyler Marshall has been a professional full-stack developer since 2013. He started working at a small web development company specializing in Drupal for e-commerce. Since then, he has worked in a variety of fields and gained experience at many different software companies. As of 2019, Tyler now works full time for his own software development company at Dovetail Digital Inc. He is currently focusing on building projects using the MACH architecture and building automation software for his 3D printing company, Gamer Gadgetry. During his time off, you can find him training in Brazilian jiu-jitsu, fishing, spending time with loved ones, or thinking about his next big software project to take on.

Francesco Placella is a software engineer with over 15 years of experience in web design and development. He has been contributing to Drupal core since 2009. Having performed foundational work in terms of entities, language negotiation, and content translation, he has served as a subsystem maintainer and subsequently as a core committer since 2020. He currently works for Tag1 Consulting, which he joined after running his own web agency for 7 years in Venice, Italy.

Table of Contents

2

Content Building Experience   25

3

Displaying Content through Views   43

4

Extending Drupal with Custom Code   71

5

Creating Custom Pages   103

6

Accessing and Working with Entities   127

7

Creating Forms with the Form API   155

8

Plug and Play with Plugins   177

9

Creating Custom Entity Types   211

10

Theming and Frontend Development   257

11

12

13

Writing Automated Tests in Drupal   343

14

Migrating External Data into Drupal   375

Index   407

Other Books You May Enjoy   418

Preface

Drupal is a popular content management system used to build websites for small businesses, e-commerce, enterprise systems, and much more. Created by over 4,500 contributors, Drupal 10 brings many new features to Drupal. Whether you are new to Drupal or an experienced Drupalista, *Drupal 10 Development Cookbook* contains recipes to dive into what Drupal 10 has to offer. We begin by helping you create and maintain your Drupal site. Next, familiarize yourself with configuring content structure and editing content. You can also find out about all new updates for this edition. These include creating custom pages, accessing and manipulating entities, running and creating tests using Drupal, and migrating external data to Drupal. As you progress, you'll learn how to customize Drupal's functionality using out-of-the-box modules, provide extensions, and write custom code to extend Drupal. You will also learn how to design a digital experience platform with robust content management and editorial workflows.

You can adapt Drupal to your needs by writing custom modules to create custom plugins, entity types, and pages. You can also power your Drupal site with modern front-end development build tools. You'll be able to create and manage code bases for Drupal sites. You can take advantage of Drupal by making Drupal your API platform, and serving content to your consumers.

What this book covers

Chapter 1, Up and Running with Drupal, walks through how to create a new Drupal site and the system requirements for running Drupal, and then run the Drupal site locally using modern local development tools based around Docker.

Chapter 2, Content Building Experience, dives into how to set up your content editing experience and add an editorial review workflow.

Chapter 3, Displaying Content through Views, walks through creating a page to list blogs and a companion block to display five of the most recent blogs using the views module, a visual query builder.

Chapter 4, Extending Drupal with Custom Code, explores how to create a custom module that can be installed onto your Drupal site.

Chapter 5, Creating Custom Pages, demonstrates how to create custom pages with controllers and routes. Creating custom pages allows you to extend Drupal beyond just content pages.

Chapter 6, Accessing and Working with Entities, covers **create, read, update, and delete (CRUD)** operations when working with entities in Drupal. We will create a series of routes to create, read, update, and delete nodes that are articles.

Chapter 7, Creating Forms with the Form API, covers the usage of the Form API, which is used to create forms in Drupal without writing any HTML.

Chapter 8, Plug and Play with Plugins, covers implementing a block plugin. We will use the Plugin API to provide a custom field type along with a widget and a formatter for the field. The last recipe will show you how to create and use a custom plugin type.

Chapter 9, Creating Custom Entity Types, explains how to create custom entity types for custom data models.

Chapter 10, Theming and Frontend Development, covers how to create a theme, work with the Twig templating system, and harness Drupal's responsive design features.

Chapter 11, Multilingual and Internationalization, demonstrates the multilingual and internationalization features of Drupal 10,

Chapter 12, Building APIs with Drupal, walks through how to create RESTful APIs in Drupal with JSON:API, showing you how to read and manipulate data through HTTP requests.

Chapter 13, Running and Writing Tests with Drupal, dives into running and writing automated tests with PHPUnit for your custom module code.

Chapter 14, Migrating External Data into Drupal, explains how to migrate from an older version of Drupal to Drupal 10, and walks through using the Migration module to migrate content and data from CSV files and HTTP APIs.

What you need for this book

In order to work with Drupal 10 and to run the code examples found in this book, the following software will be required:

Software	Operating system requirements
A local web server running in Docker (DDEV, Lando, Docksal, or Docker4Drupal) or an alternative such as MAMP	Windows, macOS, or Linux
PhpStorm or VS Code for code editing	Windows, macOS, or Linux
Terminal, iTerm, or a similar command-line tool	Windows, macOS, or Linux
NodeJS, npm, and Laravel Mix	Windows, macOS, or Linux

Note that there are several free open source tools that you can use to run Drupal locally – DDEV, Lando, Docksal, and Docker4Drupal are the top four community solutions. You are advised to use the one you are most comfortable with or already established with. This book's first chapter covers running Drupal with DDEV. Unfortunately, we cannot cover all possible solutions in depth.

It is a good idea to keep the documentation of whichever solution you use handy when using this book, as examples may be generalized, particularly when it comes to running commands.

Who this book is for

This book is for those who have been working with Drupal, such as site builders, backend and frontend developers, and those who are eager to see what awaits them when they start using Drupal 10.

Sections

In this book, you will find several headings that appear frequently (*Getting ready*, *How to do it…*, *How it works…*, *There's more…*, and *See also*).

To give clear instructions on how to complete a recipe, we use these sections as follows.

Getting ready

This section tells you what to expect in the recipe, and describes how to set up any software or preliminary settings required for the recipe.

How to do it...

This section contains the steps required to follow the recipe.

How it works...

This section usually consists of a detailed explanation of what happened in the previous section.

There's more...

This section consists of additional information about the recipe in order to make you more knowledgeable about the recipe.

See also

This section provides helpful links to other useful information for the recipe.

Download the color images

We also provide a PDF file that has color images of the screenshots and diagrams used in this book. You can download it here: `https://packt.link/N7EpQ`.

Download the example code files

You can download the example code files for this book from GitHub at https://github.com/PacktPublishing/Drupal-10-Development-Cookbook. If there's an update to the code, it will be updated in the GitHub repository.

We also have other code bundles from our rich catalog of books and videos available at https://github.com/PacktPublishing/. Check them out!

Conventions used

In this book, you will find a number of text styles that distinguish between different kinds of information. Here are some examples of these styles and an explanation of their meaning.

Code words in text, database table names, folder names, filenames, file extensions, pathnames, dummy URLs, user input, and Twitter handles are shown as follows: "Create a file named Announcement.php in the newly created directory so that we can define the Announcement class for our entity type."

A block of code is set as follows:

```
{% for tag in node.getTags %}
  <div>Tag: {{ tag.label }}</div>
{% endfor %}
```

Any command-line input or output is written as follows:

```
mkdir -p src/Entity
```

New terms and **important words** are shown in bold. Words that you see on the screen, for example, in menus or dialog boxes, appear in the text like this: "You will see the generated permissions on the **Permissions** form."

> **Tips or important notes**
> Appear like this.

Get in touch

Feedback from our readers is always welcome.

General feedback: If you have questions about any aspect of this book, email us at customercare@ packtpub.com and mention the book title in the subject of your message.

Errata: Although we have taken every care to ensure the accuracy of our content, mistakes do happen. If you have found a mistake in this book, we would be grateful if you would report this to us. Please visit www.packtpub.com/support/errata and fill in the form.

Piracy: If you come across any illegal copies of our works in any form on the internet, we would be grateful if you would provide us with the location address or website name. Please contact us at copyright@packt.com with a link to the material.

If you are interested in becoming an author: If there is a topic that you have expertise in and you are interested in either writing or contributing to a book, please visit authors.packtpub.com.

Share Your Thoughts

Once you've read *Drupal 10 Development Cookbook*, we'd love to hear your thoughts! Scan the QR code below to go straight to the Amazon review page for this book and share your feedback.

https://packt.link/r/1-803-23496-2

Your review is important to us and the tech community and will help us make sure we're delivering excellent quality content.

Download a free PDF copy of this book

Thanks for purchasing this book!

Do you like to read on the go but are unable to carry your print books everywhere? Is your eBook purchase not compatible with the device of your choice?

Don't worry, now with every Packt book you get a DRM-free PDF version of that book at no cost.

Read anywhere, any place, on any device. Search, copy, and paste code from your favorite technical books directly into your application.

The perks don't stop there, you can get exclusive access to discounts, newsletters, and great free content in your inbox daily

Follow these simple steps to get the benefits:

1. Scan the QR code or visit the link below

https://packt.link/free-ebook/9781803234960

2. Submit your proof of purchase
3. That's it! We'll send your free PDF and other benefits to your email directly

1

Up and Running with Drupal

In this chapter, we will walk through how to create a new Drupal site and the system requirements for running Drupal. We'll also walk through running the Drupal site locally using modern local development tools based on Docker.

Then, we'll cover adding and managing module and theme extensions with the site running, as well as managing your Drupal code base in Git version control and finally deploying that Drupal site. By the end of this chapter, you will know how to create a Drupal site, run it locally on your machine, and add modules and themes to that Drupal site. You will also understand how to manage the Drupal code base in version control and deploy the Drupal site. This chapter will lay the foundations for working with the rest of the chapters in this book, and experimenting on your own with Drupal.

In this chapter, we are going to cover the following topics:

- Creating a new Drupal code base for a new site
- Running a Drupal site locally
- Using Drush to manage Drupal
- Adding and managing modules and themes with Composer
- Using version control with your Drupal code base
- Successfully deploying your Drupal site

Technical requirements

This chapter will help you start working with Drupal locally on your computer.

You will require the following:

- PHP 8.1 or higher
- Docker and DDEV installed on your machine

- Composer, the PHP package management tool
- Docker, for running local environments
- An editor, such as Visual Studio Code or PhpStorm

> **Important note**
> Go to the Composer documentation to learn how to install Composer globally on your system.
> Linux/Unix/macOS: `https://getcomposer.org/doc/00-intro.md#installation-linux-unix-osx`
> Windows: `https://getcomposer.org/doc/00-intro.md#installation-windows`

Creating a Drupal site

Create a new Drupal site using the **Composer** project template and run the **Quick Start** command to create a preview site. The instructions provided in this section are based on the recommended installation instructions at `https://www.drupal.org/download`.

Getting ready

The **Quick Start** command uses SQLite as the database for Drupal. With most operating system PHP installations, this is readily available and installed. If SQLite is not available, the installation script will error. If this happens, that is okay! In *Running your Drupal site locally*, we will run Drupal using a local development environment with a database.

Drupal also requires several PHP extensions. These are typically available with most PHP distributions. The up-to-date list of required PHP extensions can be found online: `https://www.drupal.org/docs/system-requirements/php-requirements#extensions`.

How to do it...

1. Open a terminal and navigate where you would like to create your new Drupal site.
2. Use the `create-project` command to create a new Drupal site in the `mysite` directory:

```
composer create-project drupal/recommended-project mysite
```

> **Important note**
> If your PHP installation is missing any required extensions for Drupal, this command will fail. The `Composer` command output will explain what extensions are missing.

3.   Move into the newly created `mysite` directory, which contains the Drupal site's code base:

```
cd mysite
```

4.   Run the **Quick Start** command to install a sample Drupal site using the **Umami Maganize** demo:

```
php web/core/scripts/drupal quick-start demo_umami
```

5.   Once the installation script has finished, your browser will open your Drupal site. If your browser does not open, a login link will be printed in the terminal:

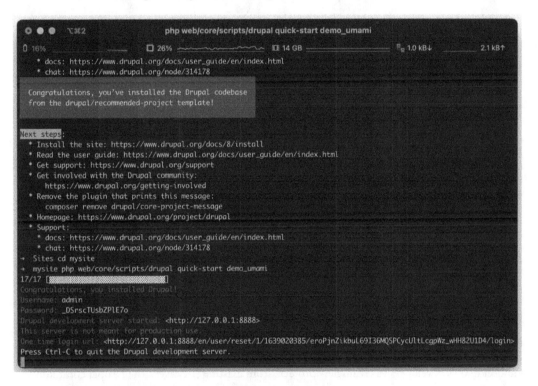

Figure 1.1 – Output from running the Quick Start command

6.   Press *Ctrl + C* to exit the **Quick Start** server at any time.

7.   Next, open `web/sites/default/settings.php` in your editor. We will modify this file to modify the configuration synchronization directory and add local setting overrides.

8.   Set the configuration synchronization directory (where Drupal's site configuration can be exported) to `../config`. The path is relative to the web directory.

The installer from the **Quick Start** command will have generated a default value. At the bottom of your file, find a line similar to the following:

```
$settings['config_sync_directory'] =
   'sites/default/files/config_....';
```

Replace it with the following line:

```
$settings['config_sync_directory'] = '../config';
```

This ensures your exported Drupal configuration is not within the web document root folder.

9. At the bottom of your file, add the following snippet of code to allow the creation of a `settings.local.php` file to override the settings in the `settings.php` file in different environments:

```
/**
 * Include local environment overrides.
 */
if (file_exists($app_root . '/' . $site_path .
   '/settings.local.php')) {
      include $app_root . '/' . $site_path .
         '/settings.local.php';
}
```

This checks whether there is also a `settings.local.php` file alongside your `settings.php` file and includes it if it exists. By using local settings files, you can add sensible defaults to your Drupal settings file but have per-environment configurations and database connection settings.

10. With that, you have set up a Drupal code base and a sample development site that we will use throughout this chapter and the rest of this book.

How it works...

Composer allows developers to create new projects from existing packages. The Drupal community provides the `drupal/recommended-project` package as scaffolding for a Drupal site. When running `create-project`, it copies the `drupal/recommended-project` package and installs our dependencies for us, making our copy of the package to use on our own.

Drupal has a configuration management system that allows exporting and importing configuration. This allows you to make configuration changes locally and push them up into production, without having to make changes on your live site. That is what `config_sync_directory` is for; it will be covered in more detail in the *Managing your Drupal code with version control* and *Successfully deploying your Drupal site* recipes.

The **Quick Start** command was added in **Drupal 8.6** to create a development environment for Drupal for new developers quickly. It installs Drupal programmatically, starts PHP's built-in web server, and uses SQLite for database access.

The **Quick Start** command is also re-entrant. If you rerun the command, it will use the existing SQLite database file. This allows you to run a development environment with one command quickly. We will cover running a full-fledged environment in the *Running your Drupal site locally* recipe.

There's more...

While `drupal/recommended-project` is the primary way to create a new Drupal site, there are other options. Other project templates include a community alternative and various distribution templates, and various agencies that work with Drupal have provided their own (internally and publicly.)

Community Composer project template

Before `drupal/recommended project`, Drupal did not have a standard Composer project template. The community drove this initiative forward and still maintains a more opinionated Drupal project template. The project can be found at `https://github.com/drupal-composer/drupal-project`.

The project adds the following enhancements:

- Support for environment files and environment variables
- Patching support for dependencies
- Drush (while a de facto tool, it is not provided by the recommended project template)

Drupal distribution templates

Drupal has a concept of installation profiles, often referred to as distributions. They are referred to as distributions because they provide an opinionated build of Drupal. There are several distribution projects templates available:

- **Open Social** is a community engagement software built on top of Drupal: `https://github.com/goalgorilla/social_template/`
- **Commerce Kickstart**, a preconfigured eCommerce store built on top of Drupal with Commerce: `https://github.com/centarro/commerce-kickstart-project`
- **Contenta CMS**, an API-first decoupled CMS built on top of Drupal: `https://github.com/contentacms/contenta_jsonapi_project`

See also

- Composer documentation: `https://getcomposer.org/doc/`

Running your Drupal site locally

To work with Drupal, you need to have a local development environment. The local development environment should be able to help you mimic your production environments, such as having access to specific PHP versions, database versions, Redis, and other services.

To achieve this, we will be using **Docker**. We will not be interacting directly with Docker but through a tool called **DDEV**. DDEV is an abstraction on top of Docker that provides sensible defaults for running a Drupal site locally yet the flexibility to extend and add additional services.

DDEV is similar to **Laravel's Sail** but supports various PHP projects that originated from the Drupal community.

Getting ready

You will need to install Docker:

- macOS and Windows require the use of Docker Desktop since containers do not run natively on either operating system: `https://www.docker.com/products/docker-desktop`

- Linux runs Docker natively; it is best to see DDEV's curated installation steps: `https://ddev.readthedocs.io/en/stable/users/docker_installation/#linux-installation-docker-and-docker-compose`

Next, you can install DDEV:

- **macOS and Linux**: Installation is done through the Homebrew package manager: `https://ddev.readthedocs.io/en/stable/#homebrew-macoslinux`

- **Windows**: Windows requires WSL2 and has detailed instructions: `https://ddev.readthedocs.io/en/stable/#installation-or-upgrade-windows-wsl2`

The DDEV installation guide covers how to install Docker and itself for each operating system in depth: `https://ddev.readthedocs.io/en/stable/#installation`.

How to do it...

1. Make sure Docker is running.
2. Open a terminal and navigate to your Drupal code base.
3. Run the `config` command to begin the setup:

```
ddev config
```

4. The first prompt is to choose a project name. Use the default name, inferred from the current directory name, or provide a custom one. Press *Enter* to continue.

5. Select the document root for the Drupal site. DDEV's default value is automatically detected. Press *Enter* to use the default value of web.

6. The next prompt is for the project type. DDEV provides platform detection and defaults to drupal10. Press *Enter* to select it.

7. The DDEV setup is now complete! We can start the local environment by using the **Start** command:

```
ddev start
```

8. Access the Drupal site with the launch command, which will bring us to the interactive site installer:

```
ddev launch
```

9. Finish installing Drupal by pressing **Save and continue** on the first two forms.

10. Once the installation has finished, fill out the site's configuration form and press **Save**.

11. Your Drupal site is now running!

How it works...

DDEV allows you to build a customizable local development environment without having to be a Docker pro but still allows you to leverage Docker specifics. DDEV is a layer above the Docker Compose tool and is used to run multi-container Docker applications. It generates the Compose file and runs docker-compose commands for you. This makes it perfect for sharing with teams, as it takes away any intricacies of Docker.

The configuration for your DDEV site is located in the config.yaml file in the .ddev directory of your Drupal directory. The PHP version, database type, version, and more can be customized in this configuration file.

When running Composer or other commands, you will need to SSH into the web application container. This can be achieved with the ssh command:

```
ddev ssh
```

By SSHing into the web application, you can run commands directly in your local environment.

There's more...

Multiple options can be changed with DDEV and other tools that are similar to DDEV.

Changing the site's PHP version

To modify the PHP version used on your project, edit .ddev/config.yaml and change the php_version property. The **Drupal 10** project type defaults to **PHP 8.1**, which is the minimum required PHP version for Drupal. But you may choose to use newer PHP versions as they are released and supported by Drupal.

Changing the database version or type

DDEV supports MySQL and MariaDB databases, but it does not support Postgres (although it is supported by Drupal). By default, DDEV uses **MariaDB 10.3**:

- To change your MariaDB version, edit .ddev/config.yaml and change the mariadb_ version property to your desired version

- To use MySQL instead of MariaDB, edit .ddev/config.yaml and replace the mariadb_ version property with mysql_version: "8.0"

You cannot change database types or downgrade database versions once there is data in the database. You must first delete the project's database using ddev delete.

Check the online documentation to learn what versions of each database type are supported: https:// ddev.readthedocs.io/en/stable/users/extend/database_types/.

Adding custom services

DDEV allows you to add custom services by writing Docker Compose files in the .ddev directory. DDEV will aggregate all Docker Compose files in the .ddev directory that follow the naming convention of docker-compose.*.yml, where * is a unique word.

For example, to add Redis, we would create a file called docker-compose.redis.yaml in the .ddev directory. It would contain the following Docker Compose manifest, which defines the Redis service and links it to the web application service:

```
version: "3.6"
services:
  redis:
    container_name: ddev-${DDEV_SITENAME}-redis
    image: redis:6
    ports:
      - 6379
    labels:
      com.ddev.site-name: ${DDEV_SITENAME}
      com.ddev.approot: $DDEV_APPROOT
  web:
    links:
      - redis:redis
```

The documentation for additional services can be found at `https://ddev.readthedocs.io/en/stable/users/extend/additional-services/`.

Running Composer with DDEV

DDEV allows you to run Composer inside of the web application container. This is beneficial if you have a different version of PHP on your host machine or have missing extensions required by the project that exists in the web application container.

To run Composer commands, use `ddev composer`. For example, the following would add a new module to a Drupal site:

```
ddev composer require drupal/token
```

You can provide any Composer commands and arguments.

See also

- **Awesome DDEV**: A collection of blogs, tutorials, tips, and tricks for DDEV: `https://github.com/drud/awesome-ddev`
- **DDEV Config**: A collection of contributed recipes and snippets for customizing DDEV sites: `https://github.com/drud/ddev-contrib`
- **Official local development guide**: `https://www.drupal.org/docs/official_docs/en/_local_development_guide.html`

Using the Drush command-line tool

Drush is a command-line tool that interacts with Drupal to perform actions such as installing Drupal or performing various maintenance tasks. In this recipe, we will add Drush to our Drupal site and use it to install the Drupal site.

> Warning
> This example uses commands that will cause data loss if you have an existing installed site.

Getting ready

When using DDEV, you must SSH into the web application container using `ddev ssh` to interact with Drush.

How to do it...

1. Open a terminal and navigate to your Drupal code base.

2. Add **Drush** via **Composer** using the `require` command:

   ```
   composer require drush/drush
   ```

3. Execute the `site:install` command to install Drupal:

   ```
   php vendor/bin/drush site:install --account-pass=admin
   ```

4. Once the installation has finished, use the `user:login` command to generate a one-time login link to access the Drupal site. Your browser should automatically open if you do not click the returned link:

   ```
   php vendor/bin/drush user:login
   ```

5. Install the **Layout Builder** module using the `pm:enable` command. Press *Enter* to confirm this to install **Layout Builder** and its dependencies:

   ```
   php vendor/bin/drush pm:enable layout_builder
   ```

6. Rebuild Drupal's caches using the `cache:rebuild` command:

   ```
   php vendor/bin/drush cache:rebuild
   ```

How it works...

Drush has been part of the Drupal community since **Drupal 4.7** and has become a must-have tool for every Drupal developer. The project can bootstrap Drupal on the command line and perform interactions with a site.

Drush has a plethora of commands, which can be found by running the `list` command:

```
php vendor/bin/drush list
```

Modules can provide their own Drush commands as well. As you add modules to your Drupal sites, new commands may be available. In the *Extending Drupal with custom code* recipe, we will cover creating your own Drush command.

There's more...

There is a plethora of Drush commands and ways that Drush can make working with your Drupal site much easier.

Running Drush with DDEV

DDEV provides a way to run Drush without using the `ssh` command to SSH into the web application container, just like it does for Composer. To run Drush commands with DDEV, use `ddev drush`. For example, the following command would generate a link to log into your Drupal site:

```
ddev drush user:login
```

You can provide any Drush command and arguments.

Checking whether there are pending security updates

It is important to keep your installed modules and themes up to date, especially if there are security releases. Drush provides the `pm:security` command, which checks for any pending security releases for installed modules or themes:

```
php vendor/bin/drush pm:security
```

Exporting or importing a SQL file to your Drupal database

Drush has a variety of SQL commands for interacting with your database directly.

The `sql:dump` command allows you to create a database dump that can be imported into another database. By default, the SQL statements are printed unless the `--result-file` option is passed. The file path is relative to Drupal's document root (the `web` directory):

```
php vendor/bin/drush sql:dump --result-file=../db-dump.sql
```

`sql:cli` allows you to execute SQL statements, including importing a SQL dump file. For example, you can use this command to import a SQL dump from your production Drupal database into your local development environment:

```
php vendor/bin/drush sql:cli < db-dump.sql
```

See also

- Drush home page: `https://www.drush.org/latest/`

Adding and managing module and theme extensions

Drupal is extremely versatile due to its composable design and its large ecosystem of contributed modules and themes. Composer is used for installing and upgrading extensions on your Drupal site using its `require` and `update` commands. In this recipe, we will add the popular **Pathauto** module (`https://www.drupal.org/project/pathauto`) and the **Barrio** theme (`https://www.drupal.org/project/bootstrap_barrio`), a Bootstrap 5 theme.

How to do it...

1. Open a terminal and navigate to your Drupal code base.

2. First, we will add the Pathauto module using the require command:

   ```
   composer require drupal/pathauto
   ```

   Composer will output some data as it begins resolving the Pathauto package. You will notice that the module dependencies for Pathauto were also downloaded: Token and Chaos Tools.

   The modules will be installed into the web/modules/contrib directory.

3. Next, we will add the Barrio theme:

   ```
   composer require drupal/bootstrap_barrio
   ```

   This will download the Barrio theme and place it into the web/themes/contrib directory.

4. Now, we will install the Pathauto module using the Drush pm:enable command:

   ```
   php vendor/bin/drush pm:enable pathauto
   ```

   This Drush command will prompt us to install Pathauto with the required module dependencies (Chaos Tools and Token) as well, with a default option of yes. Hit *Enter* to continue.

   The command will return the following:

   ```
   [success] Successfully enabled: pathauto, ctools,
     token
   ```

5. Next, we will enable the Barrio theme using the Drush theme:enable command and set it as the default theme using the config:set command:

   ```
   php vendor/bin/drush theme:enable bootstrap_barrio
   ```

   This only enables the theme; it does not make it the default theme used by your Drupal site. To make it the default theme, we need to modify the site's configuration with the config:set command:

   ```
   php vendor/bin/drush config:set system.theme default
     bootstrap_barrio
   ```

   This modifies the system.theme config so that it uses Barrio as the default theme setting.

6. Let's assume there was a new release of Pathauto that we needed to update. We can use the update command to update our package:

   ```
   composer update drupal/pathauto
   ```

This will update the `Pathauto` module to the next version. However, it will not update its dependencies – that is, `Chaos Tools` or `Token`. Using the `--with-dependencies` option ensures direct dependencies for `Pathauto` are also updated.

7. Finally, we will cover removing modules that we have added to the Drupal site. First, we must *uninstall* the module from Drupal before we remove it from the code base:

```
php vendor/bin/drush pm:uninstall pathauto ctools
    token
```

Notice how `Chaos Tools` and `Token` are added as arguments? These modules were added to our code base and installed as dependencies for `Pathauto`. We need to uninstall these modules as well before removing `Pathauto`.

8. Next, we can use the `remove` command to remove `Pathauto` from the code base:

```
composer remove drupal/pathauto
```

How it works...

By default, Composer can only add packages available on **Packagist** (`https://packagist.org/`). The Drupal.org website provides a **Composer** endpoint that exposes all Drupal projects as Composer packages under the `drupal/` namespace. The Drupal project template adds the Composer template's `composer.json` so that these packages become available:

```
"repositories": [
    {
        "type": "composer",
        "url": "https://packages.drupal.org/8"
    }
],
```

Drupal follows a pattern of having projects downloaded from `Drupal.org` go into a `contrib` directory and `custom` code go into a custom directory.

Once modules and themes have been added to a Drupal code base, they still need to be installed. Having the code present does not make them immediately activated. This also means that removing modules from your code base must be a two-part process. Drupal will throw errors if you remove a module's code before it is uninstalled.

There's more...

Drupal is a project that was created before Composer and only recently became **Composer** compatible halfway through the Drupal 8 life cycle. There are some additional items to cover.

Composer Library Installer and Drupal extensions

Composer will install packages to the vendor directory by default. The **Composer Library Installer** is a package that frameworks can use to modify the installation paths of specific package types.

The composer/installers package is added as part of Drupal's project template and supports the following package types and their destinations:

- drupal-core: The package type used for Drupal's core code base. It is installed in the web/core directory.
- drupal-module: The package type used for modules. It is installed in the web/modules/contrib directory.
- drupal-theme: The package type used for themes. It is installed in the web/themes /contrib directory.
- drupal-profile: The package type used for profiles. It is installed in the web/modules/profiles directory.
- drupal-library: A special package type used to help download frontend libraries to the web/libraries directory.

These mappings can be found in the composer.json file for your Drupal project.

Updating Drupal core

Updating the core Drupal code base is a bit more involved than updating the drupal/core-recommended package. As stated, Drupal has recently added support for true Composer build support. There is also the drupal/core-composer-scaffold package, which copies over the required files.

Composer allows us to use wildcards to update dependencies. The easiest way to upgrade Drupal core is by using a wildcard and the -with-dependencies option:

```
composer update 'drupal/core-*' -with-dependencies
```

The apostrophes are used to escape the * character. This command will update drupal/core-recommended and drupal/core-composer-scaffold at the same time, as well as all of Drupal core's dependency packages.

See also

- The official documentation for using Composer to download and update files: https://www.drupal.org/docs/user_guide/en/install-composer.html

- The official documentation for downloading and installing a theme from Drupal.org: `https://www.drupal.org/docs/user_guide/en/extend-theme-install.html`

Managing your Drupal code with version control

Now that we have a Drupal code base, it is time to put that code into version control with Git. We will also export our Drupal site's configuration to YAML files that allow us to track the site configuration in version control.

Tracking your code in version control makes it easier to collaborate with other developers, track changes, and integrate with continuous integration and deployment tools. It is highly recommended, even if you are the only developer working on the project.

Getting ready

This recipe requires that you have Git on your machine. If you do not already have Git, see the following resources:

- Git official downloads page: `https://git-scm.com/downloads`
- GitHub's *Install Git* guide: `https://github.com/git-guides/install-git`

How to do it...

1. Open a terminal and navigate to your Drupal code base.
2. Initialize a new Git repository with the `init` command:

   ```
   git init
   ```

   You will see a message about an initialized empty repository, similar to the following:

   ```
   Initialized empty Git repository in /Users/
      mglaman/Sites/mysite/.git/
   ```

3. Before we add files to Git to be tracked in version control, we must create a `.gitignore` file to specify files we do not want to be tracked. Create a `.gitignore` file in your project's root directory.

4. We want to ignore directories that contain code that is managed by Composer, user-managed files (such as uploads), and sensitive directories. Add the following to your `.gitignore` file:

```
# Ignore directories generated by Composer
/drush/contrib/
/vendor/
/web/core/
/web/modules/contrib/
/web/themes/contrib/
/web/profiles/contrib/
/web/libraries/


# Ignore local settings overrides.
/web/sites/*/settings.local.php


# Ignore Drupal's file directory
/web/sites/*/files/
```

This excludes all the directories where Composer may install dependencies, local override settings, and the file uploads directory. We do not exclude web/sites/default/settings.php but ensure we exclude settings.local.php files.

5. Now, we can add our files to be tracked by Git using the add command:

```
git add .
```

We use a period (.) for the add command's argument to add all files within the current directory.

6. Verify that the files were added to be tracked by Git by using the status command:

```
git status
```

You should see multiple lines of files colored green. Green means the files are staged to be tracked:

```
●  ●  ●      ⌥⌘1              mglaman@Matts-MacBook-Pro: ~/Sites/mysite
🔋 72% _____  ⚡ 🖥 15% _____  ⊞ 20 GB _____  🖧 7.2 kB↓ _____ 3.1 kB↑
→  mysite git:(main) ✗ git status
On branch main

No commits yet

Changes to be committed:
  (use "git rm --cached <file>..." to unstage)
        new file:   .ddev/config.yaml
        new file:   .editorconfig
        new file:   .gitattributes
        new file:   .gitignore
        new file:   composer.json
        new file:   composer.lock
        new file:   web/.csslintrc
        new file:   web/.eslintignore
        new file:   web/.eslintrc.json
        new file:   web/.ht.router.php
        new file:   web/.htaccess
        new file:   web/INSTALL.txt
        new file:   web/README.md
        new file:   web/autoload.php
        new file:   web/example.gitignore
        new file:   web/index.php
        new file:   web/modules/README.txt
        new file:   web/profiles/README.txt
        new file:   web/robots.txt
        new file:   web/sites/README.txt
        new file:   web/sites/default/default.services.yml
        new file:   web/sites/default/default.settings.php
        new file:   web/sites/default/settings.php
```

Figure 1.2 – Output from the status command, with green files representing items tracked in Git

7. Now, it is time to commit the changes using the commit command:

    ```
    git commit -m "Initial commit"
    ```

    The commit command records changes to the repository. Commits require a commit message. The -m flag allows you to provide a message.

8. With our code now tracked in Git, we want to export Drupal's configuration and track that as well. We can do this with the config:export command from Drush:

    ```
    php vendor/bin/drush config:export
    ```

    For the first import, all configurations will be exported. Afterward, you will be prompted to export the configuration as it will overwrite the existing files.

9. Add the exported configuration files to Git:

    ```
    git add config
    ```

    You may use git status to verify that the files were staged for commit.

10. Commit the configuration files:

```
git commit -m "Add configuration files"
```

11. Your Drupal site is now managed in Git and can be pushed to a GitHub or GitLab repository!

How it works...

Git is a free and open-source version control system. In this recipe, we created a new Git repository for the files that make up our Drupal site. When files are added to a Git repository, they are tracked to monitor changes to the files. Changes are then committed and create a new revision in the version control history. The Git repository can then be added to GitHub, GitLab, or other services to host the project code.

Version control is beneficial as it makes it easy to work with other developers without creating conflicting code changes. It also makes the code transportable. The Drupal site code does not live just on your machine, but also on the remote repository (GitHub, GitLab, or another service).

Nearly all **Platform-as-a-Service** (**PaaS**) hosting providers that provide continuous integration and deployment for Drupal sites require code to exist in a Git repository.

See also

- Git docs: https://git-scm.com/docs
- Drupal.org documentation for Git: https://www.drupal.org/docs/develop/git

Successfully deploying your Drupal site

So far, we have created a Drupal code base, set up a local development environment, and put our code base into version control. Now, it is time to cover deploying your Drupal site to a server.

Deploying your Drupal site involves more than just copying over the code files as you may need to run schema updates and configuration imports. In this recipe, we will use **rsync**, an efficient file transfer tool, to copy our Drupal site code base to a server and use Drush to create a successful Drupal deployment.

Getting ready

This recipe requires access to a virtual machine over **SSH** that has a **Linux, Apache, MySQL, and PHP** (**LAMP**) stack installed. Many cloud providers, such as **Digital Ocean** and AWS **Lightsail**, have one-click installations for LAMP stack virtual machines:

- A virtual machine with 1 GB of memory and one CPU will suffice, usually the lowest virtual machine tier.

- You must be able to access the virtual machine using SSH key-based authentication or password authentication.

- This recipe uses the `root` user, which is not the best security practice. Server security practices and management are outside the scope of this book.

This recipe uses an IP address of `167.71.255.26` for accessing the server. Replace `167.71.255.26` with the IP address for your server.

At the time of writing, the MySQL PHP library does not support the new `caching_sha2_authentication` authentication implemented by MySQL. You will need a user that has access to the database with the `mysql_native_password` authentication method.

Here is a summary of the SQL commands for creating a `drupaldb` database that is accessible to the `dbuser` user with a password of `dbpass`:

```
CREATE DATABASE drupal
CREATE USER 'dbuser'@'%' IDENTIFIED WITH
  mysql_native_password BY 'dbpass';
GRANT ALL ON drupal.* TO 'dbuser'@'%';
```

How to do it...

1. Open a terminal and navigate to your Drupal code base.

2. Create an ignore file for `rsync` to exclude directories named `.rsyncignore` with the following code:

```
.git/
.ddev/
.vscode/
.idea/
web/sites/*/files/
web/sites/*/settings.local.php
web/sites/*/settings.ddev.php
*.sql
```

This will be used to reduce the number of files transferred to the production server, including developer tool configuration, local development files, and any SQL dumps.

3. Now, we will deploy our Drupal code base to the remote server using `rsync`:

```
rsync -rzcEl . root@167.71.255.26:/var/www/html --
  exclude-from=".rsyncignore" --delete
```

The `rzCE` flags control how files are copied to the remote server. `r` is for recursive copying, `z` compresses files during transfer, `C` uses a checksum to see if files have been modified and should be copied, `E` preserves the executability of files, and `l` preserves links. The `E` and `l` flags are important for Composer's vendor/bin executables.

`.` represents our current working directory as the source, where `root@167.71.255.26:/var/www/html` is our destination. Replace `root@167.71.255.26` with your virtual machine's user and IP address.

The `exclude-from` option uses our `.rsyncignore` file to skip files from being uploaded, while `delete` removes old files from the destination that are no longer valid.

4. We also need to create a database SQL dump for a one-time import using the `sql:dump` command from Drush:

    ```
    php vendor/bin/drush sql:dump --result-file=../db-
       dump.sql
    ```

    We can also copy it over to the server for import later on using, **secure file copy** (**SFC**). We will upload it to the home directory of the user, not the Drupal directory:

    ```
    scp db-dump.sql root@167.71.255.26:db-dump.sql
    ```

5. To finish setting up, SSH into your virtual machine:

    ```
    ssh root@167.71.255.26
    ```

6. After copying the files, we also need to make sure writeable directories are accessible to the web server, such as writing CSS and JS aggregated files and compiled **Twig** templates. This is a one-time operation when setting up the Drupal site after the first file transfer:

    ```
    mkdir -p /var/www/html/web/sites/default/files/
    chown -R www-data:www-data /var/www/html
       /web/sites/default/files/
    ```

    This ensures the `web/sites/default/files` directory is owned by the web server user so that it can write files.

7. Next, we need to update the document root used by Apache, which defaults to `/var/www/html`. The new document root is `/var/www/html/web`. We will use the `sed` command to replace the value for us:

    ```
    sed -i "s,/var/www/html,/var/www/html/web,g"
       /etc/apache2/sites-enabled/000-default.conf
    ```

    The `sed` command stands for stream editor and makes finding and replacing text in files very easy.

8. We need to make Apache aware of our configuration changes. Use the following command:

```
systemctl reload apache2
```

This will reload the Apache service's configuration and make it aware of the new document root.

9. Before we set up our site, we will need to create our settings.local.php file on the server so that Drupal knows how to connect to the database. We will use the nano command-line editor to create and edit the file:

```
nano /var/www/html/web/sites/default
  /settings.local.php
```

10. Add the following code to your settings.local.php file:

```php
<?php

$databases['default']['default'] = [
   'driver' => 'mysql',
   'database' => 'drupal',
   'username' => 'dbuser',
   'password' => 'dbpass',
   'host' => 'localhost',
   'port' => 3306,
];
```

Be sure to change the database credentials so that they match the ones created with your server. Drupal will also try to create the database for you if it does not exist.

11. Save the file by using *CTRL + X*, then *Y*, and finally clicking *Enter*.

Verify the database connection settings using Drush:

```
cd /var/www/html
php vendor/bin/drush status
```

The database credentials should match what you added to settings.local.php.

12. Next, we need to populate our database. We will use the sql:cli command to import our initial database from the local development environment:

```
php vendor/bin/drush sql:cli < ~/db-dump.sql
```

13. Then, we can go through the deployment steps with Drush by using the `deploy` command to run any schema updates and configuration imports:

```
php vendor/bin/drush deploy
```

14. You may now access your Drupal site and view it!

How it works...

This recipe involved various components: a virtual server to host our code and serve our Drupal site, the `rsync` tool for transferring files, and Drush to perform the required deployment steps.

A benefit of using rsync over FTP or even scp, another command-line-based file transfer tool, is that rsync works incrementally. If a file has not been modified, rsync will not transfer that file. It will also ensure that deleted files are also deleted on the remote server, something other file transfer tools do not do.

The `deploy` command from Drush ensures that your Drupal site's database and configuration are up to date. It is a command that operates various processes in a best-practice fashion. The command runs all of Drupal's update hooks to ensure they are executed (schema updates and state changes provided by modules), and that configuration is synchronized from the exported configuration files. The `deploy` command should always be run, just as you would run migrations for a Symfony or Laravel application.

There's more...

Next, we will cover more about hosting and deploying your Drupal sites.

Platform-as-a-service hosting provider

You can avoid this process completely by leveraging one of the PaaS hosting providers for Drupal (listed alphabetically):

- Acquia Cloud: `https://www.acquia.com/products/drupal-cloud/cloud-platform/drupal-hosting`
- Pantheon: `https://pantheon.io/product/drupal-hosting`
- Platform.sh: `https://platform.sh/marketplace/drupal/`

Automating deployments

Using continuous integration, this deployment process can be automated in GitHub Actions, GitLab CI, or other continuous integration providers with your repository on commit. You will need to configure an additional set of private keys that are added to your continuous integration tool so that the service can SSH into your server.

See also

- Hosting partners on Drupal.org: `https://www.drupal.org/hosting`
- Documentation for the Drush `deploy` command: `https://www.drush.org/latest/deploycommand/`

2
Content Building Experience

As you know, Drupal is a content management system that excels in its editorial capabilities and content modeling. In this chapter, we will cover how to set up your content editing experience and add an editorial review workflow.

This chapter dives into creating custom types and harnessing different fields to create advanced structured content. We will walk through customizing the forms used for creating content and learn how to customize the content's display. The next thing we will learn is how to build custom landing pages using the `Layout Builder` module. We'll also learn how to add and manage content and utilize menus for linking to content. At the end of this chapter, you will be able to create a custom authoring experience for your Drupal site.

So, let's take a look at what topics we will cover in this chapter:

- Configuring the WYSIWYG editor
- Creating an editorial workflow with content moderation
- Creating a custom content type with custom fields
- Customizing the form display for editing content
- Customizing the display output of content
- Using layouts to build landing pages
- Creating menus and linking content
- Using Workspaces to create content staging areas

Configuring the WYSIWYG editor

Drupal is integrated with **CKEditor 5** as the default **What You See Is What You Get (WYSIWYG)** editor. The `Editor` module provides an API to integrate WYSIWYG editors, although CKEditor (the default editor) contributed modules can provide integrations with other WYSIWYG editors.

Text formats control the formatting of content and the WYSIWYG editor configuration for content authors. The standard Drupal installation profile provides a fully configured text format with the enabled CKEditor. We will walk through the steps of recreating this text format.

In this recipe, we will create a new text format with a custom CKEditor WYSIWYG configuration.

Getting ready

Before getting started, make sure the CKEditor module is installed. This module is automatically installed with Drupal's standard installation.

How to do it...

Let's create a new text format with a custom CKEditor WYSIWYG configuration:

1. Visit **Configuration** from the administrative toolbar and head to **Text formats and editors** under the **Content Authoring** heading.

2. Click on **Add text format** to begin creating the next text format.

3. Enter a name for the text format, such as the Editor format.

4. Select which roles have access to this format – this allows you to have granular control over what users can use when authoring content.

5. Select **CKEditor** from the **Text editor** select list. The configuration form for **CKEditor** will then be loaded.

6. You may now use an in-place editor to drag buttons onto the provided toolbar to configure your **CKEditor** toolbar:

Figure 2.1 – The text format edit form

7. Select any of the **Enabled filters** options, as shown in *Figure 2.2*, except for **Display any HTML as plain text**. That would be counterintuitive to using a WYSIWYG editor:

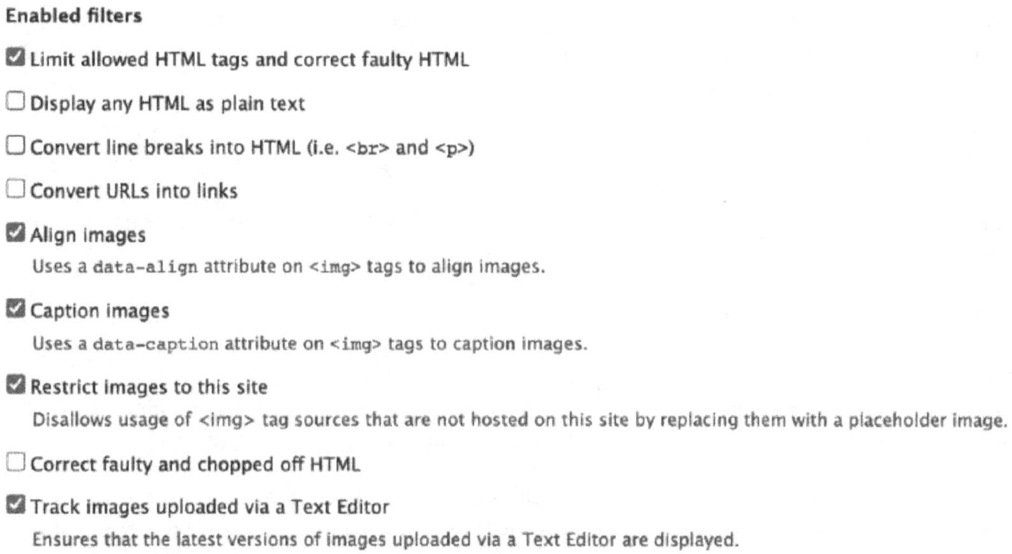

Enabled filters

☑ Limit allowed HTML tags and correct faulty HTML

☐ Display any HTML as plain text

☐ Convert line breaks into HTML (i.e.
 and <p>)

☐ Convert URLs into links

☑ Align images
  Uses a `data-align` attribute on <img> tags to align images.

☑ Caption images
  Uses a `data-caption` attribute on <img> tags to caption images.

☑ Restrict images to this site
  Disallows usage of <img> tag sources that are not hosted on this site by replacing them with a placeholder image.

☐ Correct faulty and chopped off HTML

☑ Track images uploaded via a Text Editor
  Ensures that the latest versions of images uploaded via a Text Editor are displayed.

Figure 2.2 – The Enabled filters checkboxes

8. Once you're satisfied, click on **Save configuration** to save your configuration and create the text filter. It will now be available to users when adding content to rich text fields.

How it works...

The `Filter` modules provide text formats that control how rich text fields are presented to the user. Drupal will render rich text saved in a text area based on the defined text format for the field. Text fields with *"formatted"* in their title will respect text format settings; others will render in plain text.

> **Important note**
>
> The text formats and editor's screen warns of a security risk due to improper configuration. This is because you could grant an anonymous user access to a text format that allows full HTML or allows image sources to be from remote URLs. This may leave your site open to **Cross-Site Scripting** (**XSS**) attacks. A cross-site scripting attack is when attackers can inject malicious client-side scripts into your site.

The `Editor` module provides a bridge to WYSIWYG editors and text formats. It alters the text format form and rendering to allow the integration of WYSIWYG editor libraries. This allows each text format to have a configuration for its WYSIWYG editor.

Out of the box, the `Editor` module alone does not provide an editor. The `CKEditor` module works with the Editor API to enable the usage of the WYSIWYG editor.

Contributed modules can provide support for other WYSIWYG editors. For instance, the `TinyMCE` module (`https://www.drupal.org/project/tinymce`) integrates Drupal with the `TinyMCE` editor (`https://www.tiny.cloud/tinymce`).

There's more...

Drupal provides granular control of how rich text is rendered and in extensible ways, which we will discuss further.

Filter module

When string data is added to a field that supports text formats, the data is saved and preserved as it was originally entered. Enabled filters for a text format will not be applied until the content is viewed. Drupal works in such a way that it saves the original content and only filters on display.

With the `Filter` module enabled, you can specify how text is rendered based on the roles of the user who created the text. It is important to understand the filters that are applied to a text format that uses a WYSIWYG editor. For example, if you selected the **Display any HTML as plain text** option, the formatting done by the WYSIWYG editor would be stripped out when viewed.

Improved links

A major component of WYSIWYG editing is the ability to insert links into other pieces of content or external sites. The default link button integrated with CKEditor allows for basic link embedding. This means that your content editors must know their internal content URLs ahead of time to link to them. A solution to this issue is the `Linkit` module at `https://www.drupal.org/project/linkit`.

The `LinkIt` module can be installed with the following Composer and Drush commands:

```
dd  /path/to/drupal
composer require drupal/linkit
php vendor/bin/drush en linkit -yes
```

The `Linkit` module provides a drop-in replacement for the default link functionality. It adds an auto-complete search for internal content and adds additional options for displaying the field. `Linkit` works by creating different profiles that allow you to control what content can be referenced, what attributes can be managed, and which users and roles can use a Linkit profile.

CKEditor plugins

The `CKEditor` module provides a plugin type called **CKEditorPlugin**. Plugins are small pieces of swappable functionality within Drupal. Plugins and plugin development will be covered in *Chapter 8, Plug and Play With Plugins*. This type provides integration between CKEditor and Drupal.

The image and link capabilities are plugins defined within the `CKEditor` module. Additional plugins can be provided through contributed projects or custom development.

Refer to the `\Drupal\ckeditor5\Annotation\CKEditor5Plugin` class (`https://git.drupalcode.org/project/drupal/-/blob/10.0.x/core/modules/ckeditor5/src/Annotation/CKEditor5Plugin.php`) for the plugin definition and the `\Drupal\ckeditor5\Plugin\CKEditor5Plugin\ImageUpload` class (`https://git.drupalcode.org/project/drupal/-/blob/10.0.x/core/modules/ckeditor5/src/Plugin/CKEditor5Plugin/ImageUpload.php`) `as a working example.`

See also

Refer to *Chapter 8, Plug and Play With Plugins*, for the CKEditor 5 documentation (`https://www.drupal.org/docs/core-modules-and-themes/core-modules/ckeditor-5-module`).

Creating an editorial workflow with content moderation

Many organizations have an editorial workflow that must be followed before content can be published on the website. The `Content Moderation` module allows content created in Drupal to go through an editorial process before it is published. In this recipe, we will create a content moderation workflow that puts content in a draft state and then reviews, approves, and publishes it. The content remains in a draft state and is hidden from site visitors until it is published.

Getting ready

In this recipe, we will be using the standard installation, which provides the Article content type. Any content type will suffice.

How to do it...

1. Begin by installing the `Content Moderation` module and its dependent module, `Workflows`:

    ```
    php vendor/bin/drush en content_moderation –yes
    ```

2. Visit **Configuration** and then **Workflows**. This page lists all configured content moderation workflows. Click **Add workflow** to create a new workflow.

3. In the **Label** field, give it a label of **Approval workflow** and select **Content moderation** for **Workflow type**.

4. The workflow has two default states of **Draft** and **Published**. We need to add **Review** and **Approval** states. For each of our new states, click the **Add a new state** link. Fill in the **State** label and press **Save**. Leave the **Published** and **Default revision** checkboxes unchecked. Those should only be used for a published state.

5. Rearrange the states' ordering so that it is **Draft**, **Review**, **Approval**, **Published**. Press **Save** at the bottom of the form so that our ordering is saved.

6. Next, we need to create a transition to move a **Draft** to **Review**. Click **Add a new transition**. Set the **Transition** label to **Ready for review**. Select **Draft as a From state**. Then, select **Review as the To state** and press **Save**.

7. Now, we will create the Review to Approval transition. Click **Add a new transition**. Set the **Transition** label to **Needs approval**. Select **Review as a From state**. Then, select **Approval as the To state** and press **Save**.

8. We must edit the default Publish transition. Uncheck **Draft from the From checkboxes** and select **Approval**.

9. Finally, we must assign this workflow to content entities. Under **This workflow applies to**, look for **Content types**. Press **Select** and a dialog will open. Check **Article**, then press **Save** in the dialog.

10. Press **Save** at the bottom of the form. Our content moderation workflow is now complete!

How it works...

Without `Content Moderation`, publishable content entities only have two states: unpublished or published. There also are no permissions to control who can make an unpublished piece of content published or vice versa. `Content Moderation` solves this problem.

The `Workflows` module provides an API for defining states and transitions. It is up to modules such as `Content Moderation` to provide Workflow Type plugins to bring meaningful functionality. The `Content Moderation` module integrates with the revision capabilities of Drupal content entities.

When editing a content entity that uses `Content Moderation`, there will be a **Moderation State** field. This field contains the states that a piece of content can transition to, based on the current user's permissions.

See also

- Content Moderation module documentation on `Drupal.org`: `https://www.drupal.org/docs/8/core/modules/content-moderation/overview`

- Workflows module documentation on `Drupal.org`: `https://www.drupal.org/docs/8/core/modules/workflows/overview`

Creating a custom content type with custom fields

Drupal excels in the realm of content management by allowing different types of content. In this recipe, we will walk you through creating a custom content type. We will create a Services type that has some basic fields and can be used in a scenario that brings attention to a company's provided services.

You will also learn how to add fields to a content type in this recipe, which generally goes hand in hand with making a new content type on a Drupal site.

How to do it...

1. Go to **Structure** and then **Content types**. Click on **Add content type** to begin creating a new content type.

2. Enter `Services` as the name, and an optional description.

3. Select **Display settings** and uncheck the **Display author and date information** checkbox. This will hide the author and submitted time from services pages.

4. Click on the **Save and manage fields** button to save the new content type and manage its fields.

5. By default, new content types have a **Body** field automatically added to them. We will keep this field in place.

6. We will add a field that will provide a way to enter a marketing headline for the service. Click on **Add field**.

7. Select **Text (plain)** from the dropdown and enter **Marketing headline** as the label.

> **Important note**
> The **Text (plain)** option is a regular text field. The **Text (formatted)** option will allow you to use text formats on the displayed text in the field.

8. Click on **Save field settings** on the next form. On the following form, click on **Save settings** to finish adding the field.

9. The field has now been added, and content of this type can be created.

How it works...

In Drupal, content entities can have different bundles. A bundle refers to a different type of that entity type. The word *bundle* comes from it being a bundle of fields since each bundle of a content entity type can have different fields. When working with nodes, they are synonymous with content, and bundles for nodes are referred to as content types.

When a content type is created, a default body field is created for it. This is performed by calling the `node_add_body_field()` function in the `node.module` file. It is a great reference point for those who wish to see the steps for programmatically defining a bundle field outside of the user interface.

Fields can only be managed or added if the `Field UI` module is enabled. The `Field UI` module exposes the **Manage Fields**, **Manage Form Display**, and **Manage Display** options for entities, such as **Nodes**, **Blocks**, and **Taxonomy Terms**.

Customizing the form display for editing content

Form modes allow a site administrator to customize the edit form when modifying a content entity. In the case of nodes, you can rearrange the order of fields and change the form elements used for a fields node edit form. There is also the `Field Group` module. The `Field Group` module allows you to group fields into fieldsets.

In this recipe, we will install `Field Group` and modify the form display to create an `Article` content type.

How to do it...

1. First, we must add the `Field Group` module to the Drupal site using Composer and then install it with Drush:

    ```
    composer require drupal/field_group
    php vendor/bin/drush en field_group -yes
    ```

2. To customize the form's display mode, go to **Structure** and then **Content Types**.

3. We will modify the Article content type's form. Click on and expand the **Operations** button and select **Manage form display**.

4. Click **Add field group** to begin adding a new field group.

5. Select **Details Sidebar** from **Add a new group**, give this a **Label** of **Metadata**, and click **Save** and continue.

6. Press **Create group** on the next form and use the default values to finish creating the group.

7. Drag the newly created **Metata** group (as shown in *Figure 2.3*) up from the **Disabled** section so that is it enabled. Directly above the **Disabled** label is fine.

8. Take the **Tags** field and drag it so that it is nested under the **Metadata** group – below it, and slightly to the right:

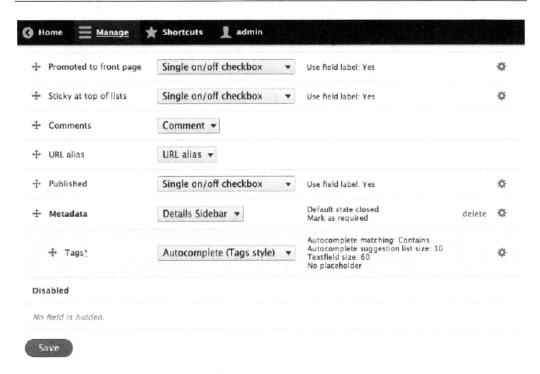

Figure 2.3 – The Manage Display form with the Tags widget moved
underneath the Metadata field group component

9. Click on the **Save** button at the bottom of the page to save your changes.

10. Go to **Create a New Article**; you will find the **Metadata** tab in the sidebar, which contains the **Tags** field:

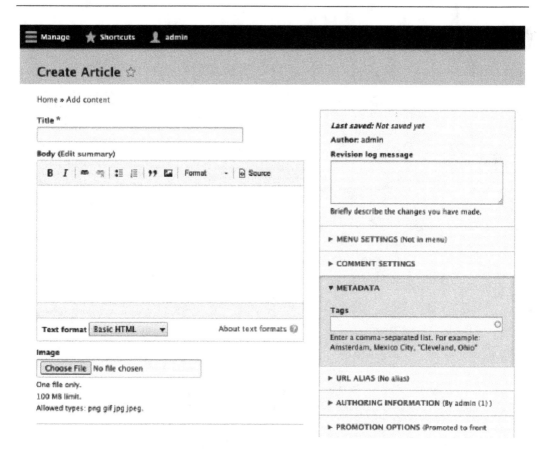

Figure 2.4 – The Article edit form, with the Tags element in the sidebar

How it works...

When a content entity form is built, the form is aware of the display mode to be used. Then, it invokes the display mode to build the components for each field using the specified field widgets.

This allows you to customize specific parts of the form without having to replace the entire form. Developers can create new field widgets or leverage ones from contributed modules to enhance the functionality of forms.

`Field Group` does not create field widgets, but a new structure inside of the form display. It will then arrange field widgets into groupings. This provides a more organized content editing experience.

There's more...

We will discuss more items for managing the form of a content entity in the following section.

Managing form display modes

Additional form display modes can be added by visiting **Structure** and then **Display Modes** under **Form Modes**. Each content entity type has a hidden default form mode that always exists. Additional form display modes can be added and configured using the display management form.

On their own, these forms and their configured field widgets are not directly integrated with Drupal. Using custom code, or even contributed projects, they can be used to embed for special uses.

For instance, there is the Register form mode for users. The user registration form is built using this display mode and the configured widgets instead of what is normally available when editing an existing user.

Customizing the display output of content

Drupal provides display view modes that allow you to customize the fields and other properties attached to an entity. In this recipe, we will adjust the teaser display mode of an `Article` content type. Each field or property has controls for displaying the label, the format to display the information in, and additional settings for the format.

Harnessing view displays allows you to have full control over how content is viewed on your Drupal site.

How to do it...

1. Now, it is time to customize the form display mode by navigating to **Structure** and then **Content Types**.

2. We will modify the `Article` content type's display. Click on the drop button arrow and select **Manage display**.

3. Click on the **Teaser view mode** option to modify it. **Teaser view mode** is used in node listings, such as the default home page.

4. Drag the **Tags** field to the hidden section. The tags on an article will no longer be displayed when viewing a **Teaser view mode**.

5. Click on the settings cog icon for the **Body** field to adjust the trimmed limit. The trim limit is a fallback for the summary or trimmed format when the summary of a text-area field is not provided. Modify this by changing it from `600` to `300`.

6. Click on **Save** to save all the changes that you have made.

7. View the home page and review the changes that have taken effect.

How it works...

The default rendering system for an entity uses view displays. View display modes are configuration entities. Since view display modes are configuration entities, they can be exported using configuration management.

When a content entity is rendered, the view display goes through each field formatter configured in the display. The field formatter is the option chosen from the **Format** property of the **Manage Display** form and identifies what code should be used to render the field value. The field value is retrieved from the entity and passed to the field formatter plugin that has been instantiated with the configuration provided to the view display. This collection of render data is then passed through the rest of Drupal's render pipeline.

There's more...

We will discuss more items for managing the form of a content entity in the following section.

Managing view display modes

Additional form display modes can be added by visiting **Structure** and then **Display Modes** under **View Modes**. Each content entity type has a hidden default view mode that always exists. Additional view display modes can be added and configured using the display management form.

These view modes can then be leveraged when displaying content with views, the Rendered entity field formatter for entity references, or when rendering entities with custom code.

Using layouts to build landing pages

The Layout Builder module allows content creators to use a drag-and-drop interface to customize how content is displayed on a page. Unlike using field formatters in view display modes, this does not require a developer and can be customized for individual pieces of content. With Layout Builder, content creators select from different layouts available in the system and place blocks in them to build the page's content. In this recipe, we will walk through installing Layout Builder and setting up the layout for the Article content type.

Getting ready

In this recipe, we will be using the standard installation, which provides the Article content type. Any content type will suffice.

How to do it...

1. Begin by installing the Layout Builder module and its dependent module, Layout Discovery:

```
php vendor/bin/drush en layout_builder -yes
```

2. We must opt into using Layout Builder for the display mode of our content type. Visit **Structure** and then **Content Types** and use the drop button for **Article** to click **Manage Display**.

3. Find the section labeled **Layout options** and check the **Use Layout Builder** checkbox.

4. Click **Save** to enable **Layout Builder**.

5. The **Manage Display** form should now show a **Manage layout** button.

6. Click the **Manage layout** button to enter the `Layout Builder` user interface to customize the **Article** layout.

7. By default, the **Show content preview** checkbox is turned on. Uncheck this checkbox to turn off the generated sample preview content.

8. Click **Add section** to create a new section and select **Two column layout**.

9. Select **33%/67%** for the **Column** width and click **Add section**, leaving the administrative label empty.

10. Now that we have added our two-column section, we can move fields into those layout parts. Drag the **Image** field to the left part and the **Body** field to the right part of the new section.

11. Click **Save** layout to save the changes.

12. Without using code, we have now created a layout for Articles that places the image in a sidebar next to the article content.

How it works...

The `Layout Builder` module provides an alternative render system for entity types. Using `Layout Builder` is an opt-in process for each display mode of a content entity type. If the entity type's display mode is not managed by `Layout Builder`, it falls back to the regular render system using field formatters.

Layouts are provided by layout plugins, which have matching Twig templates. Modules and themes can define new templates that can be used. `Layout Builder` leverages blocks to display content. The kinds of blocks available to be embedded in `Layout Builder` are based on blocks available to the system.

`Layout Builder` also exposes each field on the content entity as a block, allowing you to place each field in a different section.

Like custom nodes or other entity templates, if you make changes to the layout plugin or nested elements without updating the corresponding Twig templates for the layout, you may see things render incorrectly. Be sure to review the Twig template accordingly when making such changes.

There's more...

`Layout Builder` was an exciting addition to Drupal when it first arrived and has many more features and customizations far beyond what was covered in this recipe.

Accessible

The Layout Builder user interface went through rigorous accessibility testing. The entire Layout Builder user interface can be navigated using a keyboard or other accessibility devices.

Custom layouts for each piece of content

When configuring the layout options, the **Allow each content item to have its layout customized** option allows content editors to override the default layout for their content. When a piece of content is created, it will use the default layout. Content editors will see a **Layout** tab that allows them to customize the display of their content in the Layout Builder user interface.

The layout override is also stored in field data attached to the content entity, making it tracked with revisions! That means new drafts can be created for a piece of content with layout changes and they can be published through Content Moderation workflows.

Additional modules to extend Layout Builder

There are a copious number of modules that extend Layout Builder to customize its experience and provide default layouts. For instance, if you use the Bootstrap front-end framework, the **Bootstrap Layout Builder** (https://www.drupal.org/project/bootstrap_layout_builder) module provides a user interface for building layouts that use Bootstrap's styling.

A list of modules that extend Layout Builder can be found on Drupal.org: https://www.drupal.org/docs/8/core/modules/layout-builder/additional-modules.

See also

- Layout Builder module documentation on Drupal.org: https://www.drupal.org/docs/8/core/modules/layout-builder

Creating menus and linking content

Drupal allows you to link content being authored to a specified menu on the website, generally the main menu. You can, however, create a custom menu to provide links to content. In this recipe, we will show you how to create a custom menu and link content to it. We will then place the menu as a block on the page, in the sidebar.

Getting ready

This recipe assumes that you have installed the standard installation profile and have the default node content types available for use. You should have some content created to create a link.

How to do it...

1. Visit **Structure** and click on **Menus**.

2. Click on **Add menu**.

3. Provide a title of **Sidebar menu** and an optional summary and then click on **Save**.

4. Once the menu has been saved, click on the **Add link** button.

5. Enter a link title and then type in the title for a piece of content. The form will provide autocomplete suggestions for linkable content.

6. Click on **Save** to save the menu link.

7. With the menu link saved, go to **Structure**, and then **Block layout**.

8. Click on **Place block next to Sidebar first**. In the model, search for `Sidebar menu` and click on **Place block**.

9. In the following form, click on **Save block**.

10. View your Drupal site by clicking on **Home** in the administration menu.

How it works...

Menus and links are part of Drupal core. The ability to make custom menus and menu links is provided through the `Menu UI` module. This module is enabled on the standard installation but may not be in others.

The Link input of the menu link form allows you to begin typing content titles and easily link them to existing content. It will automatically convert the title into the internal path for you. Link input also accepts a regular path, such as `/node/1` or an external path. You may use `<front>` to link to the home page, `<nolink>` to render a non-linked anchor tag, and `<button>` for a keyboard-accessible text-only link.

There's more...

Links can be managed through the content edit form itself, which will be covered next.

Managing a contents menu link from its form

A piece of content can be added to a menu from the add or edit form. The menu settings section allows you to toggle the availability of a menu link. The menu link title will reflect the content's title by default.

The parent item allows you to decide which menu and which item it will appear under. By default, content types only have the main menu allowed. Editing a content type can allow for multiple menus or only choosing a custom menu.

This allows you to populate the main menu or complimentary menu without having to visit the menu management screens.

Using Workspaces to create content staging areas

The `Workspaces` module provides a new way of working with content on your Drupal site. It allows you to have a live version of your site's content and parallel draft versions. Normal content workflows involve multiple pieces of content that may be drafted and published at various times. The `Workspaces` module provides a way to create and prepare published drafts that release at the same time.

For example, during a big sporting event, articles are prepared based on whichever team wins. Once the winner is announced, that version of the site's content can be published. In this recipe, we will install the `Workspaces` module and walk through using site versions.

> **Important note**
>
> At the time of writing, the `Workspaces` module is an `Experimental` module. Modules that are marked as experimental are under active development and not considered stable. Experimental modules provide a way of adding new functionality to Drupal core more easily. You can read more about the experimental module policy on `Drupal.org`: `https://www.drupal.org/about/core/policies/core-change-policies/experimental/policy-and-list`.

Getting ready

In this recipe, we will be using the Standard installation, which provides the `Basic Page` content type. Any content type will suffice.

How to do it...

1. Begin by installing the `Workspaces` module:

   ```
   php vendor/bin/drush en workspaces --yes
   ```

2. Visit your Drupal site; you will notice the **Live** tab on the right of the toolbar; this is the current workspace identifier.

3. Click on **Live** to open the **Workspaces** menu.

4. Click on the Stage workspace's name and then click **Confirm** in the modal asking if we would like to activate and switch to the Stage workspace.

5. Create three or four new basic pages while using the Stage workspace and be sure to check **Promoted to front page** in the **Promotion options** group.

6. When you visit the front page of your Drupal site, you should see the pages you created in the front page list.

7. Now, open your Drupal site in another browser, or private mode, where you are not logged in. You will see that the home page shows **No front-page content has been created yet.** This shows that the content is only published in the Stage workspace, not the live site.

8. Back in your Drupal site, click on the **Stage** tab in your toolbar to open the workspace menu.

9. Click **Publish content** to begin publishing your Stage content into the Live site.

10. A confirmation form will appear. Click **Publish items to Live** to finish the process.

11. If you test your site in another browser, or private mode, again, you will see the home page now lists all your new pages!

How it works...

The `Workspace` module uses the existing revision capabilities of content entities. Revisions are then tracked against a workspace until they are published to the Live workspace. The `Workspace` module also adds safeguards. Forms that manipulate site configuration cannot be saved unless in the Live workspace; the module displays a warning and disables the **Submit** button. When using multiple workspaces, the `Workspace` module only allows a piece of content to be edited in one workspace.

Workspaces also have a user account associated with them. This allows segmented workspaces for specific users. This allows content creators to create a new workspace, but not view or modify another content creator's workspace.

There's more...

The `Workspaces` module provides other user interfaces not covered in this recipe, and there is another way to use a workspace beyond just content.

When will Workspaces become a stable module?

Effort is being made to make the `Workspaces` module stable. These issues are tagged in the Drupal core issue queue as **WI critical** (short for **Workflow Initiative Critical**). The list of issues can be found here: `https://www.drupal.org/project/issues/search/drupal?status%5B%5D=Open&issue_tags_op=%3D&issue_tags=WI+critical`.

Managing content changes in a workspace

When the workspace menu is open in the toolbar, you can click the **Manage workspace** link to see all of the active changes in the workspace. This makes it easier for a content manager to review what content has been modified in a workspace. It also allows for deleting those changes to revert to the original content.

This overview is useful for reviewing all the changes that may be published to the Live workspace.

Creating child workspaces

A workspace may also have a parent workspace. This allows you to maintain a centralized Stage workspace but forces content creators to have their child workspace under Stage. All content modifications can then merge into Stage instead of each contributor's workspace publishing to Live.

Using a workspace to test a new site redesign

Drupal has a mechanism for determining the active theme, which, by default, is the default theme. Code can be written to override the current theme based on specific conditions. The `Workspace Theme` module (`https://www.drupal.org/project/workspace_theme`) does just that.

It adds a new field to a workspace that allows you to specify a different theme to be used when that workspace is active. This allows you to preview a site's redesign with a new theme without making it the default theme on the production site, or purely relying on a test server.

See also

- The Workspaces module documentation on `Drupal.org`: `https://www.drupal.org/docs/8/core/modules/workspace/`

3

Displaying Content through Views

The **Views** module in Drupal is a visual query builder that enables you to build dynamic content displays without writing any code. We will walk through how to create a page to list blogs and a companion block to display five of the most recent blogs. Then, we will move into creating exposed filters to allow end users to control the view results. You will also learn some more advanced topics using contextual filters and custom entity reference widget output. Finally, we will cover how to use the **Charts** module to output a chart of data with Views.

In this chapter, we are going to cover the following recipes:

- Creating a blog landing page
- Creating a block of recent blogs
- Exposing filters and sorts to users to control listings
- Contextual filters for filtering by path parameters
- Adding related data in a view with relationships
- Providing an entity reference result view
- Displaying charts using Views

Creating a blog landing page

The Views module does one thing, and it does it well – listing content. The power behind the Views module is the amount of configurable power it gives to end users to display content in various forms. This recipe will cover the process of how to create a content listing and link it to the main menu. We will use the **Article** content type to create a blog landing page.

How to do it...

1. Go to **Structure** and then **Views**. This will bring you to the administrative overview of all the views created. Click on **Add view** to create a new view:

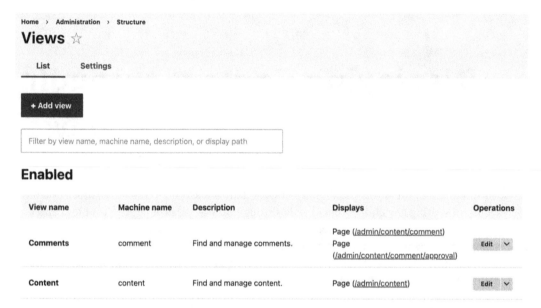

Figure 3.1 – The Views listing overview

2. The first step is to provide the view name of **Blog**, which will serve as the administrative and (by default) displayed title.

3. Next, we will modify the **View settings** section. We want to display **Content** of the **Article** type and leave the **tagged with** field empty. This will force the view to only show content of the **Article** content type.

4. Check the **Create a page** option. The **Page title** and **Path** fields will be automatically populated based on the view name and can be modified as desired. For now, leave the display and other settings at their default values:

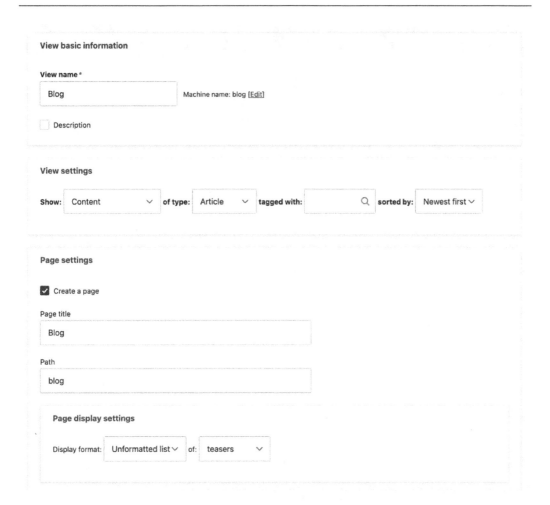

View basic information

View name *

Blog   Machine name: blog [Edit]

☐ Description

View settings

Show: Content ∨   of type: Article ∨   tagged with: [   ] 🔍   sorted by: Newest first ∨

Page settings

☑ Create a page

Page title

Blog

Path

blog

Page display settings

Display format: Unformatted list ∨   of: teasers   ∨

Figure 3.2 – Overview of the view creation form

5.   Click on **Save and edit** to continue modifying your new view.

6.   In the middle column, under the **Page Settings** section, we will change the **Menu item** settings. Click on **No menu** to change the menu option.

7.   Select **Normal menu entry**. Provide a menu link title and an optional description. Set **Parent** to **<Main Navigation>**:

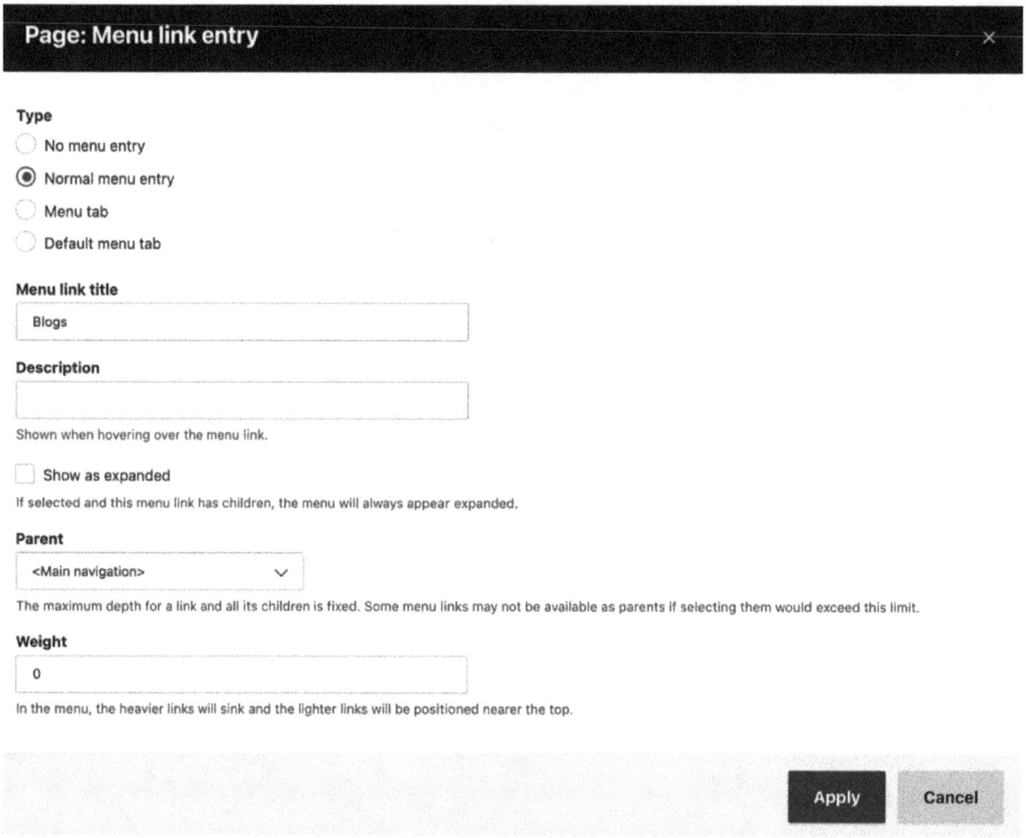

Figure 3.3 – The menu settings form for the view

8.   Click on **Apply** at the bottom of the form in the dialog.

9.   Click on **Save** to save your view.

10. Once your view has been saved, click on **Back to site** from the administrative menu. You will now see the link in your Drupal site's main menu.

How it works...

The first step for creating a view involves selecting the type of data you will be displaying. This is referred to as the base table, which can be any type of entity or data specifically exposed to Views.

> **Content and nodes**
>
> **Nodes** are labeled as **Content** in Views, and you will find this interchanged terminology throughout Drupal.

When creating a Views page, we add a menu path that can be accessed. It tells Drupal to invoke Views to render the page, which will load the view you created and render it. Then, the Views module registers that path as a route in Drupal's routing system to a controller provided by itself, which renders the view display.

There are display style and row plugins that format the data to be rendered. Our recipe used the unformatted list style to wrap each row in a simple `div` element. We could have changed this into a table for a formatted list. The row display controls how each row is outputted.

There's more...

The Views module is one of the most versatile and used modules in Drupal core. In the following section, we will dive further into some components of Views.

Views and displays

When working with Views, you will see some different terminologies. One of the key concepts to be grasped is what a display is. A view can contain multiple displays. Each display is of a certain type. The Views module comes with the following display types:

- **Attachment**: This is a display that becomes attached to another display in the same view. These are placed in the Header or Footer sections of another view display.

- **Block**: This allows you to place the view as a block on your Drupal site.

- **Embed**: The display is meant to be embedded programmatically.

- **Entity Reference**: This allows Views to provide results for an entity reference field.

- **Feed**: This display returns an XML-based feed that can be attached to another display to render a feed icon so that users can subscribe to the content.

- **Page**: This allows you to display the view from a specific path.

Each display can have its own configuration, too. However, each display will share the same base table (content, files, and more). This allows you to take the same data and present it in different ways within the same view.

Format style plugins – style and row

Within Views, there are two types of style plugins that represent how your data is displayed: **style** and **row**:

- The style plugin represents the overall format of the view
- The row plugin represents the format of each row in the results for the view

For example, the **Responsive Grid** style will output the results in a grid using CSS grids and make it responsive for different screen sizes. At the same time, the Table style creates a tabular output with field labels used as table headings.

Row plugins define how to render the row. The default type of **Content** will render the entity using a selected view mode. If you choose **Fields**, you can manually select which fields will be included in your view display results and the field formatters to use for each field.

Each **style** plugin has a corresponding Twig template that is used to theme the output. Refer to the *Using Twig templates* section in your theme recipe of *Chapter 10, Theming and Frontend Development*, to learn more about Twig templates.

Using the Embed display

Each of the available display types has a method to expose itself through the user interface, except for Embed. Often, contributed and custom modules use Views to render displays instead of manually writing queries and rendering the output. Drupal provides a special display type to simplify this.

If we were to add an **Embed** display to the view created in the recipe, we could use the following render array in custom code to output our view programmatically:

```
$view_render = [
  '#type' => 'view',
  '#name' => 'blog,
  '#display_id' => 'embed_1'
];
```

When rendered, the #type key tells Drupal that this is a view element. We then point it to our new display, embed_1. The **Embed** display type has no special functionality; it is a simplistic display plugin. The benefit of this is that it does not conduct additional operations for the sake of performance.

Using an **Embed** display is beneficial when you want to use a view in a custom page, block, or even form. For example, Drupal Commerce uses this pattern for its shopping cart block and the order summary at the checkout. A view is used to display the order information within a custom block and form.

Creating a block of recent blogs

In the last recipe, we created a page using the Views module to list articles in the Drupal site to build a blog. A view can contain multiple displays. Each display inherits defaults, such as its style and row format, filters, sorts, pager, and more. Each display type might have unique settings, such as the page settings where the menu link was configured in the previous recipe. In this recipe, we will add a block display so that we can list the five most recent articles by title anywhere on the site.

How to do it...

1. Go to **Structure** and then **Views**. This will bring you to the administrative overview of all the views that are created.

2. Find the **Blog** view that was created in the previous recipe and click on **Edit**.

3. Under **Displays**, where it says **Page**, click on the **Add** button and select **Block** from the drop-down menu. This will create a new block display, which we can configure:

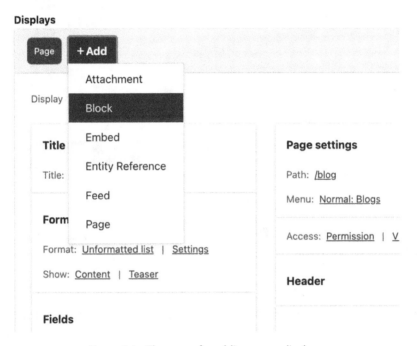

Figure 3.4 – The menu for adding a new display

4. In the **Format** section, click on **Content** (next to **Show**) to configure the row format used.

5. In the dialog that opens, we need to make sure we only modify the row format for this display. In the **For** drop-down menu, select **This block (override)** so that the changes are only for this display.

6.   Select the **Fields** option from the radio buttons and click on **Apply (this display)** to set the row format to use individual fields instead of display modes:

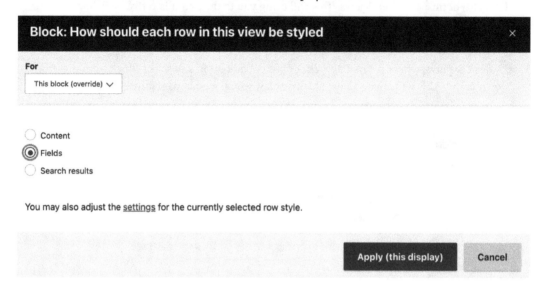

Figure 3.5 – The style format form dialog

7.   A new dialog will appear that allows you to configure options for this row format. Use the defaults and click on **Apply**.

> **Important note**
> Changing to using the **Fields** row format will automatically add the **Title** field, which has been configured to link to the piece of content.

8.   We only want this block to display the five most recent blogs. Under the **Pager** section, click on the field next to **Use Pager** to launch the dialog for configuring the pager.

9.   Just like the row format, select **This block (override)** from the **For** select list. Then, choose the **Display a specified number of items** option. Click on **Apply (this display)**:

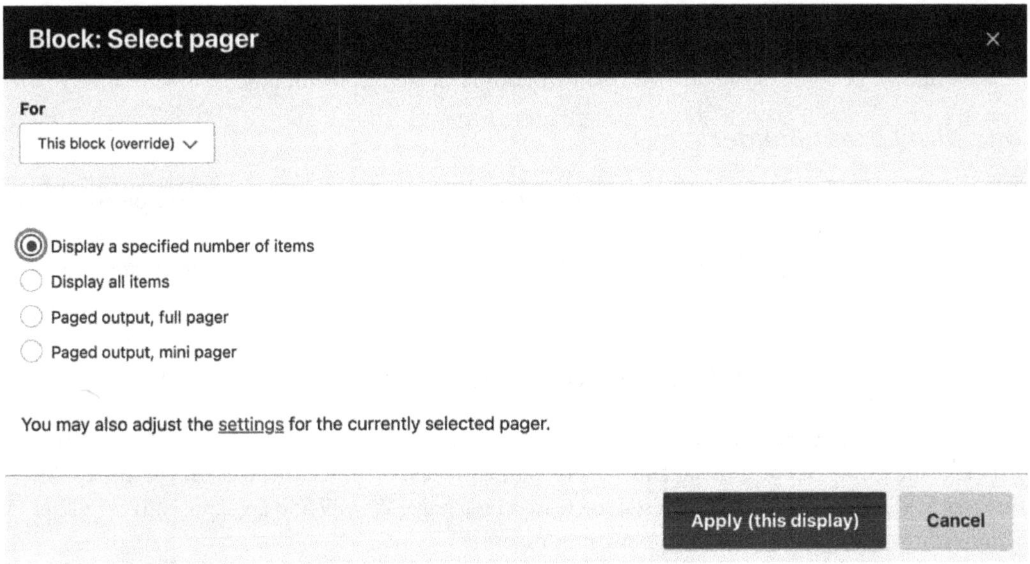

Block: Select pager   ✕

For

This block (override) ∨

◉ Display a specified number of items

○ Display all items

○ Paged output, full pager

○ Paged output, mini pager

You may also adjust the settings for the currently selected pager.

[Apply (this display)] [Cancel]

Figure 3.6 – The pager selection form dialog

10. In the next dialog, which allows you to configure the pager settings, change **Items to display** to **5**. Click on **Apply** to finish changing the pager.

11. Click on **Save** to save your changes to the view and create the block display.

12. Go to **Structure** and **Block layout** to place the block on your Drupal site. Click on **Place block** for the **Sidebar first** region.

13. Filter the list by typing in your view's name: **Blog**. Click on **Place block** to add your view's block to the block layout.

14. We do not want this block to display on our blog landing page. In the **Visibility** section, add / blog to the **Pages** textbox. Change the radio option to **Hide for the listed pages**.

15. This prevents the block from being displayed in the /blog path, which is our view for the list of articles.

16. Finally, click on the **Save** block to commit your changes.

How it works...

Blocks, in Drupal, are a type of plugin. These blocks can be embedded into the site layout and can be shown or hidden based on a variety of visibility settings. The Views module integrates with the block module to allow view displays to be placed as blocks. This empowers Drupal site builders to create dynamic content displays that can be used throughout a site.

There's more...

Now, we will explore some of the other ways in which Views interacts with blocks.

Usage with Layout Builder

In *Chapter 2, Content Building Experience*, in the *Using layouts to build landing pages* recipe, we used Layout Builder to place blocks that contained field values for content. You could place any kind of block using Layout Builder, including block displays in your view. Content creators can create landing pages using dynamic content provided by views.

Exposing filters and sorts to users to control listings

The Views module supports exposing filters and sorts on a view display for users to interact with to adjust the results. This can be done to allow users to filter by text or adjust the ordering of the results. In this recipe, we will modify the view used to create a blog page. We will add an exposed search filter and allow the user to sort articles from newest or oldest.

How to do it...

1. Go to **Structure** and then **Views**. This will bring you to an administrative overview of all the views that have been created.

2. Find the **Blog** view that was created in the first recipe and click on **Edit**.

3. Click on **Add** in the **Filter criteria** section of the form.

4. In the dialog that opens, we need to make sure we only modify the row format for this display. In the **For** drop-down menu, select **This page (override)** so that the changes are only for this page display and not the block display created in the previous recipe.

5. Select **Title** in the **Content** category and click on **Add (this display)**:

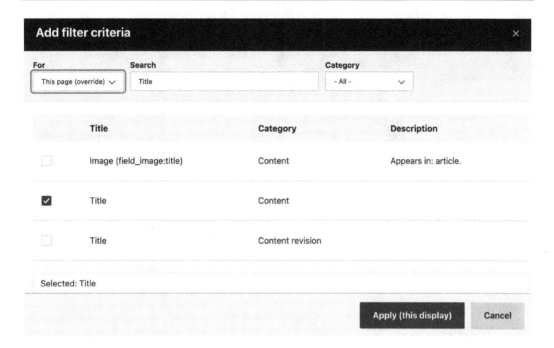

Figure 3.7 – The add filter form dialog

6.   Check the **Expose this filter to visitors, to allow them to change it** checkbox to make this an exposed filter. In the exposed filter configuration form, change **Operator** from **Is equal to** to **Contains**. This will allow for more flexible searching. Click on **Apply (this display)** to add the new filter.

7.   In the **Sort** criteria section, click on **Content: Authored on (desc)**. Select **This page (override)** from the **For** select list.

8.   Check the **Expose this sort to visitors, to allow them to change it** checkbox to make this an exposed sort.

9.   Click on **Apply (this display)** to update the sorting configuration.

10. Click on **Save** to save your changes to the view.

11. Now, when you view /blog, you can search the articles and change their sort order:

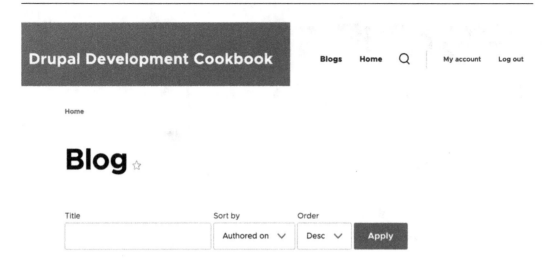

Figure 3.8 – The Blog landing page with exposed filters and sorts

How it works...

When a filter or sort is exposed, the Views module attaches a form to the view display. This form is controlled by the `\Drupal\views\Form\ViewsExposedForm` class. This reads query parameter values from the URL and maps them to known exposed filters and sorts. It applies the values to the filter and sort handlers, overriding their default values so that the query is adjusted.

There's more...

We will now explore the extra options that are available when using exposed filters and sorts.

Exposed versus non-exposed filters and sorts

Filters allow you to narrow the scope of the data displayed in a view. Filters can either be exposed or not; by default, a filter is not exposed. An example would be using the **Content: Publishing status** option set to **Yes (published)** to ensure that a view always contains published content. This is an item you would configure to display content to site visitors. However, if it were for an administrative display, you might want to expose that filter. This way, content editors can easily view what content has not been published yet or has been unpublished.

All filter and sort criteria can be marked as exposed.

Filter identifiers

Exposed filters work by parsing query parameters in the URL. On our blog page, when you search by title and submit the exposed form, the URL will now have a query parameter for `title`, `sort_by`, and `sort_order`.

Exposed filters have a **Filter identifier** option that can change the URL component. This can be modified when editing your filter or sort.

Exposed forms as blocks

If your view utilizes exposed filters, you have the option to place the exposed form in a block. With this option enabled, you could place the block anywhere on the page, even pages not for your view.

An example of using an exposed form in a block is for a search result view. You can add an exposed filter for keywords that control the search results. With the exposed filters in a block, you can easily place them within your site's header. When an exposed filter block is submitted, it will direct users to your view's display. In this recipe, it will allow users to search for articles without having to be on the `/blog` page.

To enable the exposed filters as a block, first, you must expand the **Advanced** section on the right-hand side of the Views edit form. Click on the **Exposed form in block** option from the **Advanced** section. In the options modal that opens, select the **Yes** radio button, and click on **Apply**. You can then place the block from the **Block layout** form.

Contextual filters for filtering by path parameters

Views can be configured to accept contextual filters, also known as arguments. Contextual filters allow you to provide a dynamic or fixed argument that modifies the view's query. Think of it as the root condition in the query. By default, the value is expected to be provided from the URL; otherwise, a default operation can be chosen if it is not present.

In this recipe, we will create a new page called **My Content**, which will display a user's authored content in the `/user/{user_id}/content` path. The value of `{user_id}` will be any user ID that is available in Drupal.

How to do it...

1. Go to **Structure** and then **Views**. This will bring you to an administrative overview of all the views that have been created. Click on **Add view** to create a new view.

2. Set **View name** to **My Content**.

3. Next, we will modify the **View settings** section. We want to show **Content** of the **All** type and leave the **tagged with** field empty. This will allow all content types to be displayed.

4.   Check the **Create a page** checkbox. Keep the **Page title** field as the default provided. We will need to change the **Path** field to user/%user/content. Click on **Save and edit** to move to the next screen:

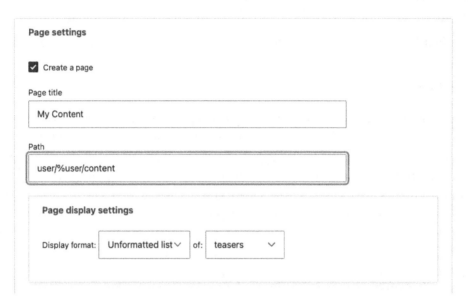

Page settings

✓ Create a page

Page title

    My Content

Path

    user/%user/content

Page display settings

Display format: Unformatted list ∨   of: teasers   ∨

Figure 3.9 – Page settings with path variable

> **Percentages in the path**
>
> When there is a percentage sign used in a view page display path, the Views module understands this as a placeholder for a value that will be used as a contextual filter. For example, given the /user/1234/content path, the value of %user will be 1234.

5.   Toggle the **Advanced** portion of the form on the right-hand side of the page. Click on **Add** in the **Contextual filters** section.

6.   Select **Authored by** from the **Content** category and then click on the **Add and configure contextual filters** button.

7.   Change the default value of **When the filter value is not in the URL** to **Display "Access denied"** to prevent all content from being displayed with an incorrect route value. Click on **Apply** to add the contextual filter and close the dialog:

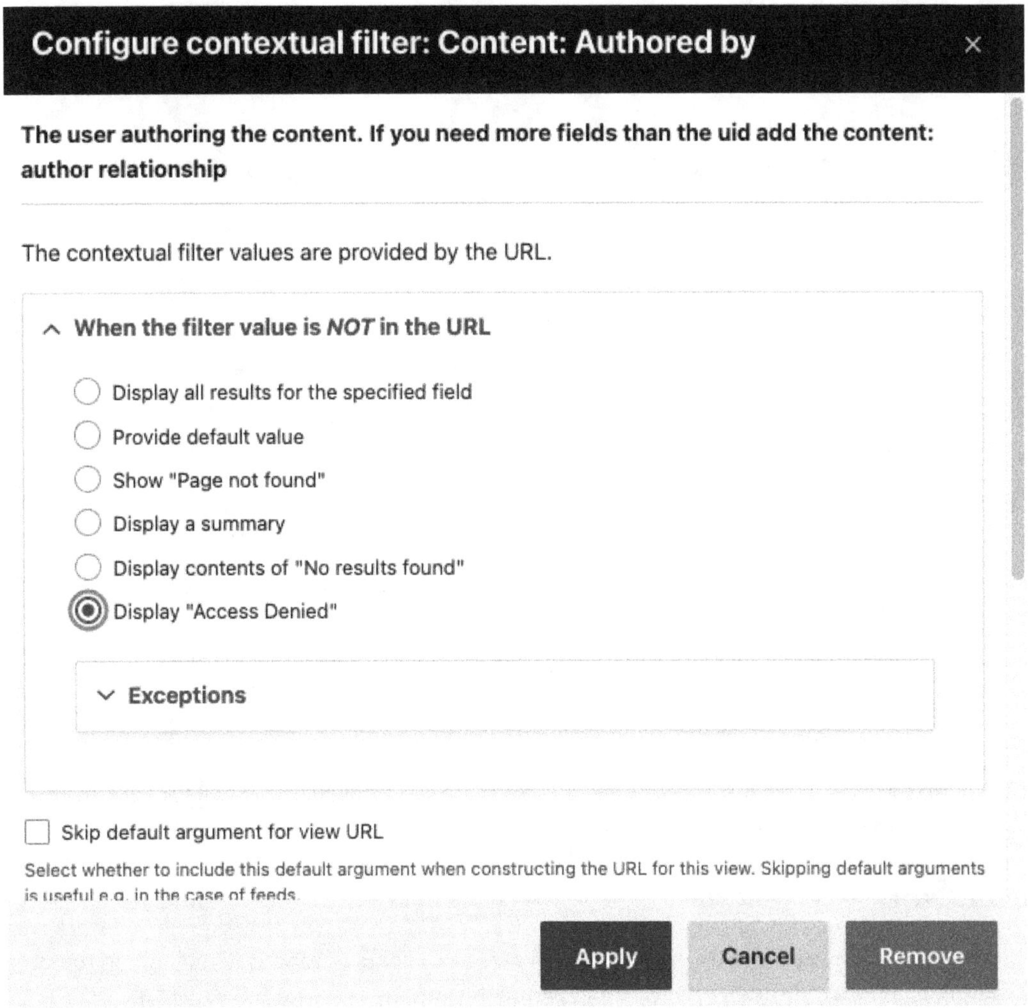

Configure contextual filter: Content: Authored by   ✕

The user authoring the content. If you need more fields than the uid add the content: author relationship

The contextual filter values are provided by the URL.

∧ **When the filter value is *NOT* in the URL**

- ◯ Display all results for the specified field
- ◯ Provide default value
- ◯ Show "Page not found"
- ◯ Display a summary
- ◯ Display contents of "No results found"
- ◉ Display "Access Denied"

∨ **Exceptions**

☐ Skip default argument for view URL

Select whether to include this default argument when constructing the URL for this view. Skipping default arguments is useful e.g. in the case of feeds.

Apply   **Cancel**   **Remove**

Figure 3.10 – The contextual filter settings

8. Under **Page settings**, the default access is for the **View published content** permission. Click on **View published content** to change the permission to **View user information**. Click on **Apply** to set the permissions for the page display.

9. Next, we will add the page as a menu tab on the user page. Click on **No Menu** from the **Menu** option.

10. Select **Menu tab** and provide a **Menu link** title, such as **My Content**. Click on **Apply** to change the menu settings:

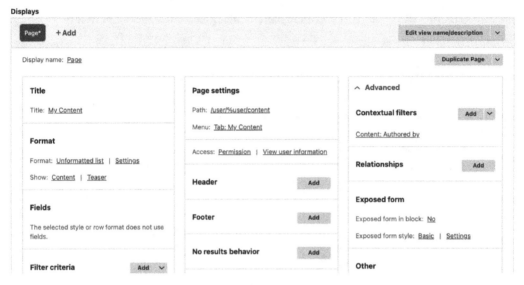

Figure 3.11 – Configured view overview

11. Then, click on **Save** to save the view.

12. Go to `/user/1/content`, and you will see the content created by the first user. It will also be listed as a tab next to **View** and **Edit**.

How it works...

Contextual filters are similar to using route parameters in Drupal's routing system, built on top of the routing component from Symfony. Route parameters are represented by percentage signs as placeholders in the view's page display path. Views will match up each placeholder with the contextual filters by order of their placement. This allows you to have multiple contextual filters, so you just need to ensure they are ordered properly.

> **Using contextual filters on other display types**
>
> When using other display types, such as blocks, you will need to use the **Provide a default value** option.

Most fields that can be used as regular filters are allowed as contextual filters. The benefit of this is that they can receive dynamic values without forcing them to be exposed filters to the end user.

There's more...

Now we will explore the extra options available when using contextual filters.

Previewing with contextual filters

You are still able to preview a view from the edit form. You can simply add the contextual filter values to the text form concatenated by a forward slash (/). In this recipe, you could replicate navigating to /user/1/content by simply inputting 1 into the preview form and updating the preview.

Providing a default value

There is an option to provide a default value when the filter value is not available. For instance, a fixed value could be provided as a fallback, or the view can try to get the content ID from the current URL or use the currently logged-in user. Some of the options are always available, and some will differ based on the data being displayed in the view.

When using a view with a block display, the default value option allows you to leverage contextual filters without a path being available to provide the parameter value. This is especially useful when creating landing pages with Layout Builder.

Altering the page title

With contextual filters, you can manipulate the current page's title. You can check the **Override title** option in the **When the filter value is present in the URL or a default is provided** section.

This textbox allows you to enter a new title that will be displayed. The **Replacement patterns** section contains tokens that could be used for dynamic title content.

Validation of contextual filter arguments

Contextual filters can have validation requirements attached. Without specifying extra validation, the Views module will take the expected argument and try to make it just work. You can add validation to help limit this scope and filter out invalid route parameters.

You can enable validation by checking **Specify validation criteria** from the **When the filter value is in the URL or a default is provided** section. The default is set to **Basic validation**, which allows you to specify how the view should react if the data becomes invalid. Based on our recipe, this would be if the user for the ID in the route parameter is not found.

The list of **Validator** options is not filtered by the contextual filter item you selected. So, some might not be applicable. For our recipe, you might want the **User ID** option. This validator would make sure that the user ID exists.

This gives you granular control over how the view operates and executes its query when using contextual filters.

Multiple arguments and exclusion

You might configure the contextual filter to allow AND or OR operations, along with using the context filter value for exclusion rather than inclusion. These options are under the **More** section when adding or editing a contextual filter.

The **Allow multiple values** option can be checked to enable AND or OR operations. If the contextual filter argument contains a series of values concatenated by plus (+) signs, it acts as an OR operation. If the values are concatenated by commas (,) it acts like an AND operation.

When the Exclude option has been checked, the value will be excluded from the results rather than limiting results based on that value. For example, with the user ID provided in this recipe, we could exclude content created by that user to display content created by all other users.

Adding related data in a view with relationships

As stated at the beginning of the chapter, Views is a visual query builder. When you first create a view, a base table is specified from which to pull data. The Views module automatically knows how to join tables for field data, such as body text or custom-attached fields.

When using an entity reference field, you can display the value as the identifier, the referenced entity's label, or the entire rendered entity. However, if you add a relationship based on a reference field, you will have access to display any of that entity's available fields.

In this recipe, we will update the **Files** view, used for administering files, to display the username of the user who uploaded the file.

How to do it...

1. Go to **Structure** and then **Views**. This will bring you to the administrative overview of all the views that have been created.

2. Find the **Files** view and click on **Edit**:

Custom block library	block_content	Find and manage custom blocks.	Page (/admin/structure/block/block-content)	Edit	⌄
Files	files	Find and manage files.	Page (/admin/content/files/usage/%) Page (/admin/content/files)	Edit	⌄
Frontpage	frontpage	All content promoted to the front page.	Feed (/rss.xml) Page (/node)	Edit	⌄
My Content	my_content		Page (/user/%user/content)	Edit	⌄

Figure 3.12 – The Files view in the Views listing

3. Click on **Advanced** to expand the section and then click on **Add**, which is next to **Relationships**.

4. Search for **User**. Select the **User who uploaded** relationship option and click on **Apply (this display)**.

5. Next, we will be presented with a configuration form for the relationship. Click on **Apply (this display)** to use the defaults.

6. Add a new field by clicking on **Add** in the **Fields** section.

7. Search for **Name** and select the **Name** field from the **User** category. Then, click on **Apply (all displays)**:

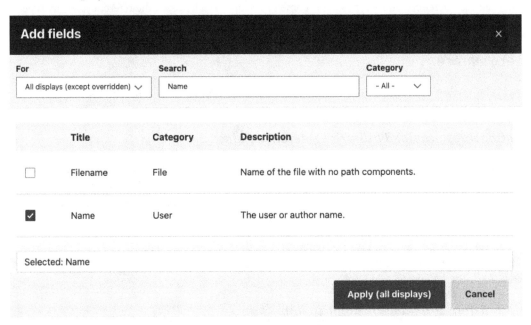

Figure 3.13 – The Name field from the User category

8. This view uses aggregation, which presents a new configuration form when you first add a field. Click on **Apply and continue** to use the aggregation defaults.

9. We will use the default field settings that will provide the label **Name** and format as the username and link to the user's profile. Click on **Apply (all displays)**.

10. Click on **Save** to finish editing the view and commit your changes.

11. When viewing the files list in /admin/content/files, the username of the user that uploaded the file will now be displayed.

How it works...

Drupal stores data in a normalized format. In short, database normalization involves the organization of data in specifically related tables. Each entity type has its own database table, and all fields have their own database table. When you create a view and specify what kind of data will be shown, you are specifying a base table in the database that Views will query. Views will automatically associate fields that belong to the entity and its relationship to those tables for you.

When an entity has an entity reference field, you can add a relationship to the referenced entity type's table. This is an explicit definition, whereas fields are implicit. When the relationship is explicitly defined, all the referenced entity type's fields come into scope. The fields on the referenced entity type can then be displayed, filtered, and sorted.

There's more...

Using relationships in Views allows you to create some powerful displays. Now we will discuss additional information about relationships.

Relationships provided by entity reference fields

The Views module uses a series of hooks to retrieve data that it then uses to represent ways to interact with the database. One of these is the hook_field_views_data hook, which processes a field storage configuration entity and registers its data with Views. The Views module implements this on behalf of the Drupal core to add relationships and reverse relationships, for Entity reference fields.

Since Entity reference fields have set schema information, Views can dynamically generate these relationships by understanding the field's table name, the destination entity's table name, and the destination entity's identifier column.

Relationships provided through custom code

There are times when you will need to define a relation in the database with your own custom code. One example of exposing a database table to the Views module is in the **Database Logging** module. The Database Logging module defines a custom database table schema for storing logs. It then uses the hook_views_data hook to expose information about its database to the Views module.

For instance, the dblog_schema hook implementation returns a uid column for the watchdog database table. This is a foreign key to the user table to associate the log with a user. That column is then exposed to Views using the following definition:

```
$data['watchdog']['uid'] = [
    'title' => t('UID'),
    'help' => t('The user ID of the user on which the log
        entry was written.'),
```

```
    'field' => [
      'id' => 'standard',
    ],
    'filter' => [
      'id' => 'numeric',
    ],
    'argument' => [
      'id' => 'numeric',
    ],
    'relationship' => [
      'title' => t('User'),
      'help' => t('The user on which the log entry as
          written.'),
      'base' => 'users_field_data',
      'base field' => 'uid',
      'id' => 'standard',
    ],
  ];
```

This array tells Views that the `watchdog` table has a column named `uid`. It is numeric in nature for its display, filtering capabilities, and sorting capabilities. The relationship key is an array of information that instructs Views how to use this to provide a relationship (`LEFT JOIN`) on the `users` table. The user entity uses the `users` table and has a primary key of `uid`.

Providing an entity reference result view

Entity reference fields allow you to reference other entities. Often, this is used with content to reference taxonomy terms or related content. By default, the entity reference will display all the available entities that can be referenced. However, using the Views module and its entity reference view display type, you can provide a more controlled result.

In this recipe, we will create an entity reference view that filters references based on content created by the current author. We will then add a field to the user account form, allowing users to select their favorite contributed content.

How to do it...

1. Go to **Structure** and then **Views**. This will bring you to the administrative overview of all the views that have been created. Click on **Add view** to create a new view.

2. Set **View name** to **My Content Reference View** and keep the current **View settings** configuration.

3. Do not choose to create a page or block. Click on **Save and edit** to continue working on your view.

4. Click on the **Add** button to create a new display. Select the **Entity Reference** option to create the new display:

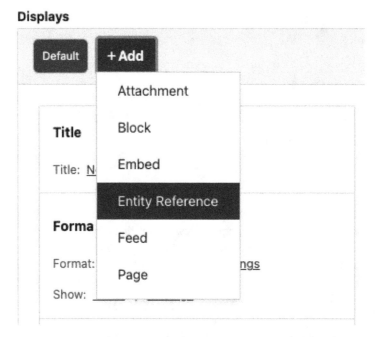

Figure 3.14 – The Add a display drop-down menu

5. The style format will automatically be set to **Entity Reference List**, which sets the row format to **Entity Reference inline fields**. Click on **Settings** next to **Entity Reference List** to modify the style format settings.

6. For **Search Fields**, check the **Content: Title** option and then click on **Apply**. This is what the field will perform the autocomplete search on:

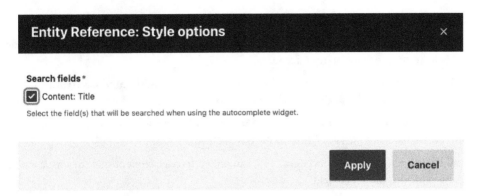

Figure 3.15 – Entity reference style options

7. We will then use a contextual filter to limit the results to the currently logged-in user. Click on **Add** from **Contextual filters** in the **Advanced** section.

8. Select the **Authored by** option in the **Content** category and click on **Add and configure contextual filters**.

9. Change the **When the filter value is not available** setting to **Provide a default value**. Select **User ID from the logged in user** from the **Type** select list. Click on **Apply** to add the contextual filter:

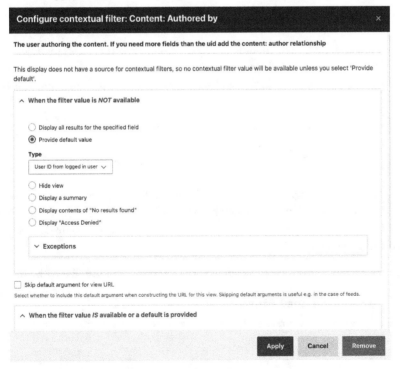

Figure 3.16 – User contextual filter with the default value provided

10. Click on **Save** to save the view.

11. Go to **Configuration** in the administrative toolbar, then **Account settings** to click on **Manage Fields** to configure fields on user accounts.

12. Add a new **Reference** field that references **Content**. Call it **Highlighted Contributions** and allow it to have unlimited values. Click on the **Save field settings** button.

13. Change the **Reference type** method to use **View: Filter by an entity reference view** and select the view we have just created. Click on the **Save settings** button.

14. Now, when a user edits their account, they can only reference content that they have created as values for this reference field.

How it works...

The entity reference field definition provides selection plugins. The Views module provides an entity reference selection plugin. This allows entity reference to gather data into a view to receive available results.

The display type for Views requires you to select which fields will be used to search against when using the autocomplete widget. If you are not using the autocomplete widget and instead use the select list or checkboxes and radio buttons, then it will return the view display's entire results.

Displaying charts using Views

In this recipe, we will use the **Charts** module to create graphs using the Views module. The Charts module integrates different graphing libraries with the Views module. The view created in this recipe will display a graph based on statistics generated from the Statistic modules to graph visits to content on the Drupal site.

Leverage the Charts module to create a view that renders a chart of data.

Getting ready

This recipe requires having enough data available to put into a graph. We will be using data available from the Statistics module, which tracks content page views. To generate content and view statistics, we will use the **Devel** (for Development) module. This module provides the means of generating sample content and populating statistics.

To use `Devel` to generate content, we must add it with Composer and install it with **Drush**:

```
composer require drupal/devel
php vendor/bin/drush en devel_generate statistics --yes
```

Now, we can generate content. Log in to your Drupal site and visit /admin/config/development/generate/content. Check the checkbox for **Article** to generate articles. Ensure the **Add statistics for each node (node_counter table)** checkbox is checked so that statistics are generated. Press **Generate** to generate the sample content.

How to do it...

1. First, we must add the Charts module to the Drupal site using Composer and install it along with its Google Charts submodule with Drush:

   ```
   composer require drupal/charts
   php vendor/bin/drush en charts charts_google --yes
   ```

2. Go to **Structure** and then **Views**. This will bring you to the administrative overview of all the views that have been created. Click on **Add view** to create a new view.

3. Set **View name** to **Content Statistics** and keep the default **View settings** values.

4. Check the **Create a page** checkbox to create a page. Use the default values provided. Under **Page display settings**, change the display format to **Chart of fields**:

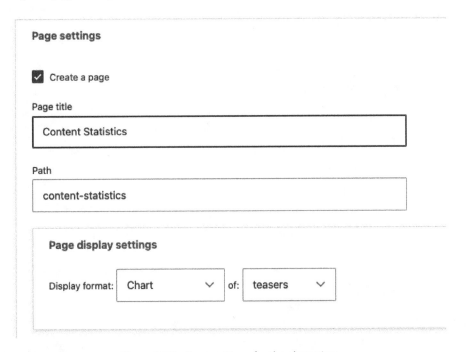

Figure 3.17 – Page settings for the chart view

5. Click on **Save and edit** to continue working on your view.

6. In the **Fields** section, click on **Add**. Search for **Total views** under the **Content statistics** category. Click on **Add and configure fields** to continue.

7. Check the **Create a label** checkbox and set the **Label** to **Total views**. Click on **Apply** to finish adding the field.

8. Next, we need to configure the chart to use our **Total views** field as the data for the chart. In the **Format** section, click on **Settings** next to **Chart**.

9. Select **Google** from the **Charting library** drop-down menu.

10. Keep the **Label field** option set to **Content: Title**. In the **Provides data** column, check the **totalcount** checkbox:

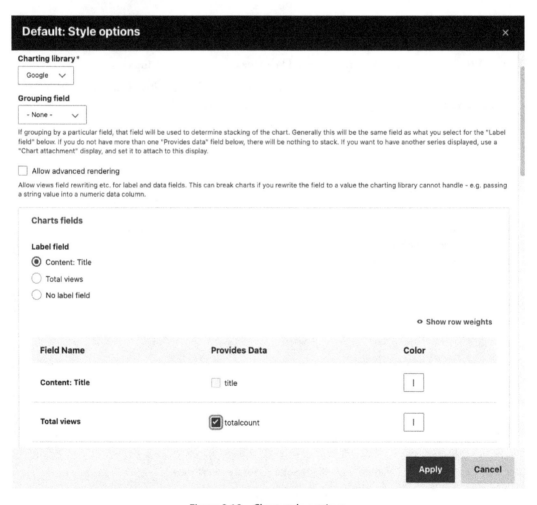

Figure 3.18 – Chart style settings

11. Click on **Apply** to set the chart settings.

12. Click on **Save** to save your view.

13. Visit `/content-statistics` to see the chart of usage statistics.

How it works...

The Charts module provides an API to integrate with various charting libraries such as Google Charts, Highcharts, and more. Developers can create charts with custom code, but one of the greatest features is its integration with Views.

The Charts module allows you to display values as various chart types. It also allows you to provide multiple data types to create advanced graphs. Each chart library has various settings that can be configured.

See also

- The Charts module project page on Drupal.org: `https://www.drupal.org/project/charts`

- Charts module documentation: `https://www.drupal.org/docs/contributed-modules/charts`

4

Extending Drupal with Custom Code

The greatest component of Drupal is its extensibility through modules. In this chapter, we will explore how to create a custom module that can be installed on your Drupal site. This chapter will explain how PSR-4 autoloading works with extensions and how to leverage class autoloading. You will be able to create a controller for a custom page and specify additional permissions to check whether the user has them. You will also understand what hooks and events in Drupal are, and how to interact with them. This chapter also lays the foundations for the following chapters.

The following recipes will be covered in this chapter:

- Creating a module
- Providing configuration settings for your module
- Defining permissions and checking whether a user has access
- Hooking into Drupal to react to entity changes
- Creating an event subscriber to react to events
- Creating a custom Drush command

Technical requirements

You can find the full code used in this chapter on GitHub: `https://github.com/PacktPublishing/Drupal-10-Development-Cookbook/tree/main/chp04`

Creating a module

The first step to extending Drupal is to create a custom module. Although the task sounds daunting, it can be accomplished in a few simple steps. Modules can provide functionalities and customizations for functionalities provided by other modules, or they can be used as a way to contain the configuration and a site's state.

In this recipe, we will create a module by defining its `modulename.info.yml` file, a file containing information that Drupal uses to discover extensions and install the module.

How to do it...

1. In your `web/modules` directory, create a new directory called `custom` and then another directory named `mymodule` inside it. This will be your module's directory. Using the command line, you may create the directory with the following command:

    ```
    mkdir -p web/modules/custom/mymodule
    ```

    This will create the required directories.

2. Create a `mymodule.info.yml` file in your module's directory. This will contain the metadata that identifies the module to Drupal.

3. Add a line to the `mymodule.info.yml` file to provide a name for the module with the name key:

    ```
    name: My Module
    ```

4. We must define the type of extension with the key type. Drupal does not assume the extension type just by directory location alone:

    ```
    type: module
    ```

5. The `description` key allows you to provide extra information about your module, which will be displayed on the module's list page:

    ```
    description: This is an example module from the Drupal
    Development Cookbook!
    ```

6. Extensions are required to provide a `core_version_requirement` that identifies what versions of Drupal core the module is compatible with, using a semantic versioning constraint:

    ```
    core_version_requirement: '>=10'
    ```

7. Save the `mymodule.info.yml` file, which looks as follows:

    ```
    name: My Module
    ```

```
type: module
description: This is an example module from the Drupal
  Development Cookbook!
core_version_requirement: '>=10'
```

8. Next, create a file named `mymodule.module` in your `module` file. This is the extension file that will allow us to add hook definitions. It is a regular PHP file, but the file extension matches its extension type of module.

9. For this example, we will provide a hook that renders a message on each payload:

```php
<?php

/**
 * Implements hook_page_top().
 */
function mymodule_page_top() {
  \Drupal::messenger()->addStatus('Hello world!');
}
```

This implements `hook_page_top`, which is called whenever a page is rendered. It uses the messenger service to add a status message to the page.

10. Install your module using Drush:

```
php vendor/bin/drush en mymodule --yes
```

11. Visit your Drupal site. The `Hello world!` message will be added to each page:

Figure 4.1 – Drupal page displaying Hello world!

How it works...

Drupal utilizes `info.yml` files to define extensions. Drupal has an extension discovery system that locates these files and parses them to discover modules. The extension discovery will scan your entire Drupal code base, giving the Drupal core directory priority.

In this recipe, we provided `>=10` for the `core_version_requirement` constraint. This constraint allows your module to work with a minimum of Drupal 10.0.0 but also be compatible with Drupal 11 or greater, simplifying maintenance when the next major version of Drupal core is released. If you know your code is not compatible with a previous minor version, it could be updated to `>=10.1.0` or even a specific patch value of `>=10.2.1`.

One method to integrate with Drupal is through its hook system. During runtime, other modules may invoke a hook that other modules can implement to perform actions or modify data. Our recipe implemented the `hook_page_top` hook. This hook is part of the page rendering life cycle and allows you to add renderable content at the very top of the page.

Module namespaces

Drupal uses the PSR-4 standard developed by the **PHP Framework Interoperability Group** (**PHP-FIG**). The PSR-4 standard is for package-based PHP namespace autoloading of classes and is used by most libraries and frameworks, including Laravel and Symfony. It defines a standard to understand how to automatically include classes based on a namespace and class name. Drupal modules have their own namespaces under the Drupal root namespace.

Using the module from the recipe, our PHP namespace will be `Drupal\mymodule`, which represents the `web/modules/mymodule/src` folder.

With PSR-4, files need to contain only one class, interface, or trait. These files need to have the same filename as the containing class, interface, or trait name. This allows a class loader to resolve a namespace as a directory path and know the class's filename. The file can then be automatically loaded when it is used in a file.

Creating a composer.json file

If you are writing a custom module that will only be used on your site, this is not necessary. However, if you plan to contribute your code to Drupal.org and distribute it, you should provide a `composer.json` file.

> **Note**
>
> Projects on Drupal.org are not required to create a `composer.json` file. If a project does not, one will be automatically generated for it based on the contents of its `info.yml` file. That is why it is recommended to create one: to be explicit.

Create a `composer.json` file in your module directory. It will look similar to the `mymodule.info.yml` file but as JSON:

```json
{
    "name": "drupal/mymodule",
    "type": "drupal-module",
    "description": "This is an example module from the Dru
        pal Development Cookbook!",
    "require": {
        "drupal/core": ">=10"
    }
}
```

The `name` key should be prefixed with `drupal/` to identify it is in the Drupal package namespace. The type is prefixed with `drupal-` for compatibility with the Composer Installers package, which we covered in *Chapter 1*, *Up and Running with Drupal*.

`core_version_requirement` is converted into Composer's dependency definition and targets the `drupal/core` package.

There's more...

There are more details about Drupal modules and the module `info.yml` files that we can explore.

Module dependencies

Modules can define dependencies to ensure that those modules are installed before your module can be installed.

Here is an example from the `info.yml` file for the `Pathauto` module:

```yaml
name: 'Pathauto'
description: 'Provides a mechanism for modules to automati
    cally generate aliases for the content they manage.'
type: module
dependencies:
- ctools:ctools
- drupal:path
- token:token
```

The `dependencies` key specifies that the `ctools` path from Drupal core and `token` module must be installed first before the `Pathauto` module can be installed. In the *Adding and managing modules and themes with Composer* recipe from *Chapter 1, Up and Running with Drupal*, they were automatically installed when we installed the `Pathauto` module.

Drupal has always supported modules that contain additional submodules, an uncommon practice in other systems. As Drupal adopted Composer, it enforced namespaced dependencies in the `info.yml` file. This identifies the root package and the specific module it contains to be installed.

If your module has dependencies and you plan to contribute it, remember to create a `composer.json` file and define your dependencies so that they will be downloaded with Composer.

See more...

- Refer to the *PSR-4: Autoloading specification*: `https://www.php-fig.org/psr/psr-4/`

- Changing a record by adding `core_version_requirement` and the reasonings behind its addition: `https://www.drupal.org/node/3070687`

- `Drupal.org` documentation for creating a module: `https://www.drupal.org/docs/creating-custom-modules`

Providing configuration settings for your module

Modules can leverage configuration settings to allow end users to modify how they operate. These pieces of configuration are YAML files. Modules can also provide default configuration for other modules when they are installed. Once the module has been installed, the default configuration it provides is imported into Drupal. Modules may also modify existing configurations programmatically through an installation hook or update hooks.

In this recipe, we will provide a configuration that creates a new contact form and then manipulates it through an update hook.

Getting ready

This recipe requires a custom module, like the one created in the first recipe. We will refer to the module as `mymodule` throughout this recipe. Use your module's appropriate name where necessary.

How to do it...

1. Create a `config` folder in your module's directory. Then, in that directory, create an `install` directory. Drupal looks for YAML configuration in this installation directory:

```
mkdir -p config/install
```

2. In the `install` directory, create a `contact.form.contactus.yml` file to store the YAML definition of the contact form, `Contact Us`.

3. Add the following YAML content to the `contact.form.contactus.yml` file:

```
langcode: en
status: true
dependencies: { }
id: contactus
label: 'Contact Us'
recipients:

- webmaster@example.com
reply: ''
weight: 0
```

This YAML file represents the exported configuration object for a contact form. `id` is the contact form's machine name and `label` is the human display name for the user interface. The `recipients` key is a YAML array of valid email addresses. The `reply` key is a string of text for the `Auto-reply` message. Finally, `weight` defines the ordering of the form on the administrative list.

> **Note**
>
> Normally, you do not manually write configuration YAML like this. You will generally export it individually from the Drupal site if needed.

4. Install the module using Drush:

```
php vendor/bin/drush en mymodule --yes
```

5. The **Contact Us** form will now be located on the **Contact forms** overview page, located under **Structure**.

6. Create a `mymodule.post_update.php` file in the module's directory. This file contains update hooks to be run after schema changes.

7. We will create a function called `mymodule_post_update_change_contactus_reply()` that will be executed by the update system to modify the contact form's configuration:

```php
<?php

/**
 * Update "Contact Us" form to have a reply message.
```

```
 */
function mymodule_post_update_change_contactus_reply()
  {
  $contact_form = \Drupal\contact\Entity\Contact
    Form::load('contactus');
  $contact_form->setReply(t('Thank you for contacting
    us, we will reply shortly'));
  $contact_form->save();
}
```

This function uses the entity's class to load the contact form entity object. It loads the **Contact Us** contact form, which our module has provided, and sets the reply property to its new value.

8. Run updates for the Drupal site using Drush:

```
php vendor/bin/drush updb
```

Drush will list the updates to be applied, including the one you just wrote. The function comment of an `update` function will be output in the list of updates to be applied. After reviewing the changes, you can tell Drush to proceed by entering yes on the command line.

9. Review the **Contact Us** form settings and verify that the reply message has been set.

How it works...

Drupal's `moduler_installer` service, provided through `\Drupal\Core\Extension\ModuleInstaller`, ensures that configuration items defined in the module's `config` folder are processed on installation. When a module is installed, the `config.installer` service, provided through `\Drupal\Core\Config\ConfigInstaller`, is called to process the module's default configuration.

If the `config.installer` service attempts to import configuration from a module's `config/install` folder that already exists, an exception will be thrown. Modules cannot provide duplicated configuration or modify existing configuration objects via the YAML files.

Since modules cannot adjust configuration objects through YAML files provided to Drupal, they can utilize the update system to modify the configuration. The update system has two update processes: schema updates and post updates. Since we did not make schema-level changes, we used the post-update process. This allows us to make modifications to existing configuration objects.

In *Chapter 7, Creating Forms with the Form API*, we will create a form for modifying configuration settings.

There's more...

We will now dive into some important notes when working with modules and configurations.

Configuration subdirectories

There are three directories that the configuration management system will inspect in a module's `config` folder, which are as follows:

- `install`
- `optional`
- `schema`

The `install` folder specifies the configuration that will be imported. If the configuration object exists, the installation will fail. The `optional` folder contains the configuration that will be installed if the following conditions are met:

- The configuration does not already exist
- It is a configuration entity
- Its dependencies can be met

If any one of the conditions fails, the configuration will not be installed, but it will not halt the module's installation process. The `schema` folder provides configuration object definitions.

Modifying the existing configuration on installation

The configuration management system does not allow modules to provide configuration on an installation that already exists. For example, if a module tries to provide `system.site` and defines the site's name, it would fail to install. This is because the `system` module provides this configuration object when you first install Drupal.

Modules may also have a `.install` file, such as `mymodule.install` for our recipe's module. This file is where modules may implement the `hook_install` hook provided by Drupal, along with schema update hooks.

`hook_install()` is executed during the module's installation process. The following code will update the site's title to `Drupal Development Cookbook!` on the module's installation:

```php
<?php

/**
 * Implements hook_install().
 */
```

```
function mymodule_install() {
  // Set the site name.
  \Drupal::configFactory()
    ->getEditable('system.site')
    ->set('name', 'Drupal Development Cookbook!')
    ->save();
}
```

Configurable objects are immutable by default, meaning they cannot be changed or saved when loaded by the default config service. To modify a configuration object, you will need to use the configuration factory to receive an editable instance of a configuration object. This object can have set and save methods that are executed to update the configuration in a configuration object.

Schema update hooks

This recipe mentioned schema update hooks. These are intended to be used to make changes to any database schema or entity field definitions. When the update system runs, the schema hooks are run first; then, post-updates are executed.

The schema update hooks are defined as hook_update_N, where N is a numeric schema version value. When schema update hooks are executed, they are run in order of their schema version. Generally, the base schema version is based on the major version of Drupal core or the module's versioning. In custom code, it can be anything you wish.

The naming conventions for schema updates have been under discussion since Drupal 8 regarding the support of semantic versioning in contributed projects. These naming conventions are discussed in the following issues:

- https://www.drupal.org/project/drupal/issues/3106712
- https://www.drupal.org/project/drupal/issues/3010334

See also

- Update API documentation on Drupal.org: https://www.drupal.org/docs/drupal-apis/update-api
- *Chapter 7, Creating Forms with the Form API*

Defining permissions and checking whether a user has access

In Drupal, roles and permissions are used to define robust access control lists for users. Modules use permissions to check whether the current user has access to perform an action, view specific items, or do other operations. Modules then define the permissions that are used so that Drupal is aware of them. Developers can then construct roles, which are made up of enabled permissions.

In this recipe, we will define new permission(s) in a module that is used to check if the user can mark content as promoted to the front page or sticky at the top of lists. This permission will be used in an entity field access hook to deny access to the fields if the user is missing the permission.

Getting ready

Create a new module, as we did in the first recipe. We will refer to the module as `mymodule` throughout this recipe. Use your module's name in the following recipe as appropriate.

Create a new Drupal user with the Content editor role. Drupal bypasses access checks for the first user. The secondary user will be required to demonstrate the permission.

How to do it...

1. Permissions are stored in a `permissions.yml` file. Add a `mymodule.permissions.yml` file to the base directory of your module.

2. First, we will need to define the internal string used to identify this permission, such as `can promote nodes`:

   ```
   can promote nodes:
   ```

3. Each permission is a YAML array of data. We will need to provide a `title` key that will be displayed on the permissions page:

   ```
   can promote nodes:
     title: 'Can promote content'
   ```

4. Permissions have a `description` key to provide details of the permission on the permissions page:

   ```
   can promote nodes:
     title: 'Can promote content'
     description: 'Determines if the user can change pro
       motion fields on content.'
   ```

5. Save your `mymodule.permissions.yml` file and edit the module's `mymodule.module` file so that we may write our hook to use the permission.

6. In your `mymodule.module` file, add a function named `mymodule_entity_field_access` to implement `hook_entity_field_access`. This is invoked to control access at a granular level per field on entity forms:

```
function mymodule_entity_field_access(
    $operation,
    \Drupal\Core\Field\FieldDefinitionInterface
        $field_definition,
    \Drupal\Core\Session\AccountInterface $account
) {
    return \Drupal\Core\Access\AccessResult::neutral();
}
```

Drupal uses access result value objects to handle access results. Access results may be neutral, forbidden, or allowed. Hooks implementing `hook_entity_field_access` must return an access result and cannot return `null`.

7. In our hook, we will check the field name being checked. If the field name is `promote` or `sticky`, we will check whether the user has the `can promote nodes` permission and return that access result:

```
function mymodule_entity_field_access(
    $operation,
    \Drupal\Core\Field\FieldDefinitionInterface
        $field_definition,
    \Drupal\Core\Session\AccountInterface $account
) {
    $field_name = $field_definition->getName();
    if ($field_name === 'promote' || $field_name ===
        'sticky') {
        $can_promote_nodes = $account->hasPermission('can
            promote nodes');
        return Drupal\Core\Access\AccessResult::allowedIf
            ($can_promote_nodes);
    }
    return \Drupal\Core\Access\AccessResult::neutral();
}
```

The access result object has an `allowedIf` method that returns an appropriate result based on the parameter provided. In this case, it will return `AccessResult::allowed()` if the user has the permission or `AccessResult::neutral()` if not.

> **Note**
>
> Drupal's access system requires explicit allowance. If an access result is neutral, the system will keep processing access results. If an access result is returned as forbidden or allowed, the access checks stop, and that result is used. If the ending result is neutral, access is not granted since it was not explicitly allowed.

8. New permissions are not granted to roles automatically. In another browser or guest tab, log in as a user with the Content editor role and create a piece of content. The **Promotion options** section of the sidebar will be missing since we do not have field access:

Figure 4.2 – Promotion options are hidden due to missing permissions

9. As your administrative user, go to **People** and then to **Permissions** to add your permission for the Content editor role in the **My Module** section:

Permission	Content editor
My Module	
Can promote content Determines if the user can change promotion fields on content.	☑

Figure 4.3 – Adding the permission to the Content editor role

10. Using your Content editor user, try and create a piece of content once more. The **Promotion options** section in the sidebar will be present:

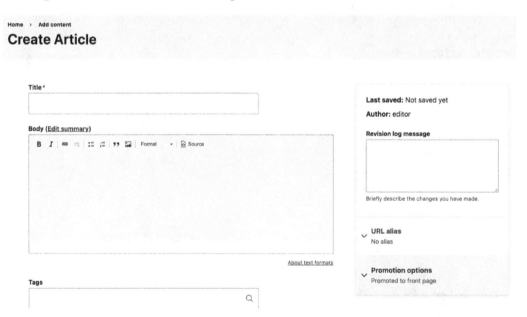

Figure 4.4 – The Promotion options section appears once the permission has been granted

How it works...

Permissions and roles are provided by the User module. The user.permissions service discovers the permissions.yml file provided by installed modules. By default, the service is defined through the \Drupal\user\PermissionHandler class.

Drupal does not save a list of all available permissions. The permissions for a system are loaded when the permissions page is loaded. Roles contain an array of permissions.

When checking a user's access for permission, Drupal checks all the user's roles to see whether they support that permission.

> **Note**
>
> You can pass undefined permissions to a user access check and not receive an error. The access check will simply fail unless the user is UID 1, which bypasses access checks. In Drupal, user UID 1 is the root user and is not beholden to security checks or permissions. Be careful when granting access to that account or using user 1 in testing.

There's more...

We will cover more ways to work with permissions in your modules in the upcoming sections.

Restricting access flag for permissions

Permissions can be flagged as having a security risk if enabled; this can be done via the restrict access flag. When this flag is set to `restrict access: TRUE`, it will add a warning to the permission's description.

This allows module developers to provide more context regarding the amount of control a permission may give a user:

Permission	Anonymous user	Authenticated user	Administrator	Author	Editor
Administer content *Warning: Give to trusted roles only; this permission has security implications.* Promote, change ownership, edit revisions, and perform other tasks across all content types.	☐	☐	☑	☐	☐
Administer content types *Warning: Give to trusted roles only; this permission has security implications.* Maintain the types of content available and the fields that are associated with those types.	☐	☐	☑	☐	☐
Bypass content access control *Warning: Give to trusted roles only; this permission has security implications.* View, edit and delete all content regardless of permission restrictions.	☐	☐	☑	☐	☐

Figure 4.5 – Example of permissions with the restrict access flag

The permission definition from our recipe would look like this:

```
can promote nodes:
  title: 'Can promote content'
  description: 'Determines if the user can change promotion
    fields on content.'
  Restrict access: TRUE
```

Defining permissions programmatically

Permissions can be defined by a module programmatically or statically in a YAML file. A module needs to provide a `permission_callbacks` key in its `permissions.yml` file that contains either an array of callable methods or functions to define permissions dynamically.

For example, the `Filter` module provides granular permissions based on the different text filters created in Drupal:

```
permission_callbacks:
  -Drupal\filter\FilterPermissions::permissions
```

This tells the `user_permissions` service to execute the permissions method of the `\Drupal\Filter\FilterPermissions` class. The method is expected to return an array that matches the same structure as that of the `permissions.yml` file.

See also...

- *Chapter 5, Creating Custom Pages*

Hooking into Drupal to react to entity changes

One of the most common integration points is hooking into Drupal to react to the create, read, update, and delete operations of an entity. The entity system also has hooks to provide default values when instantiating a new entity and modifying it before it is saved.

In this recipe, we will create a hook that runs whenever new content is published and send an email to the site's email address as a notification of the new content.

How to do it...

1. First, create a file called `mymodule.module` in your `module` file. This is the module extension file that stores hook implementations.

2. Next, we will implement a hook to listen for new node entities being inserted. Create a function named `mymodule_node_insert`, which is an implementation of the `hook_ENTITY_TYPE_insert` hook:

```php
<?php

function mymodule_node_insert(\Drupal\node\
    NodeInterface $node) {

}
```

3. In our `insert` hook, we will check if the node was saved as published. If it was, we will send an email notification:

```php
<?php

function mymodule_node_insert(\Drupal\node\
    NodeInterface $node) {
  if ($node->isPublished()) {
    $site_mail = \Drupal::config('system.site')->
        get('mail');
    /** @var \Drupal\Core\Mail\MailManager
        $mail_service */
    $mail_service = \Drupal::service(
        'plugin.manager.mail');
    $mail_service->mail(
      module: 'mymodule',
      key: 'node_published',
      to: $site_mail,
      langcode: 'en',
      params: ['node' => $node],
    );
  }
}
```

First, we check if the node has been published. The node entity type implements `EntityPublishedInterface`, which provides the `isPublished` method. If the node has been published, we fetch the site's email address from the configuration. To send an email, we need to fetch the mail manager service. With the mail manager service, we invoke the `mail` method. The `module` and `key` parameters are used to invoke another hook in the module to generate the email's content. The `to` parameter is where the email should be sent. `langcode` represents what language the email should be sent in. Finally, the `params` parameter provides context values to the hook, which generates the email content.

4. We want to add a hook that listens when nodes are updated, as they may have first been saved as unpublished. Create a function named `mymodule_node_update` so that we can implement the `hook_ENTITY_TYPE_update` hook:

    ```
    function mymodule_node_update(\Drupal\node\NodeInter
        face $node) {

    }
    ```

5. In our `update` hook, we will check if the unchanged version of the node was published or not. We do not want to send duplicate emails. We only send an email if the node was previously unpublished and then became published:

    ```
    function mymodule_node_update(\Drupal\node\NodeInter
        face $node) {
      if ($node->isPublished()) {
        /** @var \Drupal\node\NodeInterface $original */
        $original = $node->original;
        if (!$original->isPublished()) {
          $site_mail = \Drupal::config('system.site')->
            get('mail');
          /** @var \Drupal\Core\Mail\MailManager
            $mail_service */
          $mail_service = \Drupal::service('plugin
            .manager.mail');
          $mail_service->mail(
            module: 'mymodule',
            key: 'node_published_update',
            to: $site_mail,
            langcode: 'en',
            params: ['node' => $node],
          );
    ```

```
        }
    }
}
```

As you can see, this hook is nearly the same as our `insert` hook, but we check the values of the original node object. The entity storage sets the original property on an entity that has unchanged values from the database. This allows us to compare the previous values to the newly modified ones. In our hook, we verify that the original node was not already published before sending our email.

> **Note**
>
> This hook uses the `node_published_update` key so that we can use different email text.

6. Now, we need to create a function named `mymodule_mail` that implements `hook_mail`. This will allow us to define the content for our email notifications:

```
function mymodule_mail($key, array &$message, $params) {
}
```

The `key` and `params` parameters are the values we passed to the mail manager's `mail` method and how we can identify what content to generate. The `message` property is an array that represents the email to be sent, such as who the email is being sent to and its content.

7. In our `mail` hook, we will provide a different subject based on whether the email is sent for a newly published node or an `update` node that became published, along with a message:

```
function mymodule_mail($key, array &$message, $params)
{
  /** @var \Drupal\node\NodeInterface $node */
  $node = $params['node'];
  if ($key === 'node_published_insert') {
    $message['subject'] = 'Newly published node: ' .
        $node->label();
  }
  elseif ($key === 'node_published_update') {
    $message['subject'] = 'Existing node published: '
        . $node->label();
  }
  else {
    // Unknown key.
    Return;
```

```
    }
    $message['body'][] = 'The following node has been
        published:';
    $message['body'][] = $node->label();
    $message['body'][] = $node->toUrl()->setAbsolute()
        ->toString();
}
```

We check the key value and set an appropriate email subject based on the keys we have defined. The body key in the message expects an array of text, which Drupal will convert into new lines.

8. Now, whenever nodes are published, an email will be sent to the site's email address, notifying the site administrator of the newly published content.

How it works...

The entity system in Drupal has various hooks that it triggers to interact with entities when they are loaded, created (instantiation for a new entity), saved, or deleted. In this recipe, we listened to two post-save hooks. Once an entity has been saved, the entity storage's post-save process invokes the insert hook for new entities or the update hook for existing entities.

In this recipe, we used hooks that targeted a specific entity type. This allowed us to be more concise in our code and also type-hint the appropriate entity interface in our hooks. Each entity operation hook can also be implemented generically. If we were to use hook_entity_insert or hook_entity_update, they would be fired for any entity type, such as taxonomy terms or blocks. When using the more generic hook implementation, you need to use \Drupal\Entity\EntityInterface for your type hint and use the getEntityTypeId method to check the entity's type.

The available hooks for the create, read, update, and delete operations of entities are documented on Drupal.org, along with details about each hook and examples: https://api.drupal.org/api/drupal/core%21lib%21Drupal%21Core%21Entity%21entity.api.php/group/entity_crud/10.0.x.

There's more...

This recipe covered hooking into the post-save hooks. In the following section, we will explore the other hooks that are available.

Changing values before an entity is saved

The insert and update hooks are triggered after an entity has been saved. There is also a pre-save hook that allows you to manipulate the entity before it is saved.

This hook is often used to populate empty values or ensure values match an expected state. For example, in the *Creating an editorial workflow with content moderation* recipe in *Chapter 2, Content Building Experience*, we used the `Content Moderation` module. The `Content Moderation` module uses the `hook_entity_presave()` hook to ensure the content is marked as published or unpublished based on the workflow's state.

Creating an event subscriber to react to events

Drupal has two ways of integrating various parts of the system: using hooks or events. Hooks have been a part of Drupal for its entire lifespan and events were introduced in Drupal 8. Unlike the hook system, which has implicit registration, the event dispatch system uses explicit registration for an event.

The events dispatcher system comes from the Symfony framework and allows components to easily interact with one another. Within Drupal, and integrated Symfony components, events are dispatched, and event subscribers can listen to the events and react to changes or other processes.

In this recipe, we will subscribe to the `RequestEvent` event, which fires when a request is first handled. If the user is not logged in, we will navigate them to the login page.

How to do it...

1. Create `src/EventSubscriber/RequestSubscriber.php` in your module.
2. Define the `RequestSubscriber` class, which implements the `EventSubscriberInterface` interface:

```php
<?php

namespace Drupal\mymodule\EventSubscriber;

use Symfony\Component\EventDispatcher\EventSubscriber
    Interface;

class RequestSubscriber implements EventSubscriber
    Interface {

}
```

3. To satisfy the interface requirements, we must add a getSubscribedEvents method. This tells the system which events we are subscribing to and the method that needs to be invoked:

```php
<?php

namespace Drupal\mymodule\EventSubscriber;

use Symfony\Component\EventDispatcher\EventSubscriber
    Interface;
use Symfony\Component\HttpKernel\Event\RequestEvent;

class RequestSubscriber implements EventSubscriber
    Interface {

  /**
   * {@inheritdoc}
   */
  public static function getSubscribedEvents() {
    return [
      RequestEvent::class => ['doAnonymousRedirect',
        28],
    ];
  }

}
```

Event names are derived from the PHP class name for the event object. In the getSubscribedEvent method, we construct an associative array to be returned. The event class name is the key and our class method to invoke when that event is dispatched.

Note

Priorities will be discussed in the *How it works...* section. It is provided in the example to resolve possible conflicts when the dynamic_page_cache module is enabled.

4. Create the `doAnonymousRedirect` method we specified, which will receive the `RequestEvent` object for the current request:

```php
<?php

namespace Drupal\mymodule\EventSubscriber;

use Drupal\Core\Url;
use Symfony\Component\EventDispatcher\EventSubscriber
    Interface;
use Symfony\Component\HttpFoundation\RedirectResponse;
use Symfony\Component\HttpKernel\Event\RequestEvent;

class RequestSubscriber implements EventSubscriber
    Interface {

  /**
   * Redirects all anonymous users to the login page.
   *
   * @param \Symfony\Component\HttpKernel\Event\
   *    RequestEvent $event
   *      The event.
   */
  public function doAnonymousRedirect(RequestEvent
    $event) {
    // Make sure we are not on the user login route.
    if (\Drupal::routeMatch()->getRouteName() ==
        'user.login') {
      return;
    }
    // Check if the current user is logged in.
    if (\Drupal::currentUser()->isAnonymous()) {
      // If they are not logged in, create a redirect
        response.
      $url = Url::fromRoute('user.login')->toString();
      $redirect = new RedirectResponse($url);
      // Set the redirect response on the event,
```

```
                 canceling default response.
            $event->setResponse($redirect);
        }
    }


    /**
     * {@inheritdoc}
     */
    public static function getSubscribedEvents() {
        return [
            RequestEvent::class => ['doAnonymousRedirect',
                28],
        ];
    }


}
```

To prevent a redirect loop, we will use the RouteMatch service to get the current route object and verify that we are not already on the user.login route page.

Then, we check whether the user is anonymous and, if they are, set the event's response to a redirect response.

5. Now that we have created our class, create a mymodule.services.yml file in your module's directory.

6. We must register our class with the service container so that Drupal recognizes that it will act as an event subscriber:

```
services:
  mymodule.request_subscriber:
    class: Drupal\mymodule\EventSubscriber\
        RequestSubscriber
    tags:
      - { name: event_subscriber }
```

The event_subscriber tag tells the container to invoke the getSubscribedEvents method and register its methods.

7. Install the module or rebuild Drupal's caches if it has been already installed.

8. Navigate to any page as an anonymous user – you will be redirected to the login form.

How it works...

Throughout Drupal and Symfony, component events can be passed to the event dispatcher. The `event_dispatcher` service in Drupal is an optimized version of the one provided by Symfony but is completely interoperable and provides backward compatibility layers with Symfony. When the container is built, all services tagged as `event_subscriber` are gathered. They are then registered into the `event_dispatcher` service, keyed by the events returned in the `getSubscribedEvents` method.

> **Note**
>
> Symfony 4.3 changed how events are dispatched. Previously, events were identified only by name, with the event object serving as a value object. With Symfony 4.3, the event name was made optional. This also aligns with the PSR-14 Event Dispatcher by the PHP-FIG.

When the `event_dispatcher` service is told to dispatch an event, it invokes the registered methods on all subscribed services. Drupal still primarily uses named events over event objects, as many events leverage the same event object class.

The `\Symfony\Component\HttpKernel\KernelEvents` class documents the events available to interact with the request life cycle to become a response and even after the response is sent, as we did with `RequestEvent`. Then, there are events, such as `ConfigEvents::SAVE` and `ConfigEvents::DELETE`, that are dispatched and allow you to react to a configuration being saved or deleted but are not able to adjust the configuration entity directly through the event object.

There's more...

Event subscribers require knowledge of creating services, registering them, and even dependency injection. We'll discuss this some more in the next section.

Using dependency injection

Drupal utilizes a service container that allows you to declare classes and services and define their dependencies. For services, a dependency is an argument that must be passed to its constructor. Dependency injection is a software design concept, and at its base level, it provides a means to use a class without having to directly reference it. In our example, we retrieved services multiple times using the `\Drupal` global static class. This is convenient but is a bad practice within services. It can make testing more difficult.

To implement dependency injection, first, we will add a constructor to our class that accepts the services used (`current_route_match` and `current_user`) and matches protected properties to store them:

```
/**
 * The route match.
 *
 * @var \Drupal\Core\Routing\RouteMatchInterface
 */
protected $routeMatch;

/**
 * Account proxy.
 *
 * @var \Drupal\Core\Session\AccountProxyInterface
 */
protected $accountProxy;

/**
 * Creates a new RequestSubscriber object.
 *
 * @param \Drupal\Core\Routing\RouteMatchInterface
 *    $route_match
 * The route match.
 * @param \Drupal\Core\Session\AccountProxyInterface
 *    $account_proxy
 * The current user.
 */
public function __construct(RouteMatchInterface
  $route_match, AccountProxyInterface $account_proxy) {
  $this->routeMatch = $route_match;
  $this->accountProxy = $account_proxy;
}
```

We can then replace any calls to `\Drupal::` with `$this->`:

```
/**
 * Redirects all anonymous users to the login page.
```

```
     *
     * @param \Symfony\Component\HttpKernel\Event\Request
         Event $event
     *     The event.
     */
    public function doAnonymousRedirect(RequestEvent $event)
{
    // Make sure we are not on the user login route.
    if ($this->routeMatch->getRouteName() == 'user.login') {
      return;
    }
    // Check if the current user is logged in.
    if ($this->accountProxy->isAnonymous()) {
      // If they are not logged in, create a redirect
        response.
      $url = Url::fromRoute('user.login')->toString();
      $redirect = new RedirectResponse($url);
      // Set the redirect response on the event, canceling
        default response.
      $event->setResponse($redirect);
    }
  }
}
```

Finally, we will update `mymodule.services.yml` to specify our constructor arguments so that they will be injected when the container runs our event subscriber:

```
services:
  mymodule.request_subscriber:
    class: Drupal\mymodule\EventSubscriber\
        RequestSubscriber
    arguments: ['@current_route_match', '@current_user']
    tags:
      - { name: event_subscriber }
```

Dependency injection feels and seems magical at first. However, with use and practice, it will begin to make more sense and become second nature when developing with Drupal.

See also

- PSR-14 Event Dispatcher by PHP-FIG: https://www.php-fig.org/psr/psr-14/

Creating a custom Drush command

Throughout this book, we have used Drush to perform operations on a Drupal site from the command line. Custom commands for Drush can be provided by modules. This allows developers to create commands that help them manage their Drupal sites. Drush requires modules to provide a composer.json file that instructs them where to load a services file that will register Drush commands.

In this recipe, we will create a new Drush command for a custom module that prints the location of where Drupal is installed.

How to do it...

1. Drush provides a command to generate the required files for creating a command file for custom commands. To begin, run the following command:

```
php vendor/bin/drush generate drush-command-file
```

2. You will be prompted to provide a value for the Module machine name; type mymodule for the name of our module.

3. Next, press *Enter* to skip converting a legacy Drush command file.

4. The command output will display the files that have been created or updated:

```
Welcome to drush-command-file generator!

Module machine name:
➤ mymodule

Absolute path to legacy Drush command file (optional – for porting):
➤

The following directories and files have been created or updated:

• modules/custom/mymodule/composer.json
• modules/custom/mymodule/drush.services.yml
• modules/custom/mymodule/src/Commands/MymoduleCommands.php
```

Figure 4.6 – Output from the command file generator

The `composer.json` file contains information about `drush.services.yml`. The `drush.services.yml` file is a service definition file that contains classes and their arguments. It has an initial definition for the created `MymoduleCommands` class. The `MymoduleCommands` class is generated with sample commands as well.

5. The `drush.services.yml` file is important. It is a services definition file that tags services as `drush.command` so that classes are collected by Drush:

```
services:
  mymodule.commands:
    class: \Drupal\mymodule\Commands\MymoduleCommands
    tags:
      - { name: drush.command }
```

6. Commands are defined as class methods in a command file. Open the `src/Commands/MymoduleCommands.php` file to create a new command.

7. Create a new method called `helloWorld`, which we will use to provide the `hello-world` command:

```
public function helloWorld() {

}
```

8. Next, add the following code to the command to output a message and display the directory of the Drupal site:

```
public function helloWorld() {
  $this->io()->writeln('Hello world!');
  $self_alias = \Drush\Drush::aliasManager()->get
    Self();
  $drupal_root = $self_alias->root();
  $this->io()->writeln("Drupal is located at: {$dru
  pal_root}");
}
```

This method uses the `io()` method to get the input/output helper to write content back to the terminal. The code then gets the current site alias from the alias manager. Drush supports using aliases to connect to remote Drupal sites, with the "self" alias being the current local Drupal site. The code then calls the `root` method to display the directory of the Drupal code base.

9. Finally, we need to provide annotations in the document block of the method. This is how Drush interprets the command name:

```
/**
 * @command mymodule:hello-world
 */
public function helloWorld() {
  $this->io()->writeln('Hello world!');
  $self_alias = \Drush\Drush::aliasManager()->get
      Self();
  $drupal_root = $self_alias->root();
  $this->io()->writeln("Drupal is located at: {
      $drupal_root}");
}
```

10. Now, we can execute the command. First, we must clear the cache so that Drupal and Drush can register the new command. Then, we can execute it:

```
php vendor/bin/drush cache-rebuild
php vendor/bin/drush mymodule:hello-world
```

How it works...

The Drush command line bootstraps Drupal when it is launched. During that launch, it takes the Drupal service container and adds and registers the \Drush\Drupal\FindCommandsCompilerPass compiler pass. This compiler pass scans the services.yml files collected by Drupal and finds services tagged with drush.command. This is why modules must have a drush.services. yml file. This defines the services and tags them appropriately to be discovered by Drush.

Since Drush wraps around Drupal, command files may also have other services injected into them as dependencies. Here is an example of a drush.services.yml file using dependency injection from the Pathauto module:

```
services:
  pathauto.commands:
    class: \Drupal\pathauto\Commands\PathautoCommands
    arguments:
      - '@config.factory'
      - '@plugin.manager.alias_type'
      - '@pathauto.alias_storage_helper'
```

```
tags:
  - { name: drush.command }
```

See also

- Drush command authoring documentation: `https://www.drush.org/latest/commands/`

5

Creating Custom Pages

In this chapter, we will make custom pages with controllers. A controller is a class that contains a method used to build a page when Drupal is accessed at a specific path. Creating custom pages allows you to extend Drupal beyond just the content pages. This chapter will cover the process of creating custom pages, receiving dynamic values from paths, and serving JSON or file download responses.

In this chapter, we will learn about the following recipes:

- Defining a controller to provide a custom page
- Using route parameters
- Creating a dynamic redirect page
- Creating a JSON response
- Serving files for download

Technical requirements

This chapter requires an existing custom module installed on your Drupal site. This custom module will contain the controllers created throughout this recipe. *Chapter 4, Extending Drupal with Custom Code*, covers how to create a custom module. You can find the full code used in this chapter on GitHub: `https://github.com/PacktPublishing/Drupal-10-Development-Cookbook/tree/main/chp05`

Defining a controller to provide a custom page

Whenever an HTTP request is made to a Drupal site, the path for the URL is routed to a controller. Controllers are responsible for returning the response for a path that has been defined as a route. Generally, these controllers return render arrays for Drupal's render system to convert into HTML.

In this recipe, we will define a controller that returns a render array to display a message on the page.

How to do it...

1. First, we need to create the `src/Controller` directory in the module's directory. We will put our controller class in this directory, which gives our `controller` class the `Controller` namespace:

    ```
    mkdir -p src/Controller
    ```

2. Create a file named `HelloWorldController.php` in the controller directory. This will hold our `HelloWorldController` controller class.

3. Our `HelloWorldController` class will extend the `ControllerBase` base class provided by Drupal core:

    ```php
    <?php

    namespace Drupal\mymodule\Controller;

    use Drupal\Core\Controller\ControllerBase;

    class HelloWorldController extends ControllerBase {

    }
    ```

    Following PSR-4 autoloading conventions, our class is in the `\Drupal\mymodule\Controller` namespace, which Drupal is able to determine as the `src/Controller` directory in our module. As per PSR-4, the filename and class name must also be the same.

    The `\Drupal\Core\Controller\ControllerBase` class provides a handful of utility methods that could be leveraged.

4. Next, we will create a method that returns a render array to display a string of text. Add the following method to our `HelloWorldController` class:

    ```php
    /**
     * Returns markup for our custom page.
     *
     * @returns array
     *   The render array.
     */
    public function page(): array {
      return [
    ```

```
      '#markup' => '<p>Hello world!</p>'
  ];
}
```

The page method returns a render array that the Drupal rendering system will parse. The `#markup` key denotes a value that does not have any additional rendering or theming and allows basic HTML elements.

5. Create the `mymodule.routing.yml` file in your module's directory. The `routing.yml` file is provided by modules to define routes.

6. The first step in defining a route is to provide a name for the route, which is used as its identifier for URL generation and other purposes:

```
mymodule.hello_world
```

7. Give the route a path:

```
mymodule.hello_world:
  path: /hello-world
```

8. Next, we register the path with our controller. This is done using the `defaults` key where we provide the controller and page title:

```
mymodule.hello_world:
  path: /hello-world
  defaults:
    _controller: Drupal\mymodule\Controller\
        HelloWorldController::page
    _title: 'Hello world!'
```

The `_controller` key is the fully qualified class name with the class method to be used. The `_title` key provides the page title to be displayed.

9. Lastly, define a requirements key to specify the access requirements:

```
mymodule.hello_world:
  path: /hello-world
  defaults:
    _controller: Drupal\mymodule\Controller\
        HelloWorldController::page
    _title: 'Hello world!'
  requirements:
    _permission: 'access content'
```

The _permission option tells the routing system to verify the current user has specific permission in order to view a page.

10. Drupal caches its routing information. We must rebuild Drupal's caches in order for it to be aware of the module's new route:

```
php vendor/bin/drush cr
```

11. Go to /hello-world on your Drupal site and view your custom page:

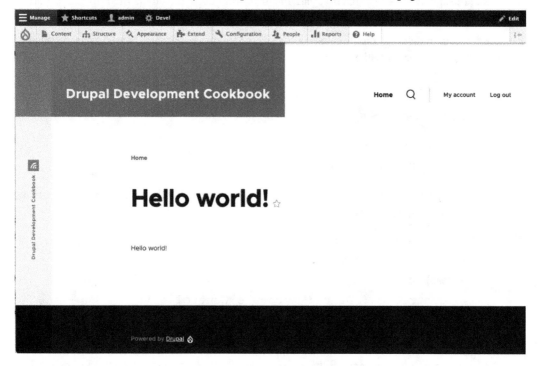

Figure 5.1 – The /hello-world page

How it works...

Drupal's routing is built on top of Symfony's routing component. Each route has a method in a controller class that returns a response. Most commonly, the returned response is a render array. Other recipes in this chapter will show you how to return response objects directly. The routes are collected into Drupal's routing system.

When an HTTP request comes to Drupal, the system tries to match the path to known routes. If a route is found, the route's definition is used to deliver the page. If a route cannot be found, a 404 page is displayed. If a route is found, Drupal performs access checks based on the requirements key. If the requirements key conditions fail, then Drupal may return a 403 page or 404 page.

After the controller has returned the response, Drupal checks whether the value is a render array or a response from Symfony's `HttpFoundation` component. The `onViewRenderArray` method of the `MainContentViewSubscriber` class checks whether the controller response is an array. If it is, the renderer is then resolved and converts the render array into an HTML response. Otherwise, it allows the returned response object to be handled.

When writing controllers, the `ControllerBase` base class is not required; but it does provide simplified access to common services without setting up dependency injection.

There's more...

In the following sections, we will cover more items about routes.

Route requirements

Routes can define different access requirements through the requirements key. Multiple validators can be added. However, there must be one that provides a true result, or else the route will return 403, access denied. This is true if the route defines no requirement validators.

Route requirement validators are defined by implementing `\Drupal\Core\Routing\Access\AccessInterface`. The following list shows some of the common requirement validators defined throughout Drupal core:

- `_access: 'TRUE'`: This always grants access to the route. Be careful when granting this instead of a permission or role check, as this means anyone can access the route.

- `_entity_access`: This validates that the current user can perform an entity operation. For example, `node.update` verifies the user can update the node in the URL parameters.

- `_permission`: This checks whether the current user has the provided permissions.

- `_user_is_logged_in`: This validates that the user is logged in. The value of `'TRUE'` requires the user to be logged in and `'FALSE'` is for the user to be logged out. An example of `'FALSE'` is for the user login page.

Providing dynamic routes

The routing system allows modules to define routes programmatically. This can be accomplished by providing a `routing_callbacks` key that defines a class and method that will return an array of the `\Symfony\Component\Routing\Route` objects.

In the module's `routing.yml` file, you will define the routing callbacks key and related class:

```
route_callbacks:
  - 'Drupal\mymodule\Routing\CustomRoutes::routes'
```

The `Drupal\mymodule\Routing\CustomRoutes` class will then have a method named routes, which returns an array of route objects:

```php
<?php

namespace Drupal\mymodule\Routing;

use Symfony\Component\Routing\Route;

class CustomRoutes {
  public function routes() {
    $routes = [];
    // Create mypage route programmatically
    $routes['mymodule.hello_world'] = new Route(
      // Path definition
      '/hello-world',
      // Route defaults
      [
        '_controller' =>
        '\Drupal\mymodule\Controller\
            HelloWorldController::page',
        '_title' => 'Hello world',
      ],
      // Route requirements
      [
        '_permission' => 'access content',
      ]
    );
    return $routes;
  }
}
```

If a module provides a class that interacts with routes, the best practice is to place it in the routing portion of the module's namespace. This helps you identify its purpose.

The invoked method is expected to return an array of initiated route objects. The Route class takes the following arguments:

- path: This is the path for the route.
- defaults: This is the array of defaults for the route and its controller.
- requirements: This is an array of validators to make sure the route is accessible.
- options: This is an array that can be passed and used optionally to hold metadata about the route.

Altering existing routes

When the routing system is being rebuilt, an event is dispatched to alter the discovered routes. This involves implementing an event subscriber. Drupal provides a base class to ease this implementation. Here, \Drupal\Core\Routing\RouteSubscriberBase implements the required interface methods and subscribes to the RoutingEvents::ALTER event.

Create a src/Routing/RouteSubscriber.php file for your module to hold the route subscriber class:

```php
<?php

namespace Drupal\mymodule\Routing;

use Drupal\Core\Routing\RouteSubscriberBase;
use Symfony\Component\Routing\RouteCollection;

class RouteSubscriber extends RouteSubscriberBase {
  /**
   * {@inheritdoc}
   */
  public function alterRoutes(RouteCollection $collection) {
    // Change path of mymodule.hello_world to just 'hello'
    if ($route = $collection->get('mymodule.hello_world')) {
      $route->setPath('/hello');
    }
  }
}
```

The preceding code extends `RouteSubscriberBase` and implements the `alterRoutes` method. We fetch the route object from the route collection, if it exists, and change the path from `/hello-world` to just `/hello`.

Then, we must register the event subscriber in the module's `mymodule.services.yml`:

```yaml
services:
  mymodule.route_subscriber:
    class: Drupal\mymodule\Routing\RouteSubscriber
    tags:
      - { name: event_subscriber }
```

After adding this change, clear the Drupal cache. This makes Drupal aware of our event subscriber so that it can react to the dispatch of the `RoutingEvents::ALTER` event.

See also

- The Symfony Routing component: `https://symfony.com/doc/current/create_framework/routing.html`

Using route parameters

In the previous recipe, we defined a route and controller that responded to the `/hello-world` path. A route can add variables to the path, called route parameters, so that the controller can handle different URLs.

In this recipe, we will create a route that takes a user ID as a route parameter to display information about that user.

Getting started

This recipe uses the route created in the *Defining a controller* recipe to provide a custom page.

How to do it...

1. First, remove the `src/Routing/RouteSubscriber.php` file and `mymodule.services.yml` from the previous section and clear the Drupal cache, so it does not interfere with what we are about to do.

2. Next, edit `routing.yml` so that we can add a route parameter of `user` to the path:

   ```yaml
   path: /hello-world/{user}
   ```

   Route parameters are wrapped with an opening bracket ({) and a closing bracket (}).

3. Next, we will update the requirements key to specify that the user parameter should be an integer for a user ID, and that the current user has access to view other profiles:

```
requirements:
  user: '\d+'
  _entity_access: 'user.view'
```

The user key under requirements represents the same route parameter. The routing system allows you to provide regular expressions to validate the value of a route parameter. This validates the user parameter as any digit value.

We then use the _entity_access requirement to verify the current user has access to perform the view operation on the entity type user.

4. Then, we add a new options key to the route definition so that we can identify what type of value the user route parameter is:

```
options:
  parameters:
    user:
      type: 'entity:user'
```

This defines the user route parameter as being of the entity:user type. Drupal will use this to convert the ID value into a user object for our controller.

5. Open the src/Controller/HelloWorldController.php file so that the page method can be updated to receive the user route parameter value.

6. Update the page method to receive the user route parameter as a user object in its method parameters:

```
/**
 * Returns markup for our custom page.
 *
 * @param \Drupal\user\UserInterface $user
 *   The user parameter.
 *
 * @returns array
 *   The render array.
 */
public function page(UserInterface $user): array {
  return [
    '#markup' => '<p>Hello world!</p>'
  ];
}
```

The routing system passes route parameter values to the method based on parameter names for the method. Our parameter's definition specifies that Drupal should convert the ID in the URL into a user object.

7. Let's adjust the returned text from `Hello world!` to replace "world" with the email of the user object:

```
return [
    '#markup' => sprintf('<p>Hello %s!</p>',
        $user->getEmail()),
];
```

We use `sprintf` to return a formatted string that contains the user's email address.

8. Drupal caches its routing information. We must rebuild Drupal's caches in order for it to be aware of the changes to the module's new route:

```
php vendor/bin/drush cr
```

9. When you visit /hello-world, the route's old path without a route parameter, Drupal will return a 404 error for page not found.

10. When you visit /hello-world/1, the page will display our formatted text with the user's email address:

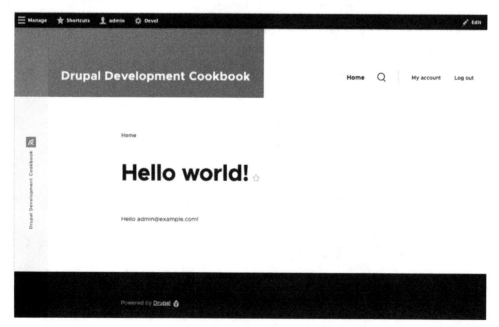

Figure 5.2 – The formatted text with the user's email address

How it works...

As discussed in the previous recipe, the routing system compares the path from the incoming HTTP request. The path is then matched against registered routes. When a route does not contain route parameters, the match is simple. To accomplish route matching based on an incoming path from a URL, the route has a matching pattern compiled. This matching pattern converts the route path and its route patterns into a regular expression that can be matched against the path from the incoming URL.

The `Drupal\Core\Routing\RouteCompiler` class extends the `RouteCompiler` from Symfony's routing component. When a route is compiled, the route's path is converted into a regular expression that is used to compare it against the path from the incoming URL. Given our route path of `/hello-world/{user}` with a requirement of `\d+`, here is the compiled regular expression the user route parameter matching the regular expression used to match our route:

```
#^/hello\-world/(?P<user>\d+)$#sDu
```

When this regular expression is evaluated through `preg_match`, the matches will return an associated array of matches. If the path from the incoming URL matches, then the matches array will contain a key of user with the value found in the path.

Drupal's routing system has a concept of parameter converters that transform route parameter values from their value raw. With the route's definition of `options.parameters.user` as `entity:user`, the `\Drupal\Core\ParamConverter\EntityConverter` class converts the user ID into a loaded user object.

After the route has been matched and the parameters converted, they are matched against the defined parameters for the controller method. The `ArgumentResolver` from Symfony's `HttpKernel` uses reflection to assemble the correct argument order before calling the controller to handle the request.

See also

- Symfony's documentation for the HttpKernel component and argument resolving: `https://symfony.com/doc/current/components/http_kernel.html#4-getting-the-controller-arguments`

- Symfony's documentation for the routing component and route parameters: `https://symfony.com/doc/current/routing.html#route-parameters`

Creating a dynamic redirect page

Controllers for routes in Drupal can return request objects provided by the Symfony `HttpFoundation` component instead of a render array. When a response object is returned, the render system is bypassed and the response object is handled directly.

In this recipe, we will create a route that redirects authenticated users to the homepage and anonymous users to the user login form.

How to do it...

1. First, we need to create the `src/Controller` directory in the module's directory. We will put our controller class in this directory, which gives our controller class the `Controller` namespace:

   ```
   mkdir -p src/Controller
   ```

2. Create a file named `RedirectController.php` in the `Controller` directory. This will hold our `RedirectController` controller class.

3. Our `RedirectController` class will extend the `ControllerBase` base class provided by Drupal core:

   ```php
   <?php

   namespace Drupal\mymodule\Controller;

   use Drupal\Core\Controller\ControllerBase;

   class RedirectController extends ControllerBase {

   }
   ```

   Following PSR-4 autoloading conventions, our class is in the `\Drupal\mymodule\Controller` namespace, which Drupal can determine as the `src/Controller` directory in our module. As per PSR-4, the filename and class name must also be the same.

   The `\Drupal\Core\Controller\ControllerBase` class provides a handful of utility methods that can be leveraged.

4. Next, we will create a method that checks whether the current user is logged in or not. Update the `RedirectController` class to include the following method:

   ```php
   <?php

   namespace Drupal\mymodule\Controller;

   use Drupal\Core\Controller\ControllerBase;
   use Symfony\Component\HttpFoundation\RedirectResponse;
   ```

```
class RedirectController extends ControllerBase {

  /**
   * Returns redirect to home or user login form.
   *
   * @return \Symfony\Component\HttpFoundation\
   *     RedirectResponse
   *   The redirect response.
   */
  public function page(): RedirectResponse {
    if ($this->currentUser()->isAuthenticated()) {
      // Redirect to the homepage.
    }
    else {
      // Redirect to the user login form.
    }
  }
}
```

The `ControllerBase` class provides a `currentUser` method that accesses the current user object. We can call the `isAuthenticated` method to check whether the user is logged in or not.

5. Next, we will update the code to return a `RedirectResponse` object to a URL that is generated from a route name:

```
public function page(): RedirectResponse {
  if ($this->currentUser()->isAuthenticated()) {
    $route_name = '<front>';
  }
  else {
    $route_name = 'user.login';
  }
  $url = \Drupal\Core\Url::fromRoute($route_name);
  return new RedirectResponse($url->toString());
}
```

We set the route name in the $route_name variable. While <front> is not a typical path, it is a route name available to route to the appropriate path that is set as the homepage. Drupal core defines special slugs such as <front> and <none> for convenience in routing. See the core Url class for more information.

We then construct a new URL object with the static fromRoute method of the \Drupal\ Core\Url class. We then return a RedirectResponse object that redirects to our URL. We have to get the string for the URL using the toString method on the URL object.

6. Create the mymodule.routing.yml file in your module's directory. The routing.yml file is provided by modules to define routes.

7. The first step in defining a route is to provide a name for the route, which is used as its identifier for URL generation and other purposes:

```
mymodule.user_redirect
```

8. Give the route a path:

```
mymodule.user_redirect:
   path: /user-redirect
```

9. Next, we register the path with our controller. This is done with the defaults key where we provide the controller:

```
mymodule.user_redirect:
   path: /user-redirect
   defaults:
     _controller: Drupal\mymodule\Controller\
         RedirectController::page
```

The _controller key is the fully qualified class name with the class method to be used.

10. Lastly, define a requirements key to specify the access requirements. We want the route to always be accessible since we handle authenticated and anonymous users:

```
mymodule.user_redirect:
   path: /user-redirect
   defaults:
     _controller: Drupal\mymodule\Controller\
         RedirectController::page
   requirements:
     _access: 'TRUE'
```

The _access option allows us to specify that a route is always accessible.

11. Drupal caches its routing information. We must rebuild Drupal's caches in order for it to be aware of the module's new route:

```
php vendor/bin/drush cr
```

12. Go to /user-redirect on your Drupal site as an anonymous user and you will be redirected to the user login form. If you are authenticated, you will be redirected to the homepage.

How it works...

The RedirectResponse object comes from Symfony's HttpFoundation component and represents an HTTP redirect response. When converted into a response sent from the web server, it will set the location header to the URL provided. It also passes one of the valid 3xx HTTP status codes. The redirect response defaults to the HTTP status code of 302 Found. A 302 redirect is intended to be temporary and not cacheable by the browser.

Drupal can generate URLs from a given route name. As we have learned in previous recipes, route names are used to identify a specific path, controller, and other information. When invoking toString, the URL object invokes the URL generator to convert the route name into a URL.

See also

- The HTTP/1.1 RFC Redirection 3xx specification: https://datatracker.ietf.org/doc/html/rfc2616#section-10.3

Creating a JSON response

Routes can also return **JavaScript Object Notation (JSON)** responses. A JSON response is often used for building API routes since it is an interchange format that is supported by all programming languages. This allows exposing data to be consumed by a third-party consumer.

In this recipe, we will create a route that returns a JSON response containing information about the Drupal site.

How to do it...

1. First, we need to create the src/Controller directory in the module's directory. We will put our controller class in this directory, which gives our controller class the Controller namespace:

```
mkdir -p src/Controller
```

2. Create a file named SiteInfoController.php in the Controller directory. This will hold our SiteInfoController controller class.

3. Our `SiteInfoController` class will extend the `ControllerBase` base class provided by Drupal core:

```php
<?php

namespace Drupal\mymodule\Controller;

use Drupal\Core\Controller\ControllerBase;
use Symfony\Component\HttpFoundation\JsonResponse;

class SiteInfoController extends ControllerBase {

}
```

Following PSR-4 autoloading conventions, our class is in the `\Drupal\mymodule\Controller` namespace, which Drupal can determine as the `src/Controller` directory in our module. As per PSR-4, the filename and class name must also be the same.

The `\Drupal\Core\Controller\ControllerBase` class provides a handful of utility methods that can be leveraged.

4. Next, we will create a method that returns a `JsonResponse` object. Add the following method to our `SiteInfoController` class:

```php
/**
 * Returns site info in a JSON response.
 *
 * @return \Symfony\Component\HttpFoundation\
 *     JsonResponse
 *    The JSON response.
 */
public function page(): JsonResponse {
  return new JsonResponse();
}
```

The page method returns a `JsonResponse` object. This ensures the `Content-Type` header for the response is set to `application/json`.

5. Let's add content to our response object with data from the `system.site` configuration object:

```php
/**
 * Returns site info in a JSON response.
```

```
 *
 * @return \Symfony\Component\HttpFoundation\
      JsonResponse
 *    The JSON response.
 */
public function page(): JsonResponse {
  $config = $this->config('system.site');
  return new JsonResponse([
    'name' => $config->get('name'),
    'slogan' => $config->get('slogan'),
    'email' => $config->get('mail')
  ]);
}
```

We use the `config` method provided by `ControllerBase` to retrieve the `system.site` configuration object. Then, we provide an associative array of data to the `JsonResponse` object. The array will be converted into JSON when the response is sent.

6. Create the `mymodule.routing.yml` file in your module's directory. This file is provided by modules to define routes.

7. The first step in defining a route is to provide a name for the route, which is used as its identifier for URL generation and other purposes:

```
mymodule.site_info
```

8. Give the route a path:

```
mymodule.site_info:
  path: /site-info
```

9. Next, we register the path with our controller. This is done with the `defaults` key where we provide the controller and page title:

```
mymodule.site_info:
  path: /site-info
  defaults:
    _controller: Drupal\mymodule\Controller\
        SiteInfoController::page
```

The `_controller` key is the fully qualified class name with the class method to be used.

10. Lastly, define a requirements key to specify the access requirements:

```
mymodule.site_info:
  path: /site-info
  defaults:
    _controller: Drupal\mymodule\Controller\
        SiteInfoController::page
  requirements:
    _access: 'TRUE'
```

The _access option allows the route to always be accessible.

11. Drupal caches its routing information. We must rebuild Drupal's caches in order for it to be aware of the module's new route:

```
php vendor/bin/drush cr
```

12. Go to /site-info on your Drupal site, and you should receive a JSON response like the following:

```
{
  "name": "Drupal Development Cookbook",
  "slogan": "Practical recipes to harness the power of
    Drupal 10.",
  "email": "admin@example.com"
}
```

How it works...

The JsonResponse object is used to represent a JSON response. Its constructor receives an array or object of data and passes it to PHP's json_encode function for you. It sets the response's Content-Type header to be application/json.

There's more...

The JSON response controller can be enhanced to leverage the harness-caching capabilities of Drupal.

Caching JSON responses with Drupal

Drupal also provides \Drupal\Core\Cache\CacheableJsonResponse. This extends JsonResponse and allows the response to be cached by Drupal's page caching. However, you will want to make the system.site configuration object a cacheable dependency of the response. That way the response cache is invalidated if that configuration object is changed.

The code would be updated with the following:

```
class SiteInfoController extends ControllerBase {

  /**
   * Returns site info in a JSON response.
   *
   * @return \Symfony\Component\HttpFoundation\JsonResponse
   *   The JSON response.
   */
  public function page(): JsonResponse {
    $config = $this->config('system.site');
    $response = new \Drupal\Core\Cache\
        CacheableJsonResponse([
      'name' => $config->get('name'),
      'slogan' => $config->get('slogan'),
      'email' => $config->get('mail')
    ]);
    $response->addCacheableDependency($config);
    return $response;
  }

}
```

The main difference is that we do not directly return the response object. We set the configuration object as a cacheable dependency, first.

See also

- *Chapter 12, Building APIs with Drupal*

Serving files for download

Routes can be used to serve file downloads with the `BinaryFileResponse` response object. Using the `BinaryFileResponse` to serve a file for download allows you to keep the original file's URL private or to send dynamic content as a file download.

In this recipe, we will create a route that provides a download for a PDF.

Getting started

This recipe uses a PDF file that is located in the same directory as the module. You can use any other available file type, such as a text file. A test PDF can be found on the World Wide Web Consortium website at https://www.w3.org/WAI/ER/tests/xhtml/testfiles/resources/pdf/dummy.pdf.

How to do it...

1. First, we need to create the src/Controller directory in the module's directory. We will put our controller class in this directory, which gives our controller class the Controller namespace:

    ```
    mkdir -p src/Controller
    ```

2. Create a file named DownloadController.php in the Controller directory. This will hold our DownloadController controller class:

    ```php
    <?php

    namespace Drupal\mymodule\Controller;

    class SiteInfoController {

    }
    ```

    Following PSR-4 autoloading conventions, our class is in the \Drupal\mymodule\Controller namespace, which Drupal is able to determine as the src/Controller directory in our module. As per PSR-4, the filename and class name must also be the same.

3. Next, we will create a method that returns a BinaryFileResponse object. Add the following method to our DownloadController class:

    ```php
    /**
     * Downloads a file.
     *
     * @return \Symfony\Component\HttpFoundation\
     *       BinaryFileResponse
     *   The file response.
     */
    public function page(): BinaryFileResponse {
      // File paths are relative to the document root
          (web.)
    ```

```
        $file_path = 'modules/custom/mymodule/dummy.pdf';

        $response = new BinaryFileResponse($file_path);
        $response->setContentDisposition('attachment',
            basename($file_path));
        return $response;
    }
```

The page method returns a `BinaryFileResponse` object. We define a file path where our PDF exists. The file path may be relative to Drupal's document root (web). Our module's directory is `modules/custom/mymodule` relative to the document root. We set the `Content-Disposition` header to attachment and specify a filename so that the file automatically downloads. We use PHP's basename function to get the filename from the path.

4. The controller is almost ready. We should also provide a `Content-Type` header for the response. Using the `file.mime_type.guesser` service, we can get the correct header value:

```
    /**
     * Downloads a file.
     *
     * @return \Symfony\Component\HttpFoundation\
     *     BinaryFileResponse
     *   The file response.
     */
    public function page(): BinaryFileResponse {
      // File paths are relative to the document root
          (web.)
      $file_path = 'modules/custom/mymodule/dummy.pdf';

      /** @var \Drupal\Core\File\MimeType\
          MimeTypeGuesser $guesser */
      $guesser = \Drupal::service
            ('file.mime_type.guesser');
      $mime_type = $guesser->guessMimeType($file_path);

      $response = new BinaryFileResponse($file_path);
      $response->headers->set('Content-Type',
          $mimetype);
      $response->setContentDisposition('attachment',
```

```
        basename($file_path));
    return $response;
}
```

The `file.mime_type.guesser` service is used to determine the appropriate MIME type for a file based on its extension. In this case, it would `return application/pdf`.

5. Create `mymodule.routing.yml` file in your module's directory. The `routing.yml` file is provided by modules to define routes.

6. The first step in defining a route is to provide a name for the route, which is used as its identifier for URL generation and other purposes:

```
mymodule.pdf_download
```

7. Give the route a path:

```
mymodule.pdf_download:
  path: /pdf-download
```

8. Next, we register the path with our controller. This is done with the defaults key where we provide the controller and page title:

```
mymodule.pdf_download:
  path: /pdf-download
  defaults:
    _controller: Drupal\mymodule\Controller
        \DownloadController::page
```

The `_controller` key is the fully qualified class name with the class method to be used.

9. Lastly, define a requirements key to specify the access requirements:

```
mymodule.pdf_download:
  path: /pdf-download
  defaults:
    _controller: Drupal\mymodule\Controller
        \DownloadController::page
  requirements:
    _user_is_logged_in: 'TRUE'
```

The `_user_is_logged_in` option requires a user to be authenticated to access the route.

10. Drupal caches its routing information. We must rebuild Drupal's caches in order for it to be aware of the module's new route:

```
php vendor/bin/drush cr
```

11. Go to /pdf-download on your Drupal site, and you will be prompted to download the dummy.pdf file.

How it works...

The BinaryFileResponse stores information about the file until the response is prepared to be sent. When the response is prepared to be sent, the Content-Length header is populated based on the file size. Then, when the response is sent, the contents of the file are streamed to the visitor via the web server.

6

Accessing and Working with Entities

In this chapter, we will go through the **create, read, update, and delete** (CRUD) operations of working with entities in Drupal. We will create a series of routes to create, read, update, and delete nodes that are articles.

In this chapter, we will cover the following:

- Creating and saving an entity
- Querying and loading entities
- Checking entity access
- Updating an entity's field values
- Performing entity validation
- Deleting an entity

Technical requirements

This chapter will require a custom module that has a `routing.yml` file and a controller named `ArticleController` in the `src/Controller` directory of the module. In the following recipes, the module name is mymodule. Replace as appropriate. You can find the full code used in this chapter on GitHub: `https://github.com/PacktPublishing/Drupal-10-Development-Cookbook/tree/main/chp06`

We are using the **Article content** type created by the standard Drupal installation.

The recipes in this chapter have example HTTP requests that are used to interact with code created in each recipe. These HTTP requests can be run with any HTTP client. If you use VSCode, try the **REST Client** extension (`https://marketplace.visualstudio.com/items?itemName=humao.rest-client`), or if you have PhpStorm, use the built-in **HTTP Client** (`https://www.jetbrains.com/help/idea/http-client-in-product-code-editor.html`). If for some reason you do not have an editor or cannot get those working, you can use Postman (`https://www.postman.com/`).

Creating and saving an entity

In this recipe, we will define a route to create a new article. The route will be for an HTTP POST request sending JSON to specify the article's title and body text.

How to do it...

1. Create a `store` method in the `ArticleController` controller in your module that will receive the incoming request object:

```php
<?php

namespace Drupal\mymodule\Controller;

use Drupal\Core\Controller\ControllerBase;
use Symfony\Component\HttpFoundation\JsonResponse;
use Symfony\Component\HttpFoundation\Request;

class ArticleController extends ControllerBase {

  public function store(Request $request):
      JsonResponse {

  }
}
```

We need the request object so that we can retrieve the JSON provided in the request payload.

2. Next, we will convert the request's content from JSON to a PHP array using Drupal's JSON serialization utility class:

```php
public function store(Request $request):
  JsonResponse {
```

```
    $content = $request->getContent();
    $json = \Drupal\Component\Serialization\
        Json::decode($content);
}
```

While we could use the `json_decode` function directly, leveraging utility classes provided by Drupal standardizes the way code works.

3. Then, we get the entity type manager and retrieve the entity storage for the `node` entity type:

```
public function store(Request $request):
JsonResponse {
$content = $request->getContent();
$json = \Drupal\Component\Serialization\
    Json::decode($content);

$entity_type_manager = $this->entityTypeManager();
$node_storage = $entity_type_manager->
    getStorage('node');
}
```

The entity type manager is a repository of information for entity types and is used to get handlers for entity types, such as the storage handler. When getting an entity storage handler, you pass the entity type ID.

4. From the storage, invoke the `create` method to create a new node entity object:

```
public function store(Request $request):
JsonResponse {
$content = $request->getContent();
$json = \Drupal\Component\Serialization\
    Json::decode($content);

$entity_type_manager = $this->entityTypeManager();
$node_storage = $entity_type_manager->
    getStorage('node');

$article = $node_storage->create([
  'type' => 'article',
]);
}
```

The `create` method instantiates a new entity object with the entity type class. For the node entity type, our `$article` variable will be of the `\Drupal\node\Node` type. When instantiating a new entity, you must specify its bundle, which we do with the `type` key set to `article`.

5. Provide an associative array of `title` and `body` to the `create` method, copying values from the JSON we received from the request:

```
public function store(Request $request): JsonResponse {
  $content = $request->getContent();
  $json = \Drupal\Component\Serialization\
    Json::decode($content);

  $entity_type_manager = $this->entityTypeManager();
  $node_storage = $entity_type_manager->
    getStorage('node');

  $article = $node_storage->create([
   'type' => 'article',
   'title' => $json['title'],
   'body' => $json['body'],
  ]);
}
```

6. Invoke the `save` method on the entity object to save the entity:

```
public function store(Request $request):
  JsonResponse {
  $content = $request->getContent();
  $json = \Drupal\Component\Serialization\
    Json::decode($content);

  $entity_type_manager = $this->entityTypeManager();
  $node_storage = $entity_type_manager->
    getStorage('node');

  $article = $node_storage->create([
   'type' => 'article',
   'title' => $json['title'],
   'body' => $json['body'],
```

```
]);
$article->save();
}
```

7. We will now return a response with a Location header that has the URL to the newly created now and an HTTP status code of 201 Created:

```
public function store(Request $request):
  JsonResponse {
$content = $request->getContent();
$json = \Drupal\Component\Serialization\
    Json::decode($content);

$entity_type_manager = $this->entityTypeManager();
$node_storage = $entity_type_manager->
    getStorage('node');

$article = $node_storage->create([
  'type' => 'article',
  'title' => $json['title'],
  'body' => $json['body'],
]);
$article->save();

$article_url = $article->toUrl()->setAbsolute()->
    toString();
return new JsonResponse(
  $article->toArray(),
  201,
  ['Location' => $article_url],
);
}
```

The 201 Created status code is used to represent a successful response and signifies that an item has been created. When a 201 Created response is returned, it is recommended to return a Location header with a URL to the created item. Entity classes have a toUrl method to return a URL object, and then call its toString method to convert it to a string from an object.

8. We must create the route in our module's `routing.yml` that points to the `store` method of `ArticleController` for an HTTP POST request to the `/articles` path:

```
mymodule.create_article:
  path: /articles
  defaults:
    _controller: Drupal\mymodule\Controller\
      ArticleController::store
  methods: [POST]
  requirements:
    _access: 'TRUE'
```

Routes may specify the HTTP methods they support with the `methods` key. In this recipe, we have set `requirements` to `_access: 'TRUE'` only to bypass access checks. This should be set to `_entity_create_access: 'node'`.

9. Rebuild your Drupal site's cache to make it aware of the new route:

```
php vendor/bin/drush cr
```

10. An HTTP request such as the following can then be used to create a new node that is an article on your Drupal site:

```
POST http://localhost/articles
Content-Type: application/json
Accept: application/json


{
  "title": "New article",
  "body": "Test body"
}
```

How it works...

The `create` method is used to instantiate a new entity object and returns an object of that entity type's class. For this recipe, the node storage will return entities with the `\Drupal\node\Node` class. The values accepted in the `create` method are based on that entity type's field definitions. These include the base fields and any fields created through the user interface.

The bundle for an entity type must be specified when it is created. This is used to determine the fields available since each bundle can have different fields. For nodes, the bundle field is named `type`. That is why we provide the `article` value for the `type` key.

The `save` method then commits the entity to the database storage.

When an entity is inserted on its first save, the entity storage fires invoke the following hooks, allowing you to hook into the insert of a new entity. The entity being inserted is passed as an argument:

- `hook_ENTITY_TYPE_presave`
- `hook_entity_presave`
- `hook_ENTITY_TYPE_insert`
- `hook_entity_insert`

Querying and loading entities

In this recipe, we will use an entity query to find all published articles and return them as JSON. We will also allow specifying the sort order via a query parameter.

How to do it...

1. Create an `index` method in the `ArticleController` controller in your module that will receive the incoming `Request` object:

```php
<?php

namespace Drupal\mymodule\Controller;

use Drupal\Core\Controller\ControllerBase;
use Symfony\Component\HttpFoundation\JsonResponse;
use Symfony\Component\HttpFoundation\Request;

class ArticleController extends ControllerBase {

  public function index(Request $request):
  JsonResponse {
  }
}
```

The `request` object will be used to retrieve query parameters passed in the URL.

2. From the request, get the sort query parameter, defaulting to DESC:

```
public function index(Request $request):
  JsonResponse {
$sort = $request->query->get('sort', 'DESC');
}
```

3. Then, we get the entity type manager and retrieve the entity storage for the node entity type:

```
public function index(Request $request):
  JsonResponse {
$sort = $request->query->get('sort', 'DESC');

$entity_type_manager = $this->entityTypeManager();
$node_storage = $entity_type_manager->
    getStorage('node');
}
```

The entity type manager is a repository of information for entity types and is used to get handlers for entity types, such as the storage handler. When getting an entity storage handler, you pass the entity type ID.

4. From the storage handler, invoke the getQuery method. This returns a query object that is used to perform an entity query:

```
public function index(Request $request):
  JsonResponse {
$sort = $request->query->get('sort', 'DESC');

$entity_type_manager = $this->entityTypeManager();
  $node_storage = $entity_type_manager->
      getStorage('node');

$query = $node_storage->getQuery()
  ->accessCheck(TRUE);
}
```

Drupal requires specifying if the entity query should perform entity access checks when querying for content entities. We must call the accessCheck method and set it to TRUE or FALSE. In this case, we want entity access checks to be applied to the entity query.

5. We will add conditions to the query to make sure we only return published articles:

```
public function index(Request $request):
  JsonResponse {
$sort = $request->query->get('sort', 'DESC');

$entity_type_manager = $this->entityTypeManager();
$node_storage = $entity_type_manager->
   getStorage('node');

$query = $node_storage->getQuery();
 ->accessCheck(TRUE);
$query->condition('type', 'article');
$query->condition('status', TRUE);
}
```

The `condition` method is passed the field name and value to create a condition. The first condition ensures we only query for nodes with the type (bundle) of `article`. The second condition is to ensure the `status` field is `true` for published.

6. Then, we specify the `sort` order of the query from our URL query parameter:

```
public function index(Request $request):
  JsonResponse {
$sort = $request->query->get('sort', 'DESC');

$entity_type_manager = $this->entityTypeManager();
$node_storage = $entity_type_manager->
   getStorage('node');

$query = $node_storage->getQuery();
 ->accessCheck(TRUE);
$query->condition('type', 'article');
$query->condition('status', TRUE);
$query->sort('created', $sort);
}
```

The `sort` method is passed the field name to order the query by and a direction of ASC or DESC.

7. Calling the execute method will execute the entity query and return the available entity IDs:

```
public function index(Request $request):
  JsonResponse {
$sort = $request->query->get('sort', 'DESC');

$entity_type_manager = $this->entityTypeManager();
$node_storage = $entity_type_manager->
   getStorage('node');

$query = $node_storage->getQuery()
 ->accessCheck(TRUE);
$query->condition('type', 'article');
$query->condition('status', TRUE);
$query->sort('created', $sort);
$node_ids = $query->execute();
}
```

8. After calling execute, we have an array of node IDs that can be passed to the loadMultiple method from the entity storage to load the nodes:

```
public function index(Request $request):
  JsonResponse {
$sort = $request->query->get('sort', 'DESC');

$entity_type_manager = $this->entityTypeManager();
$node_storage = $entity_type_manager->
   getStorage('node');

$query = $node_storage->getQuery()
 ->accessCheck(TRUE);
$query->condition('type', 'article');
$query->condition('status', TRUE);
$query->sort('created', $sort);
$node_ids = $query->execute();

$nodes = $node_storage->loadMultiple($node_ids);
}
```

9. We can now use `array_map` to turn the nodes into array values and return a JSON response of articles:

```
public function index(Request $request):
  JsonResponse {
  $sort = $request->query->get('sort', 'DESC');

  $entity_type_manager = $this->entityTypeManager();
  $node_storage = $entity_type_manager->
    getStorage('node');

  $query = $node_storage->getQuery()
   ->accessCheck(TRUE);
  $query->condition('type', 'article');
  $query->condition('status', TRUE);
  $query->sort('created', $sort);
  $node_ids = $query->execute();

  $nodes = $node_storage->loadMultiple($node_ids);
  $nodes = array_map(function (\Drupal\node\
    NodeInterface $node) {
   return $node->toArray();
  }, $nodes);
  return new JsonResponse($nodes);
}
```

The `array_map` function allows you to transform the values of items in an existing array. We will use `array_map` to iterate over the returned node entities and call the `toArray` method to get their values as an array.

10. We must create the route in `routing.yml` that points to the `index` method of `ArticleController` for an HTTP GET request to the `/articles` path:

```
mymodule.get_articles:
  path: /articles
  defaults:
    _controller: Drupal\mymodule\Controller\
      ArticleController::index
  methods: [GET]
```

```
requirements:
  _permission: 'access content'
```

Routes may share the same path if they explicitly define the HTTP methods they support.

11. Rebuild your Drupal site's cache to make it aware of the new route:

```
php vendor/bin/drush cr
```

12. An HTTP request such as the following can then be used to retrieve the articles on your Drupal site:

```
GET http://localhost/articles
Accept: application/json
```

How it works...

Entity queries are an abstraction above the Database API in Drupal. Drupal stores entity and field data in normalized database tables. The entity query builds the appropriate database query to check the entity's base table, data table, and any field tables. It orchestrates all of the JOIN statements required.

When an entity query is executed, it returns the IDs of matching entities. These IDs are then passed to the loadMultiple method to retrieve entity objects.

There's more...

There are more things that can be done with entity queries.

Count queries

An entity query can also perform a count instead of returning the entity IDs. This is done by calling the count method on an entity query object:

```
$node_storage->getQuery()
  ->accessCheck(FALSE)
  ->condition('type', 'article')
  ->condition('status', FALSE)
  ->count()
  ->execute();
```

The preceding code would return the number of unpublished articles.

Checking entity access

In this recipe, we will demonstrate how to check whether the current user has access to view an **article** node. In previous recipes throughout the book, we have used the _entity_access route requirement to perform entity access checks. This recipe will use its own entity access control so that the response is a 404 Not Found response instead of a 403 Forbidden response.

How to do it...

1. Create a get method in the ArticleController controller in your module that has a parameter for the node entity object that will be provided by a route parameter:

```php
<?php

namespace Drupal\mymodule\Controller;

use Drupal\Core\Controller\ControllerBase;
use Drupal\node\NodeInterface;
use Symfony\Component\HttpFoundation\JsonResponse;
use Symfony\Component\HttpFoundation\Request;

class ArticleController extends ControllerBase {

  public function get(NodeInterface $node):
    JsonResponse {
  }
}
```

If using the same controller from previous recipes, this adds a new use statement for the Drupal\node\NodeInterface interface.

2. Then, we get the entity type manager and retrieve the access control handler for the node entity type:

```php
  public function get(NodeInterface $node):
    JsonResponse {
    $entity_type_manager = $this->entityTypeManager();
    $access_handler = $entity_type_manager->
      getAccessControlHandler('node');
  }
```

The entity type manager is a repository of information for entity types and is used to get handlers for entity types, such as the access control handler.

3. From the access control handler, invoke the `access` method:

```
public function get(NodeInterface $node):
  JsonResponse {
$entity_type_manager = $this->entityTypeManager();
$access_handler = $entity_type_manager->
  getAccessControlHandler('node');

$node_access = $access_handler->access($node,
  'view');
}
```

The first parameter of `access` is the entity. The second parameter is the operation, which is `view` for this recipe. By default, the `access` method returns a Boolean value.

4. If the result is not allowed, we want to return a `404 Not Found` response:

```
public function get(NodeInterface $node):
  JsonResponse {
$entity_type_manager = $this->entityTypeManager();
$access_handler = $entity_type_manager->
  getAccessControlHandler('node');

$node_access = $access_handler->access($node,
  'view');

if (!$node_access) {
 return new JsonResponse(NULL, 404);
 }
}
```

We will return a JSON response, but with `NULL` data and a `404` status code.

5. If the result is allowed, return a JSON response of the article node's content:

```
public function get(NodeInterface $node):
  JsonResponse {
$entity_type_manager = $this->entityTypeManager();
$access_handler = $entity_type_manager->
```

```
    getAccessControlHandler('node');

  $node_access = $access_handler->access($node,
    'view');

  if (!$node_access) {
   return new JsonResponse(NULL, 404);
  }

  return new JsonResponse(
   $node->toArray(),
  );
 }
```

6. We must create the route in our module's `routing.yml` that points to the `get` method of `ArticleController` for an HTTP GET request to the `/articles/{node}` path:

```
mymodule.get_article:
  path: /articles/{node}
  defaults:
   _controller: Drupal\mymodule\Controller\
     ArticleController::get
  requirements:
   _permission: 'access content'
```

Since our route parameter is named `node` and our controller method accepts the class for a node entity, Drupal will automatically have our node parameter converted to an entity object for us.

7. Rebuild your Drupal site's cache to make it aware of the new route:

```
php vendor/bin/drush cr
```

8. An HTTP request such as the following can then be used to retrieve an article that is on your Drupal site:

```
GET http://localhost/articles/1
Accept: application/json
```

How it works...

This recipe did not use the `_entity_access` route requirement to showcase entity validation. The `_entity_access` route requirement invokes the access method on the entity located in the route parameter against an operation.

The following operations are recognized by Drupal's entity access system:

- `view`: The user is allowed to view the entity.
- `view_label`: A less used operation. It is used to check whether the user has the privilege to at least view the entity's label/title.
- `update`: The user is allowed to update the entity.
- `delete`: The user is allowed to delete the entity.

> **Note**
>
> The access to create an entity is a different call to the access control handler since it cannot be checked against an entity object. The `createAccess` method on the access control handler is used to see if a user has access to create a new entity of the entity type.

Checking `access` of an entity can also be done by invoking the `access` method on the entity itself. This recipe is intended to showcase the access control handler as well. The recipe could check access by performing the following:

```
$node_access = $node->access('view');
```

By default, the access check uses the current user. Access checks allow passing an alternative user account to perform access checks. This may be useful when running code on the command line or in background jobs:

```
$node_access = $node->access('view', $other_user);
```

Updating an entity's field values

In this recipe, we will define a route to update the field values of an article node. The route will be for an HTTP PATCH request sending JSON to specify a new title and body text.

How to do it...

1. Create an `update` method in the `ArticleController` controller that receives the incoming request and node object:

```php
<?php

namespace Drupal\mymodule\Controller;

use Drupal\Core\Controller\ControllerBase;
use Drupal\node\NodeInterface;
use Symfony\Component\HttpFoundation\JsonResponse;
use Symfony\Component\HttpFoundation\Request;

class ArticleController extends ControllerBase {

  public function update(Request $request,
    NodeInterface $node): JsonResponse {


  }
}
```

We need the request object so that we can retrieve the JSON payload provided to this method and the node object to update.

2. Next, we will convert the request's content from JSON to a PHP array using Drupal's JSON serialization utility class:

```php
public function update(Request $request,
  NodeInterface $node): JsonResponse {
  $content = $request->getContent();
  $json = \Drupal\Component\Serialization\
    Json::decode($content);
}
```

While we could use the `json_decode` function directly, leveraging utility classes provided by Drupal standardizes the way code works.

3. First, we will update the article node's `title`, if provided in the request's JSON:

```php
public function update(Request $request,
  NodeInterface $node): JsonResponse {
```

```
$content = $request->getContent();
$json = \Drupal\Component\Serialization\
    Json::decode($content);

if (!empty($json['title'])) {
 $node->setTitle($json['title']);
 }
}
```

Some entity classes provide methods for setting specific field values like the Node class does with setTitle to modify the node's title.

4. Then, we will update the article's body field, if provided in the request's JSON:

```
public function update(Request $request,
   NodeInterface $node): JsonResponse {
$content = $request->getContent();
$json = \Drupal\Component\Serialization\
    Json::decode($content);

if (!empty($json['title'])) {
 $node->setTitle($json['title']);
}
if (!empty($json['body'])) {
 $node->set('field_body', $json['body']);
}
}
```

The set method allows us to set the value for a field. The first parameter is the field name and the second parameter is the field's value.

5. After the fields have been updated, we can save the entity and return it as a JSON response:

```
public function update(Request $request,
   NodeInterface $node): JsonResponse {
$content = $request->getContent();
$json = \Drupal\Component\Serialization\
    Json::decode($content);

if (isset($json['title'])) {
```

```
    $node->setTitle($json['title']);
  }
  if (isset($json['body'])) {
   $node->set('body', $json['body']);
  }
  $node->save();
  return new JsonResponse(
   $node->toArray()
  );
}
```

6. We must create the route in `routing.yml` that points to the `update` method of `ArticleController` for an HTTP PATCH request to the `/articles/{node}` path:

```yaml
mymodule.update_article:
  path: /articles/{node}
  defaults:
   _controller: Drupal\mymodule\Controller\
      ArticleController::update
  methods: [PATCH]
  requirements:
   _access: 'TRUE'
```

This route should have `_entity_access: 'node.update'` as its requirements. However, we have used `_access: 'TRUE'` to bypass access checks for this recipe.

7. Rebuild your Drupal site's cache to make it aware of the new route:

```
php vendor/bin/drush cr
```

8. An HTTP request such as the following can then be used to update an article that is on your Drupal site:

```
PATCH http://localhost/articles/1
Content-Type: application/json
Accept: application/json

{
  "title": "New updated title!",
  "body": "Modified body text"
}
```

How it works...

When updating an entity, the entity storage updates the field values in the database and the entity's database record. The entity storage will write the field values to the appropriate database tables that hold field values.

When an entity is updated, the entity storage fires invoke the following hooks, allowing you to hook into an update to an entity. The entity being updated is passed as an argument:

- hook_ENTITY_TYPE_presave
- hook_entity_presave
- hook_ENTITY_TYPE_update
- hook_entity_update

Entities may also be validated, to ensure their updated values are correct. This is covered in the next recipe, *Performing entity validation*.

Performing entity validation

In this recipe, we will walk through entity validation. Drupal has integrated with the **Symfony Validator** component. Entities can be validated before saving. We will build off of the last recipe, which allows updating an article node to add validation of its values.

How to do it...

1. We will be adding validation to the update method from the previous recipe:

```
public function update(Request $request,
  NodeInterface $node): JsonResponse {
$content = $request->getContent();
$json = \Drupal\Component\Serialization\
    Json::decode($content);

if (isset($json['title'])) {
  $node->setTitle($json['title']);
}
if (isset($json['body'])) {
  $node->set('body', $json['body']);
}
```

```
    $node->save();
    return new JsonResponse(
     $node->toArray()
    );
}
```

2. We will modify the `update` method to `validate` the node before saving:

```
public function update(Request $request,
  NodeInterface $node): JsonResponse {
$content = $request->getContent();
$json = \Drupal\Component\Serialization\
    Json::decode($content);

if (isset($json['title'])) {
 $node->setTitle($json['title']);
}
if (isset($json['body'])) {
 $node->set('body', $json['body']);
}

$constraint_violations = $node->validate();

$node->save();
return new JsonResponse(
 $node->toArray()
);
}
```

We will invoke the `validate` method, which runs the validation system against all constraints on the entity and its field values.

3. The `validate` method returns an object containing any constraint violations and does not throw an exception. We must check whether there are any violations:

```
public function update(Request $request,
  NodeInterface $node): JsonResponse {
$content = $request->getContent();
```

```
$json = \Drupal\Component\Serialization\
   Json::decode($content);

if (isset($json['title'])) {
 $node->setTitle($json['title']);
}
if (isset($json['body'])) {
 $node->set('body', $json['body']);
}

$constraint_violations = $node->validate();
if (count($constraint_violations) > 0) {
}

$node->save();
return new JsonResponse(
 $node->toArray()
);
}
```

The returned object, an instance of `\Drupal\Core\Entity\`
`EntityConstraintViolationListInterface`, implements `\Countable`. This
allows us to use the `count` function to see if there are any violations.

4. If there are constraint violations, we will build an array of error messages and return a `400
    Bad Request` response:

```
public function update(Request $request,
  NodeInterface $node): JsonResponse {
$content = $request->getContent();
$json = \Drupal\Component\Serialization\
   Json::decode($content);

if (isset($json['title'])) {
 $node->setTitle($json['title']);
}
if (isset($json['body'])) {
 $node->set('body', $json['body']);
}
```

```
$constraint_violations = $node->validate();
if (count($constraint_violations) > 0) {
  $errors = [];
  foreach ($constraint_violations as $violation) {
    $errors[] = $violation->getPropertyPath()
      . ': ' . $violation->getMessage();
  }
  return new JsonResponse($errors, 400);
}

$node->save();
return new JsonResponse(
  $node->toArray()
);
}
```

The `EntityConstraintViolationListInterface` object is also iterable, allowing us to loop over all of the violations. From each violation, we can use `getPropertyPath` to identify the invalid field and `getMessage` for information about the invalid value.

5. The following HTTP request would trigger a constraint violation for an empty value in the `title` field:

```
PATCH https://localhost/articles/1
Content-Type: application/json
Accept: application/json

{
  "title": "",
  "body": "Modified body text"
}
```

How it works...

Drupal utilizes the Symfony Validator component (`https://symfony.com/components/Validator`) to validate data. The Validator component has a concept of constraints that are validated, and if the validation fails a violation is reported. Drupal's entity validation works with an outside-in approach: entity-level constraints are validated and then each field is validated, going down through each field's properties.

Entity validation does not automatically run when an entity is saved. It is an explicit operation that must be invoked when manipulating entities programmatically. The only time Drupal invokes entity validation is when an entity is modified through its forms.

At the same time, the invoker of the entity invalidation must choose how to react to constraint violations, such as our recipe did to prevent the entity from being saved. An invalid entity can always be saved programmatically.

There's more...

There are more options when validating an entity's values. Let us see a few of these options in the following sections.

Validating fields directly

Field item classes have a `validate` method for directly validating a specific field instead of validating the entire entity. This can be done by using the `get` method to get the field item and then invoking the `validate` method on the field item:

```
$node->get('body')->validate();
```

Filtering constraint violations

The `EntityConstraintViolationListInterface` class extends the `Symfony\Component\Validator\ConstraintViolationListInterface` class provided by Symfony. This adds Drupal-specific methods for filtering returned violations. The following methods are available to filter the violations:

- `getEntityViolations`: Some violations may be at the entity level and not at the class level. Constraints may be applied at the entity level and not to specific fields. For example, the Workspaces module adds a constraint at the entity level to check for workspace conflicts.

- `filterByFields`: Given a series of field names, the violations are reduced to only those that apply to those fields.

- `filterByFieldAccess`: This filters the violations based on fields accessible only to the user. Drupal allows saving entities in an invalid state, especially if a workflow allows a less privileged user to modify specific fields of an entity. If using this filter, be cautious because the entity must have updated fields the user may not have had access to.

The previous methods always return a new object instance and do not have side effects on the original violations list.

Deleting an entity

In this recipe, we will walk through deleting an entity. Deleting an entity allows you to remove an entity from the database so that it no longer exists.

How to do it...

1. Create a `delete` method in the `ArticleController` controller in your module that has a parameter for the node entity object that will be provided by a route parameter:

```php
<?php

namespace Drupal\mymodule\Controller;

use Drupal\Core\Controller\ControllerBase;
use Drupal\node\NodeInterface;
use Symfony\Component\HttpFoundation\JsonResponse;
use Symfony\Component\HttpFoundation\Request;

class ArticleController extends ControllerBase {

  public function delete(NodeInterface $node):
    JsonResponse {

  }
}
```

2. To delete an entity, you will invoke the `delete` method:

```php
  public function delete(NodeInterface $node):
    JsonResponse {
    $node->delete();
  }
```

The `delete` method immediately removes the entity from the database storage.

3. We will then return an empty JSON response:

```php
  public function delete(NodeInterface $node):
    JsonResponse {
    $node->delete();
```

```
return new JsonResponse(null, 204);
}
```

When no content is returned, we will use the 204 No Content status code.

4. We must create the route in routing.yml that points to the delete method of ArticleController for an HTTP DELETE request to the /articles/{node} path:

```
mymodule.delete_article:
  path: /articles/{node}
  defaults:
   _controller: Drupal\mymodule\Controller\
      ArticleController::delete
  methods: [DELETE]
  requirements:
   _access: 'TRUE'
```

This route should have _entity_access: 'node.delete' for its requirements. However, we have used _access: 'TRUE' to bypass access checks for this recipe.

5. Rebuild your Drupal site's cache to make it aware of the new route:

```
php vendor/bin/drush cr
```

6. An HTTP request such as the following can then be used to retrieve an article that is on your Drupal site:

```
DELETE http://localhost/articles/1
Accept: application/json
```

7. A second HTTP request to get the article will return a 404 Not Found response since it has been deleted:

```
GET http://localhost/articles/1
Accept: application/json
```

How it works...

The delete method on the entity class is delegated to the delete method on the entity type's storage handler. When a content entity is deleted, the storage purges all field values from the database and the entity's database record. Deletion is permanent and cannot be reversed.

When an entity is deleted, the entity storage fires invoke the following hooks, allowing you to hook into an entity's deletion. The entity being deleted is passed as an argument:

- `hook_ENTITY_TYPE_predelete`
- `hook_entity_predelete`
- `hook_ENTITY_TYPE_delete`
- `hook_entity_delete`

Throwing an exception in a hook will roll back the database transaction and prevent the entity from being deleted, but it may also crash Drupal if not handled appropriately.

7

Creating Forms with the Form API

This chapter will cover the usage of the Form API, which is used to create forms in Drupal without writing any HTML! This chapter will walk you through creating a form to manage a custom piece of configuration with validation. You will also learn how to implement conditional form fields using the `states` property to control whether an element is hidden, visible, required, or more. We will also demonstrate how AJAX can be implemented in Drupal forms to provide dynamic form elements. Finally, you will learn how to alter other forms in Drupal to customize their application.

In this chapter, we will go through the following recipes:

- Creating a custom form and saving configuration changes
- Validating form data
- Specifying conditional form elements
- Using AJAX in a Drupal form
- Customizing existing forms in Drupal

Technical requirements

This chapter will require an installed custom module. In the following recipes, the module name is `mymodule`. Replace as appropriate. You can find the full code used in this chapter on GitHub: `https://github.com/PacktPublishing/Drupal-10-Development-Cookbook/tree/main/chp07`

Creating a custom form and saving configuration changes

In this recipe, we will create a form that allows saving the company name and phone number for the website to the configuration. Forms are defined as classes that implement \Drupal\Core\Form\FormInterface. \Drupal\Core\Form\FormBase serves as a standard base class for forms. We will extend this class to create a new form that saves the custom configuration.

How to do it...

1. First, we need to create the `src/Form` directory in the module's directory. We will put our form class in this directory, which gives our form class the `Form` namespace:

    ```
    mkdir -p src/Form
    ```

2. Create a file named `CompanyForm.php` in the `Form` directory. This will hold our `CompanyForm` form class.

3. Our `CompanyForm` class will extend the `FormBase` class provided by Drupal core:

    ```php
    <?php

    namespace Drupal\mymodule\Form;

    use Drupal\Core\Form\FormBase;
    use Drupal\Core\Form\FormStateInterface;

    class CompanyForm extends FormBase {

      public function getFormId() {}

      public function buildForm(array $form,
        FormStateInterface $form_state) {}

      public function submitForm(array &$form,
        FormStateInterface $form_state) {}

    }
    ```

    Following PSR-4 autoloading conventions, our class is in the \Drupal\mymodule\Form namespace, which Drupal can determine as the src/Form directory in our module. Per PSR-4, the filename and class name must also be the same.

The \Drupal\Core\Form\FormBase class provides internal logic for handling forms. It only requires us to implement the getFormId, buildForm, and submitForm methods, which will be explained and implemented in the following steps.

4. All forms must have a unique string that identifies the form. Let's give our form the ID of company_form by updating the getFormId method:

```
public function getFormId() {
  return 'company_form';
}
```

5. The buildForm method returns the form structure as an array of form elements. We provide a text field for a company name and telephone:

```
public function buildForm(array $form,
  FormStateInterface $form_state) {
  $form['company_name'] = [
    '#type' => 'textfield',
    '#title' => 'Company name',
  ];
  $form['company_telephone'] = [
    '#type' => 'tel',
    '#title' => 'Company telephone',
  ];
  return $form;
}
```

The buildForm method is passed the $form array argument, which is where our form structure is added. Both company_name and company_telephone in the $form array are called **form elements**. Form elements are defined with a minimum of #type (to specify what the element is) and #title (to act as the label).

6. Next, we want to load an existing configuration and pass its values to the elements:

```
public function buildForm(array $form,
  FormStateInterface $form_state) {
  $company_settings = $this->config
      ('company_settings');
  $form['company_name'] = [
    '#type' => 'textfield',
```

```
        '#title' => 'Company name',
        '#default_value' => $company_settings->
          get('company_name'),
      ];
      $form['company_telephone'] = [
        '#type' => 'tel',
        '#title' => 'Company telephone',
        '#default_value' => $company_settings->
          get('company_telephone'),
      ];
      return $form;
    }
```

We load a configuration object named `company_settings` with the `config` method, which will store our values. The `#default_value` property allows specifying an initial value that should be used for an element.

7. Then, we must add a submit button:

```
    public function buildForm(array $form,
      FormStateInterface $form_state) {
      $company_settings = $this->
          config('mymodule.company_settings');
      $form['company_name'] = [
        '#type' => 'textfield',
        '#title' => 'Company name',
        '#default_value' => $company_settings->
          get('company_name'),
      ];
      $form['company_telephone'] = [
        '#type' => 'tel',
        '#title' => 'Company telephone',
        '#default_value' => $company_settings->
          get('company_telephone'),
      ];
      $form['actions']['#type'] = 'actions';
      $form['actions']['submit'] = [
        '#type' => 'submit',
```

```
        '#value' => 'Submit',
    ];
    return $form;
}
```

We provide a submit button as a form element with the submit type. It is best practice to place the submit button and other buttons in the actions render element.

8. Fill in submitForm and save it to the mymodule.company_data object:

```
public function submitForm(array &$form,
    FormStateInterface $form_state) {
    $config = $this->configFactory()->
        getEditable('mymodule.company_settings');
    $config->set('company_name', $form_state->
        getValue('company_name'));
    $config->set('company_telephone', $form_state->
        getValue('company_telephone'));
    $config->save();
    $this->messenger()->addStatus('Updated company
        information');
}
```

In order to save our configuration, we must fetch it from the configuration factory with the getEditable method. This allows us to save changes to the configuration object.

9. Add a new route to make the form accessible at the /company-form path:

```
mymodule.company_form:
  path: /company-form
  defaults:
    _form: Drupal\mymodule\Form\CompanyForm
    _title: Company form
  requirements:
    _access: 'TRUE'
```

10. Rebuild your Drupal site's cache to make it aware of the new route:

```
php vendor/bin/drush cr
```

11. Now, you may visit /company-form and access your form:

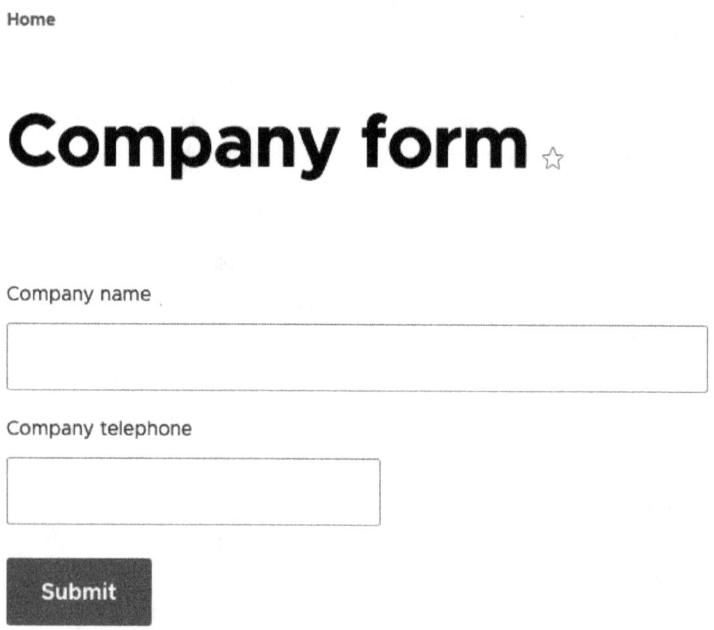

Figure 7.1 – The output of the CompanyForm form

How it works...

This recipe creates a form that is accessible from a route, using a _form property in place of the _controller property. The _form property contains the form class name. When Drupal's routing system is built, a _controller entry is added that is handled by \Drupal\Core\Controller\ HtmlFormController::getContentResult. This addition is done by the \Drupal\ Core\Routing\Enhancer\FormRouteEnhancer enhancer. The HtmlFormController passes the class name from _form into the form builder and returns the complete form render array.

The form builder is responsible for determining whether the form is being rendered or whether it is handling a submission if the request is an HTTP GET or HTTP POST.

> **Note**
> The Form API has existed in Drupal since Drupal 4.7. In fact, the render array system was born out of the Form API and created in Drupal 7.

When the form builder handles a form submission, the form structure is also built from `buildForm`. This is done to prevent additional invalid values from being submitted. Incoming input data is mapped to elements in the form and pushed to the form's `state` values, which are retrieved using `getValue` for a specific element value or `getValues` for all values. Once the values have been set in the form state, the form builder invokes the form validator service. Form validation is handled in the next recipe, *Validating form data*.

If the form has no errors, then the form build invokes the form submission service and invokes the form's `submitForm` method.

There's more...

Many components make up a form created through Drupal's Form API. We will explore a few of them in depth.

The form state

The `\Drupal\Core\Form\FormStateInterface` object represents the current state of the form and its data. The **form** state contains user-submitted data for the form along with build state information. It can also store arbitrary information between the form being built and the submissions. The form state also handles redirection after the form submission. You will interact more with the form state in the following recipes.

The form cache

Drupal utilizes a cache table for forms. This holds the build table, as identified by form build identifiers. This allows Drupal to validate forms during AJAX requests and easily build them when required. It is important to keep the form cache in persistent storage; otherwise, there may be repercussions, such as loss of form data or invalidating forms. We will cover AJAX forms in the *Using AJAX in a Drupal form* recipe.

The ConfigFormBase class

Drupal provides a base form class to simplify forms that modify a configuration object. This is the `\Drupal\Core\Form\ConfigFormBase` class. This class prevents the need to call `getEditable` from the configuration factory when retrieving your configuration object. It also adds a default submit button and messaging when the form is submitted.

Here is an updated version of our form class using `ConfigFormBase`. The `getEditableConfigNames` method contains our configuration object's name and allows it to be editable whenever loaded:

```php
<?php
```

```php
namespace Drupal\mymodule\Form;

use Drupal\Core\Form\ConfigFormBase;
use Drupal\Core\Form\FormStateInterface;

class CompanyForm extends ConfigFormBase {

  public function getFormId() {
    return 'company_form';
  }

  protected function getEditableConfigNames() {
    return ['mymodule.company_settings'];
  }

  public function buildForm(array $form, FormStateInterface
    $form_state) {
    $company_settings = $this->
        config('mymodule.company_settings');
    $form['company_name'] = [
      '#type' => 'textfield',
      '#title' => 'Company name',
      '#default_value' => $company_settings->
        get('company_name'),
    ];
    $form['company_telephone'] = [
      '#type' => 'tel',
      '#title' => 'Company telephone',
      '#default_value' => $company_settings->
        get('company_telephone'),
    ];

    return parent::buildForm($form, $form_state);
  }

  public function submitForm(array &$form,
```

```
  FormStateInterface $form_state) {
  parent::submitForm($form, $form_state);
  $this->config('mymodule.company_settings')
    ->set('company_name', $form_state->
      getValue('company_name'))
    ->set('company_telephone', $form_state->
      getValue('company_telephone'))
    ->save();
  }


}
```

See also

- Form and render elements documentation: https://www.drupal.org/docs/drupal-apis/form-api/form-render-elements

- List of available form and render elements: https://api.drupal.org/api/drupal/elements/10.0.x

Validating form data

We will expand on the form created in the last recipe to add validation. We will add validation information to form elements in the company form. There is also a validateForm method that can be used to programmatically identify errors and prevent form submission.

Getting ready

This recipe will use the form class created in the *Creating a custom form and saving configuration changes* recipe.

How to do it...

1. First, we will make the form elements required. This will prevent submitting the form without providing values. Update the form elements in buildForm to match the following:

```
$form['company_name'] = [
  '#type' => 'textfield',
  '#title' => 'Company name',
  '#required' => TRUE,
  '#default_value' => $company_settings->
```

```
          get('company_name'),
      ];
      $form['company_telephone'] = [
        '#type' => 'tel',
        '#title' => 'Company telephone',
        '#required' => TRUE,
        '#default_value' => $company_settings->
          get('company_telephone'),
      ];
```

This is achieved by adding '#required' => TRUE to the form element. When a form element is marked as required, Drupal will automatically validate that the field has a non-empty value. It also specifies the HTML5 required attribute on the input, adding client-side validation.

2. Second, we will add input constraints to the telephone form element. Even though we have an HTML5 tel element, it does not validate the input characters:

```
      $form['company_telephone'] = [
        '#type' => 'tel',
        '#title' => 'Company telephone',
        '#required' => TRUE,
        '#pattern' => '^[0-9-+\s()]*$',
        '#default_value' => $company_settings->
          get('company_telephone'),
      ];
```

The #pattern property allows specifying the HTML5 pattern attribute on the rendered input element. This pattern expression allows numbers, dashes, and parentheses to be input, but not regular alphabetical characters.

3. Next, we will override the validateForm method, which allows for programmatic validation:

```
    public function validateForm(array &$form,
  FormStateInterface $form_state) {
      $company_name = $form_state->
        getValue('company_name');
      if (str_contains($company_name, 'foo')) {
        $form_state->setErrorByName(
          'company_name',
          'Name cannot contain "foo"'
        );
```

```
    }
  }
```

We use the `getValue` method on the form state to get the submitted value for `company_name`. Using `str_contains`, we check whether the company name contains the word `foo`. If it does, we use the `setErrorByName` method to set an error on the `company_name` input.

4. When the form is submitted, the company name cannot contain the word `foo`:

Home

Company form ☆

Company name *

```
foo
```

Company telephone *

```
555-555-5555
```

Submit

Figure 7.2 – The company name field with a validation error

How it works...

When a form is submitted, the form builder creates the form state values as a mapping based on the incoming user input and the form elements. The form builder invokes the form validation service. Form validation runs from the inside out. The form validation service iterates through each form element and then invokes the `validateForm` method for the form class.

When an element is validated, this is when the #required attribute is evaluated. If the form state is missing a value for the element, it is marked as having an error. The same is true for #pattern. The backend still validates the incoming input to make sure it matches the pattern provided.

See also

- Additional properties for validation on the form and render elements documentation: https://www.drupal.org/docs/drupal-apis/form-api/form-render-elements

Specifying conditional form elements

The Form API provides a mechanism for defining form element states. These states are mapped to JavaScript interactions that can control whether an element is required, visible, and more. In this example, we will demonstrate a form that has a disabled submit button until a checkbox is checked.

How to do it...

1. Create a file named ApprovalRequiredForm.php in the src/Form directory for your module to hold the ApprovalRequiredForm form class.

2. We will define the ApprovalRequiredForm class with a form ID of mymodule_approval_form:

```php
<?php

namespace Drupal\mymodule\Form;

use Drupal\Core\Form\FormBase;
use Drupal\Core\Form\FormStateInterface;

class ApprovalRequiredForm extends FormBase {

  public function getFormId() {
    return 'mymodule_approval_form';
  }

  public function buildForm(array $form,
    FormStateInterface $form_state) {
    return $form;
  }
```

```
    public function submitForm(array &$form,
      FormStateInterface $form_state) {
    }


}
```

3. In the `buildForm` method, we will start by creating a `checkbox` element that will be required for submitting the form and controlling the state of our submit button:

```
    public function buildForm(array $form,
      FormStateInterface $form_state) {
    $form['approval'] = [
      '#type' => 'checkbox',
      '#title' => 'I acknowledge',
      '#required' => TRUE,
    ];


    return $form;
    }
```

We add a checkbox and mark it as `#required`, so that the form has client-side validation of the checkbox and backend validation.

4. Next, we add our submit button. This will contain the logic to control its state based on the checkbox:

```
    $form['actions']['#type'] = 'actions';
    $form['actions']['submit'] = [
      '#type' => 'submit',
      '#value' => 'Submit',
      '#states' => [
        'disabled' => [
          ':input[name="approval"]' => ['checked' =>
            FALSE],
        ],
      ],
    ];
```

The `#states` property of an element allows you to specify a state and the conditions that trigger it via element selectors to other inputs. We want the button to be in a `disabled` state if our checkbox `approval` is not checked.

5. Add a new route to make the form accessible at the `/approval-form` path:

```
mymodule.approval_form:
  path: /approval-form
  defaults:
    _form: Drupal\mymodule\Form\ApprovalRequiredForm
    _title: Approval form
  requirements:
    _access: 'TRUE'
```

6. Rebuild your Drupal site's cache to make it aware of the new route:

```
php vendor/bin/drush cr
```

7. Now, you may visit `/approval-form` and use the form. The submit button will be disabled until the checkbox is checked:

Figure 7.3 – Approval form with its submit button disabled until the checkbox is checked

How it works...

The Form API bridges PHP code to JavaScript code with its element states capabilities. When the form is processed, the values from the `#states` property are JSON encoded and added to the rendered element as the `data-drupal-states` attribute.

Here is the result of `data-drupal-states` on the form's submit button:

```
data-drupal-states="{&quot;disabled&quot;:{&quot;::input
   [name=\u0022approval\u0022]&quot;:{&quot;checked&quot;
      :false}}}"
```

When a form has states, the `core/misc/states.js` JavaScript file is added to the page. This file uses the `[data-drupal-states]` CSS selector to find all elements with state data. This data is then parsed as JSON and evaluated. The states provided to an element will not work if they do not provide correct CSS selectors to the element that controls their state.

The documentation for the states provides information on the available states and conditions: `https://api.drupal.org/api/drupal/core%21lib%21Drupal%21Core%21Form%21FormHelper.php/function/FormHelper%3A%3AprocessStates/10.0.x`.

Using AJAX in a Drupal form

The Form API has a mechanism to perform AJAX requests without writing any JavaScript. In this example, we will create a counter with an increment and decrement button.

How to do it...

1. Create a file named `CounterForm.php` in the `src/Form` directory for your module to hold the `CounterForm` form class.

2. We will define the `CounterForm` class with a form ID of `mymodule_counter_form`:

    ```php
    <?php

    namespace Drupal\mymodule\Form;

    use Drupal\Core\Form\FormBase;
    use Drupal\Core\Form\FormStateInterface;

    class CounterForm extends FormBase {

      public function getFormId() {
        return 'mymodule_counter_form';
      }
    ```

```php
public function buildForm(array $form,
  FormStateInterface $form_state) {
  return $form;
}


public function submitForm(array &$form,
  FormStateInterface $form_state) {


}


}
```

3. In the `buildForm` method, we will start by creating an element to display our counter value. This element will be replaced and updated after each AJAX request with the current count:

```php
public function buildForm(array $form,
  FormStateInterface $form_state) {
  $count = $form_state->get('count') ?: 0;
  $form['count'] = [
    '#markup' => "<p>Total count: $count",
  ];

  return $form;
}
```

We will use the form state storage to maintain the `count` value. The `get` method allows retrieving values from the form state storage. We use the `? :` operator to make sure the default value is zero when the form is first loaded. Otherwise, the value would be `null`, which is not an integer. The form state value for `count` will be updated in our AJAX callback.

4. In order for Drupal to properly update our element after each AJAX request, we need to wrap it with an element that has an HTML ID that we can target:

```php
$form['count'] = [
  '#markup' => "<p>Total count: $count",
  '#prefix' => '<div id="counter">',
  '#suffix' => '</div>',
];
```

We use the `#prefix` and `#suffix` keys to wrap our form element with HTML markup. This gives us a wrapper element to target for the AJAX update.

5. Next, we will add the button that will trigger the AJAX call to increment our counter:

```
$form['increment'] = [
  '#type' => 'submit',
  '#value' => 'Increment',
  '#ajax' => [
    'callback' => [$this, 'ajaxRefresh'],
    'wrapper' => 'counter',
  ],
];
```

The #ajax property allows an element to execute an AJAX request to interact with the form. The #ajax property requires specifying a callback that contains a method to invoke for specifying what parts of the form to return, which we will implement next. The wrapper property contains the target HTML ID for an element that should be updated.

6. Now, we will implement the ajaxRefresh method in our class that we specified for our #ajax callback:

```
public function ajaxRefresh(array $form,
  FormStateInterface $form_state) {
  return $form['count'];
}
```

The callback to an #ajax property is responsible for returning the subset of the form that should be replaced.

7. Then, we must update the submitForm method to increment our counter whenever the increment button is pressed:

```
public function submitForm(array &$form,
  FormStateInterface $form_state) {
  $count = $form_state->get('count') ?: 0;
  $count++;
  $form_state->set('count', $count);
  $form_state->setRebuild();
}
```

We retrieve the count value from the form state storage and then set it again after incrementing the value. We then call setRebuild on the form state. This instructs Drupal to rebuild the form, so the updated count value is shown.

8. Add a new route to make the form accessible at the /counter-form path:

```
mymodule.counter_form:
  path: /counter-form
  defaults:
    _form: Drupal\mymodule\Form\CounterForm
    _title: Counter form
  requirements:
    _access: 'TRUE'
```

9. Rebuild your Drupal site's cache to make it aware of the new route:

```
php vendor/bin/drush cr
```

10. Now you may visit /counter-form and use the form:

Counter form ☆

Total count: 2

Increment

Figure 7.4 – The counter form

How it works...

The #ajax property on a form element is processed by \Drupal\Core\Render\Element\
RenderElement::preRenderAjaxForm. This is invoked on each element as part of building
the form. It attaches the default events that will trigger the AJAX call. For buttons, the mousedown
JavaScript event is used. The mousedown event was used for buttons for accessibility, as pressing
Enter in other elements can trigger a click on a form button. Input text fields are on the blur event.
Radios, checkboxes, select lists, and date fields are on the click event.

When an AJAX button is triggered on a form, it is submitted. The form's submitForm method
is invoked. Then, the element's #ajax callback is invoked to return the form. However, if the
submitForm method calls for the form to be rebuilt, as we did with setRebuild on the form
state, the buildForm method is called before the #ajax callback. This allows the returned form
elements to match the current form state's values and storage.

There's more...

In the following sections, we will explore how the Form APIs AJAX capabilities can also be used.

Specifying the event to trigger when AJAX is fired

It is possible to change the JavaScript event that triggers when the AJAX is triggered for an element. This is accomplished by specifying the `type` property in `#ajax`. For instance, the following would cause AJAX to fire on a text element with each keystroke instead of when the text element loses focus:

```
$element['#ajax']['type'] = 'keyup';
```

> **Using AJAX in a custom template**
>
> If you are using AJAX on a page that is output with a template, note that you must render your form in the template as `{{ form|without(IDs of named form elements using AJAX) }}`.

See also

- AJAX forms documentation: `https://www.drupal.org/docs/drupal-apis/javascript-api/ajax-forms`

Customizing existing forms in Drupal

The Form API does not just provide a way to create forms. There are ways to alter existing forms through hooks in a custom module. By using this technique, new elements can be added, default values can be changed, and elements can even be hidden from view to simplify the user experience.

The altering of a form does not happen in a custom class; this is a hook defined in the module file. In this recipe, we will use the `hook_form_FORM_ID_alter()` hook to add a telephone field to the site's configuration form.

How to do it...

1. Ensure that your module has a `.module` file to contain hooks, such as `mymodule.module`.

2. We will implement `hook_form_FORM_ID_alter` for the `system_site_information_settings` form:

```php
<?php

use Drupal\Core\Form\FormStateInterface;
```

```
function mymodule_form_system_site_information
  _settings_alter(array &$form, FormStateInterface
    $form_state) {
  // Code to alter form or form state here
}
```

Drupal will call this hook and pass the current form array and its form state object. The form array is passed by reference, allowing our hook to modify the array without returning any values. This is why the $form parameter has the ampersand (&) before it. In PHP, all objects are passed by reference, which is why we have no ampersand before $form_state.

Form IDs can be found by inspecting the getFormId method of the form class.

3. Next, we add our telephone field to the form so that it can be displayed and saved:

```php
<?php

use Drupal\Core\Form\FormStateInterface;

function mymodule_form_system_site_information_
  settings_alter(array &$form, FormStateInterface
    $form_state) {
  $form['site_information']['site_phone'] = [
    '#type' => 'tel',
    '#title' => 'Site phone',
    '#default_value' => \Drupal::config('system.site')
        ->get('phone'),
  ];
}
```

We retrieve the current phone value from the system.site configuration object so that it can be modified if already set.

4. We then need to add a submit handler to the form in order to save the configuration for our new field:

```php
<?php

use Drupal\Core\Form\FormStateInterface;

function mymodule_form_system_site_information
```

```
  _settings_alter(array &$form, FormStateInterface
    $form_state) {
  $form['site_information']['site_phone'] = [
    '#type' => 'tel',
    '#title' => 'Site phone',
    '#default_value' => \Drupal::config('system.site')
        ->get('phone'),
  ];
  $form['#submit'][] = 'mymodule_system_site_
    information_phone_submit';
}


function mymodule_system_site_information_phone_submit
    (array &$form, FormStateInterface $form_state) {
  $config = Drupal::configFactory()->
    getEditable('system.site');
  $config ->set('phone', $form_state->
    getValue('site_phone'));
}
```

The $form['#submit'] modification adds our callback to the form's submit handlers. This allows our module to interact with the form once it has been submitted.

The mymodule_system_site_information_phone_submit callback is passed the form array and form state. We load the current configuration factory to receive the configuration that can be edited. We then load the system.site configuration object and save phone based on the value from the form state.

5. Rebuild your Drupal site's cache to make it aware of the new hook, so that it will be invoked when viewing the site settings form:

```
php vendor/bin/drush cr
```

6.   Visit the site settings configuration form at `/admin/config/system/site-information`:

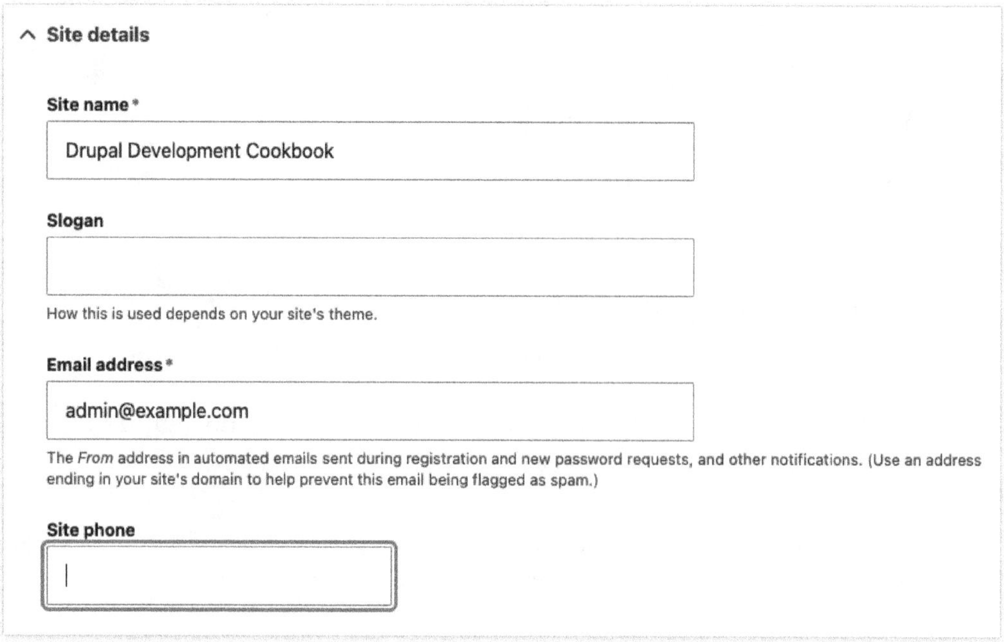

∧ **Site details**

Site name *

```
Drupal Development Cookbook
```

Slogan

How this is used depends on your site's theme.

Email address *

```
admin@example.com
```

The *From* address in automated emails sent during registration and new password requests, and other notifications. (Use an address ending in your site's domain to help prevent this email being flagged as spam.)

Site phone

Figure 7.5 – The altered site settings form

How it works...

In this recipe, we targeted the specific `hook_form_FORM_ID_alter()` alter hook. There is also the generic `hook_form_alter()` hook that is invoked for all forms and allows modifying every form when it is rendered. This allows for modules to generically modify all forms, if needed, or several different form IDs in one hook. It also allows for more explicit hook targets.

The form array is passed by reference, allowing modifications to be made in this hook and altering the original data. This allows us to add an element or modify existing items, such as titles and descriptions.

8
Plug and Play with Plugins

Plugins power many items in **Drupal**, such as blocks, field types, and field formatters. Plugins and plugin types are provided by modules. They provide a swappable and specific functionality.

In this chapter, we will implement a **block plugin**. We will use the Plugin API to provide a custom field type along with a widget and formatter for the field. The last recipe will show you how to create and use a custom plugin type.

Upcoming changes to the plugin system in Drupal minor versions

PHP 8 provides a feature called **PHP attributes** (`https://www.php.net/manual/en/language.attributes.overview.php`). With **Drupal 10**'s adoption of **PHP 8.1**, there is consideration to adopt PHP attributes over code document annotations, which are used in this chapter.

Support for PHP attributes instead of annotations may be available in **Drupal 10.1**, the first minor release of Drupal 10. Annotations will be supported throughout Drupal 10 but may become deprecated. Deprecating annotations in favor of PHP attributes is discussed in the following issue: `https://www.drupal.org/project/drupal/issues/3252386`.

In this chapter, we will dive into the Plugin API provided in Drupal with the following recipes:

- Creating blocks using plugins
- Creating a custom field type
- Creating a custom field widget
- Creating a custom field formatter
- Creating a custom plugin type

Technical requirements

This chapter will require a custom module to be installed. In the following recipes, the module name is `mymodule`. Replace as appropriate. You can find the full code used in this chapter on GitHub: `https://github.com/PacktPublishing/Drupal-10-Development-Cookbook/tree/main/chp08`

Creating blocks using plugins

In Drupal, a **block** is a piece of content that can be placed in a region provided by a theme. Blocks are used to present specific kinds of content, such as a user login form, a snippet of text, and many more.

Blocks are annotated plugins. Annotated plugins use documentation blocks to provide details of the plugin. They are discovered in the module's `Plugin` class namespace. Each class in the `Plugin/Block` namespace will be discovered by the `Block` module's plugin manager.

In this recipe, we will define a block that will display a copyright snippet and the current year and place it in the footer region.

How to do it...

1. First, we need to create the `src/Plugin/Block` directory in the module's directory. This will translate the `\Drupal\mymodule\Plugin\Block` namespace and allow block plugin discovery:

    ```
    mkdir -p src/Plugin/Block
    ```

2. Create a file named `Copyright.php` in the newly created directory so that we can define the `Copyright` class for our block.

3. The `Copyright` class will extend the `\Drupal\Core\Block\BlockBase` class:

    ```php
    <?php

    namespace Drupal\mymodule\Plugin\Block;

    use Drupal\Core\Block\BlockBase;

    class Copyright extends BlockBase {

    }
    ```

    We will extend the `BlockBase` class, which implements `\Drupal\Core\Block\BlockPluginInterface` and provides us with an implementation of nearly all of the interface's methods.

4. Next, we will write the plugin annotation in a class document block. We will provide the block's identifier, administrative label, and category as annotation tags:

```php
<?php

namespace Drupal\mymodule\Plugin\Block;

use Drupal\Core\Block\BlockBase;

/**
 * @Block(
 *   id = "copyright_block",
 *   admin_label = @Translation("Copyright"),
 *   category = @Translation("Custom"),
 * )
 */
class Copyright extends BlockBase {
}
```

Annotations are provided in code comments and are prefixed with @. The @ symbol in @Block specifies that this is a Block annotation. Drupal will parse this and create a plugin definition based on the provided properties. id is the internal machine name, admin_label is displayed on the block listing page, and category shows up in the block select list.

5. We will need to implement the build method to satisfy the \Drupal\Core\Block\ BlockPluginInterface interface. This returns the output to be displayed:

```php
<?php

namespace Drupal\mymodule\Plugin\Block;

use Drupal\Core\Block\BlockBase;

/**
 * @Block(
 * id = "copyright_block",
 * admin_label = @Translation("Copyright"),
 * category = @Translation("Custom")
 * )
```

```
  */
class Copyright extends BlockBase {

  /**
   * {@inheritdoc}
   */
  public function build() {
    $date = new \DateTime();
    return [
      '#markup' => t('Copyright @year&copy; My
        Company', [
        '@year' => $date->format('Y'),
      ]),
    ];
  }
}
```

The build method returns a render array that uses Drupal's t function to substitute @year for the \DateTime object's output that is formatted as a full year.

6. Rebuild your Drupal site's cache to rebuild the block plugin definitions cache, causing a rediscovery of plugin definitions:

```
php vendor/bin/drush cr
```

7. Go to the **Block layout** page from **Structure** in the administrative menu. In the Footer fourth region, click on **Place block**.

8. Review the block list and add the custom block to your regions, for instance, the footer region. Find the **Copyright** block and click on **Place block** in the dialog form:

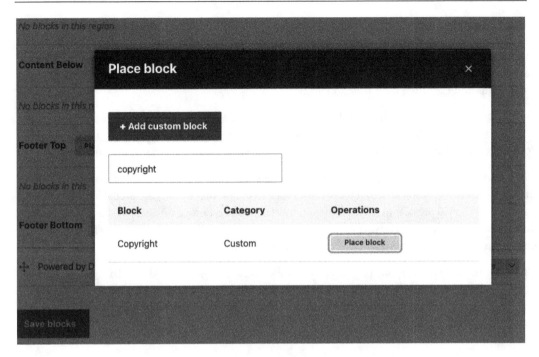

Figure 8.1 – Place block dialog for the Copyright block

9. Uncheck the **Display title** checkbox so that only our block's content will be rendered. Click on **Save blocks** and accept all other defaults.

10. Visit your Drupal site and verify that the copyright statement displays the current year:

Figure 8.2 – Copyright block in the footer of a Drupal site

How it works...

The plugin system is comprised of multiple instantiable classes that share a similar interface. Using annotations and plugin managers, Drupal makes these classes discoverable. This allows for interacting with plugins and executing their functionality.

The `\Drupal\Core\Block\BlockManager` class specifies that the block plugins must be located in the `Plugin\Block` namespace. It also defines the base interface that needs to be implemented, along with the `Annotation` class, which is to be used when parsing the class's document block.

When retrieving plugin definitions, the plugin manager first checks whether definitions have been previously discovered and cached. If there are no cached plugin definitions, the available namespaces registered in Drupal are scanned for plugins in the `\Drupal\{extension}\Plugin\Block` namespace. The discovered classes are then processed with the class documentation, which contains annotation data, and are then cached as the available plugin definitions.

When viewing the **Block layout** page to manage blocks, the `label` method on `\Drupal\Core\Block\BlockBase` is invoked to display the human-readable name defined in the plugin's annotation. When a block is displayed on a rendered page, the `build` method is invoked and passed to the theming layer to be output.

There's more...

There are more in-depth items that can be used when creating a block plugin. We will cover those in the following sections.

Altering blocks

Blocks can be altered in three different ways: the **plugin definition**, the **build array**, or the **view array output** can be altered.

A module can implement `hook_block_alter` in its `.module` file and modify the annotation definitions of all the discovered blocks. This will allow a module to change the default `user_login_block` from **User Login** to **Login**:

```
/**
 * Implements hook_block_alter().
 */
function mymodule_block_alter(&$definitions) {
  $definitions['user_login_block']['admin_label'] =
    t('Login');
}
```

A module can implement hook_block_build_alter and modify the build information of a block. The hook is passed through the build array and the instance for the current block. Module developers can use this to add cache contexts or alter the cacheability of the cache metadata:

```
/**
 * Implements hook_block_build_alter().
 */
function mymodule_block_build_alter(
  array &$build,
  \Drupal\Core\Block\BlockPluginInterface $block
) {

  // Add the 'url' cache the block per URL.
  if ($block->id() == 'myblock') {
    $build['#cache']['contexts'][] = 'url';
  }

}
```

You can test the modification of the cache metadata by altering the block created in this recipe to output a timestamp instead of a year format. With caching enabled, you will see that the value persists on the same URL, but it will be different across each page.

Finally, a module can implement hook_block_view_alter in order to modify the output of the block to be rendered. A module can add content to be rendered or removed. This can be used to remove the contextual_links item, which allows inline editing on the front page of a site:

```
/**
 * Implements hook_block_view_alter().
 */
function mymodule_block_view_alter(
  array &$build,
  \Drupal\Core\Block\BlockPluginInterface $block
) {
  // Remove the contextual links on all blocks that provide
    them.
  if (isset($build['#contextual_links'])) {
```

```
        unset($build['#contextual_links']);
    }
}
```

Block settings form

Blocks can provide a settings form. This recipe provides the text *My Company* for the copyright text. Instead of being set in code, this can be defined through a text field in the block's setting form.

Let's readdress the `Copyright.php` file that holds our block's class. We will override methods provided by our base class. The following methods will be added to the class written in this recipe.

A block can override the default `defaultConfiguration` method, which returns an array of setting keys and their default values. The `blockForm` method can then be overridden to return a Form API array to represent the settings form:

```
/**
 * {@inheritdoc}
 */
public function defaultConfiguration() {
  return [
    'company_name' => '',
  ];
}


/**
 * {@inheritdoc}
 */
public function blockForm($form,
  \Drupal\Core\Form\FormStateInterface $form_state) {
  $form['company_name'] = [
    '#type' => 'textfield',
    '#title' => t('Company name'),
    '#default_value' => $this->configuration
        ['company_name'],
  ];
  return $form;
}
```

The blockSubmit method must then be implemented, which updates the block's configuration. The following code retrieves the company_name value from the form's state, which contains submitted values, and sets it to the configuration property in its company_name key:

```
/**
 * {@inheritdoc}
 */
public function blockSubmit($form, \Drupal
   \Core\Form\FormStateInterface $form_state) {
   $this->configuration['company_name'] =
   $form_state->getValue('company_name');
}
```

Finally, the build method can be updated to use the new configuration item:

```
/**
 * {@inheritdoc}
 */
public function build()
{
   $date = new \DateTime();
   return [
     '#markup' => t('Copyright @year&copy; @company', [
       '@year' => $date->format('Y'),
       '@company' => $this->configuration['company_name'],
     ]),
   ];
}
```

You can now return to the **Block layout** form and click on **Configure** for the Copyright block. The new setting will be available in the block instance's configuration form.

Defining access to a block

Blocks, by default, are rendered for all users. The default access method can be overridden. This allows a block to only be displayed to authenticated users or based on specific permissions:

```
/**
 * {@inheritdoc}
 */
```

```
protected function blockAccess(AccountInterface $account) {
  $route_name = $this->routeMatch->getRouteName();
  if ($account->isAnonymous() && !in_array($route_name,
    ['user.login', 'user.logout'])) {
    return AccessResult::allowed()
      ->addCacheContexts(['route.name',
        'user.roles:anonymous']);
  }
  return AccessResult::forbidden();
}
```

The preceding code is taken from user_login_block. It allows access to the block if the user is logged out and is not on the login or logout page. The access is cached based on the current route name and the user's current role being anonymous. If these are not passed, the access returned is forbidden and the block is not built.

Other modules can implement hook_block_access to override the access of a block:

```
/**
 * Implements hook_block_access().
 */
function mymodule_block_access(
  \Drupal\block\Entity\Block $block,
  $operation,
  \Drupal\Core\Session\AccountInterface $account
) {
  // Example code that would prevent displaying the
    Copyright' block in
  // a region different from the footer.
  if ($operation == 'view' && $block->getPluginId() ==
    'copyright') {
    return
      \Drupal\Core\Access\AccessResult::forbiddenIf($block-
        >getRegion() != 'footer');
  }
  // No opinion.
```

```
    return \Drupal\Core\Access\AccessResult::neutral();
}
```

A module implementing the preceding hook will deny access to our Copyright block if it is not placed in the footer region. If the block operation is not view and the block is not our Copyright block, a neutral access result is passed. A neutral result allows the system to process other access results. Otherwise, AccessResult::forbiddenIf will return neutral or forbidden based on the Boolean value passed to it.

See also

- Refer to the *Creating a custom plugin type* recipe of this chapter
- Annotation-based plugin documentation: https://www.drupal.org/docs/drupal-apis/plugin-api/annotations-based-plugins
- Information about hooks provided by the Block module: https://api.drupal.org/api/drupal/core%21modules%21block%21block.api.php/10

Creating a custom field type

Field types are defined using the plugin system. Each field type has its own class and definition. A new field type can be defined through a custom class that will provide schema and property information.

Field types define ways in which data can be stored and handled through the **Field** API on entities. Field widgets provide means for editing a field type in the user interface. Field formatters provide means for displaying the field data to users. Both are plugins and will be covered in later recipes.

In this example, we will create a simple field type called realname to store the first and last names and add it to a comment type.

Getting ready

This recipe adds a field to a comment type, which requires the Comment module to be installed. The Comment module is installed by default with a standard Drupal installation.

How to do it...

1. First, we need to create the src/Plugin/Field/FieldType directory in the module's directory. The Field module discovers field types in the Plugin\Field\FieldType namespace:

   ```
   mkdir -p src/Plugin/Field/FieldType
   ```

2. Create a file named `RealName.php` in the newly created directory so that we can define the `RealName` class. This will provide our `realname` field type for the first and last names.

3. The `RealName` class will extend the `\Drupal\Core\Field\FieldItemBase` class:

```php
<?php

namespace Drupal\mymodule\Plugin\Field\FieldType;

use Drupal\Core\Field\FieldItemBase;
use Drupal\Core\Field\FieldStorageDefinitionInterface;
use Drupal\Core\TypedData\DataDefinition;

class RealName extends FieldItemBase {
}
```

We will extend the `FieldItemBase` class, which satisfies methods defined by inherited interfaces for the `FieldType` plugin type, except for the `schema` and `propertyDefinitions` methods.

4. Next, we will write the plugin annotation in a class document block. We will provide the field type's identifier, label, description, category, default widget, and formatter:

```php
<?php

namespace Drupal\mymodule\Plugin\Field\FieldType;

use Drupal\Core\Field\FieldItemBase;
use Drupal\Core\Field\FieldStorageDefinitionInterface;
use Drupal\Core\TypedData\DataDefinition;

/**
 * Plugin implementation of the 'realname' field type.
 *
 * @FieldType(
 *   id = "realname",
 *   label = @Translation("Real name"),
 *   description = @Translation("This field stores a
 *       first and last name."),
 *   category = @Translation("General"),
 *   default_widget = "string_textfield",
```

```
 *    default_formatter = "string"
 * )
 */
class RealName extends FieldItemBase {
}
```

The @FieldType annotation tells Drupal that this is a FieldType plugin. The following properties are defined:

- id: This is the plugin's machine name

- label: This is the human-readable name for the field

- description: This is the human-readable description of the field

- category: This is the category where the field shows up in the user interface

- default_widget: This is the default form widget to be used for editing

- default_formatter: This is the default formatter with which you can display the field

5. The RealName class needs to implement the schema method defined in \Drupal\ Core\Field\FieldItemInterface. This returns an array of the database API schema information. Add the following method to your class:

```
/**
 * {@inheritdoc}
 */
public static function schema(FieldStorage
  DefinitionInterface $field_definition)  {
  return [
    'columns' => [
      'first_name' => [
        'description' => 'First name.',
        'type' => 'varchar',
        'length' => '255',
        'not null' => TRUE,
        'default' => '',
      ],
      'last_name' => [
        'description' => 'Last name.',
        'type' => 'varchar',
        'length' => '255',
```

```
                'not null' => TRUE,
                'default' => '',
            ],
        ],
        'indexes' => [
          'first_name' => ['first_name'],
          'last_name' => ['last_name'],
        ],
      ];
    }
```

The `schema` method defines the database columns in the field's data table. We define a column to hold the `first_name` and `last_name` values.

6. We will also need to implement the `propertyDefinitions` method. This returns a data definition of the values defined in the `schema` method. Add the following method to your class:

```
/**
 * {@inheritdoc}
 */
public static function propertyDefinitions
    (FieldStorageDefinitionInterface
        $field_definition) {
  $properties['first_name'] =
      DataDefinition::create('string')
    ->setLabel(t('First name'));
  $properties['last_name'] =
      DataDefinition::create('string')
    ->setLabel(t('Last name'));
  return $properties;
}
```

This method returns an array that is keyed with the same column names provided in the schema. It returns data definitions to represent the properties in the field type.

7. We will override one more method, the `mainPropertyName` method, to specify that `first_name` is the main property:

```
/**
 * {@inheritdoc}
 */
```

```
public static function mainPropertyName() {
    return 'first_name';
}
```

This method allows specifying the main property to be used for retrieving the field value automatically when there are multiple values.

8. Rebuild your Drupal site's cache to build the field type plugin definitions cache, causing a rediscovery of plugin definitions:

```
php vendor/bin/drush cr
```

9. The field will now appear on the field type management screen. To use it, go to **Structure** and then to **Comment types**. You can now go to **Manage fields** and click on **Add field** to add a real name entry for your comments:

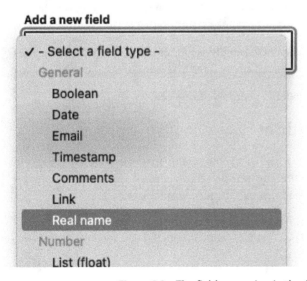

Figure 8.3 – The field appearing in the Add a new field list

How it works...

The plugin manager for field types is the `plugin.manager.field.field_type` service. This plugin manager defines that field type plugins must be in the `Plugin\Field\FieldType` namespace and implement `\Drupal\Core\Field\FieldItemInterface`.

When adding a new field to an entity type, the definitions are retrieved from the field type manager to populate the list of field types. When a field is added to an entity type, that entity type's database storage is updated based on the properties provided by the field in `propertyDefinitions` with the schema from the `schema` method.

There's more...

Field types can implement a method to define whether the value is empty or not. We will cover this in the next section.

Defining whether a field is empty

Field type classes have an `isEmpty` method that is used to determine whether the field has no values.

Field types extend `Drupal\Core\TypedData\Plugin\DataType\Map`, which is a class representation of an associative array in Drupal's **Typed Data** API. This in turn implements the `\Drupal\Core\TypedDate\ComplexDataInterface` interface, which provides the `isEmpty` method.

The default functionality is that a field is not considered empty as long as one property has values. For instance, our real name field would not be considered empty if the first name or last name had values.

Field types can provide their own implementations to provide a more robust verification.

Creating a custom field widget

Field widgets provide the form component to a field in an entity form. These integrate with the Form API to define how a field can be edited and the way in which the data can be formatted before it is saved. Field widgets are chosen and customized through the form display interface.

In this recipe, we will create a widget for the field created in the *Creating a custom field type* recipe in this chapter. The field widget will provide two text fields for entering the first and last name items.

Getting ready

This recipe provides a field widget for the field type created in the previous recipe, *Creating a custom field type*.

How to do it...

1. First, we need to create the `src/Plugin/Field/FieldWidget` directory in the module's directory. The `Field` module discovers field widgets in the `Plugin\Field\FieldWidget` namespace:

```
mkdir -p src/Plugin/Field/FieldWidget
```

2. Create a `RealNameDefaultWidget.php` file in the newly created directory so that we can define the `RealNameDefaultWidget` class. This will provide a custom form element to edit the first and last name values of our field.

3. The `RealNameDefaultWidget` class will extend the `\Drupal\Core\Field\WidgetBase` class:

```php
<?php

namespace Drupal\mymodule\Plugin\Field\FieldWidget;

use Drupal\Core\Field\FieldItemListInterface;
use Drupal\Core\Field\WidgetBase;
use Drupal\Core\Form\FormStateInterface;

class RealNameDefaultWidget extends WidgetBase {
}
```

4. We will extend the `WidgetBase` class, which satisfies methods defined by inherited interfaces for the `FieldWidget` plugin type, except the `formElement` method.

5. We will provide the field widget's identifier, label, and supported field types in the plugin's annotation:

```php
<?php

namespace Drupal\mymodule\Plugin\Field\FieldWidget;

use Drupal\Core\Field\FieldItemListInterface;
use Drupal\Core\Field\WidgetBase;
use Drupal\Core\Form\FormStateInterface;

/**
 * Plugin implementation of the 'realname_default'
```

```
       widget.
   *
   * @FieldWidget(
   *   id = "realname_default",
   *   label = @Translation("Real name"),
   *   field_types = {
   *     "realname"
   *   }
   * )
   */
  class RealNameDefaultWidget extends WidgetBase {


  }
```

@FieldWidget tells Drupal that this is a field widget plugin. It defines id to represent the machine name, the human-readable name as label, and the field types that the widget interacts with as the field_types property.

6. We need to implement the formElement method to satisfy the remaining interface methods after extending \Drupal\Core\Field\WidgetBase. Add the following method to your class:

```
  /**
   * {@inheritdoc}
   */
  public function formElement(
    FieldItemListInterface $items,
    $delta,
    array $element,
    array &$form,
    FormStateInterface $form_state
  ) {
    $element['first_name'] = [
      '#type' => 'textfield',
      '#title' => t('First name'),
      '#default_value' => '',
      '#size' => 25,
      '#required' => $element['#required'],
    ];
```

```
    $element['last_name'] = [
      '#type' => 'textfield',
      '#title' => t('Last name'),
      '#default_value' => '',
      '#size' => 25,
      '#required' => $element['#required'],
    ];
    return $element;
}
```

The `formElement` method returns the Form API array structure, which should be added to an entity form for each field item. The names of the element items – `first_name` and `last_name` – map to the field property names so that they are saved correctly.

7. Next, we will need to modify our original `RealName` field type plugin class to use the default widget that we created. Modify the `src/Plugin/FieldType/RealName.php` file, and update the `default_widget` annotation property as `realname_default`:

```
/**
 * Plugin implementation of the 'realname' field type.
 *
 * @FieldType(
 *    id = "realname",
 *    label = @Translation("Real name"),
 *    description = @Translation("This field stores a
 *        first and last name."),
 *    category = @Translation("General"),
 *    default_widget = "realname_default",
 *    default_formatter = "string"
 * )
 */
class RealName extends FieldItemBase {
```

8. Rebuild your Drupal site's cache to update the field type definition and discovery of the new field widget plugin:

```
php vendor/bin/drush cr
```

9.   The field added to **Comment type** will now use the field widget:

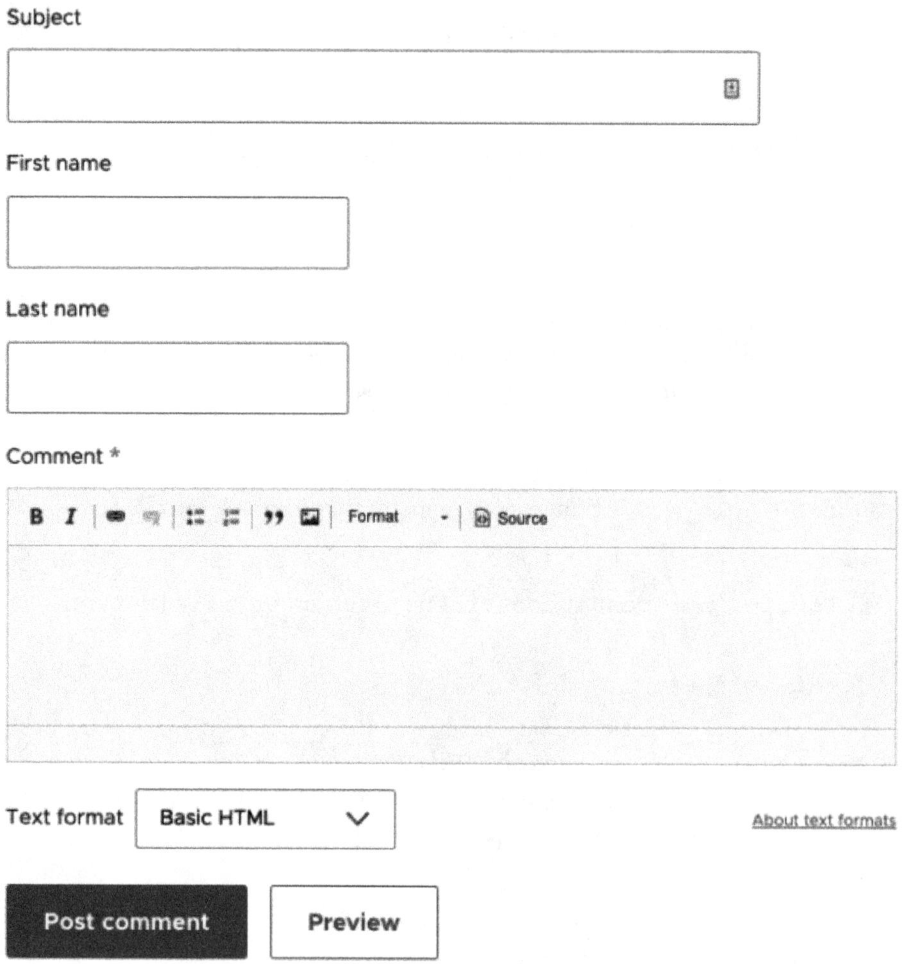

Subject

First name

Last name

Comment *

| B | *I* | | | | | | **99** | | Format | ▾ | Source |

Text format   Basic HTML ⌄   About text formats

Post comment   Preview

Figure 8.4 – Real name widget on a comment form

How it works...

The plugin manager for field types is the `plugin.manager.field.widget` service. This plugin manager defines that field type plugins must be in the `Plugin\Field\FieldWidget` namespace and implement `\Drupal\Core\Field\WidgetInterface`.

The entity form display system uses the plugin manager to load field definitions as options on the form display configuration form. When the entity form is built using the form display configuration, the form-building process adds the element returned from the `formElement` method to the entity form.

There's more...

Field widgets have additional methods to provide more information; they are covered in the next section.

Field widget settings and summary

The `\Drupal\Core\Field\WidgetInterface` interface defines three methods that can be overridden to provide a settings form and a summary of the current settings:

- `defaultSettings`: This returns an array of the setting keys and default values
- `settingsForm`: This returns a Form API array that is used for the settings form
- `settingsSummary`: This allows an array of strings to be returned and displayed on the manage display form for the field

Widget settings can be used to alter the form presented to the user. A setting can be created that allows the field element to be limited to only entering the first or last name with one text field.

Creating a custom field formatter

Field formatters define the way in which a field type will be presented. These formatters return the render array information to be processed by the theming layer. Field formatters are configured on the display mode interfaces.

In this recipe, we will create a formatter for the field created in the *Creating a custom field type* recipe in this chapter. The field formatter will display the first and last name values inline, as a full name.

Getting ready

This recipe provides a field formatter for the field type created in the previous recipe, *Creating a custom field type*.

How to do it...

1. First, we need to create the `src/Plugin/Field/FieldFormatter` directory in the module's directory. The `Field` module discovers field formatters in the `Plugin\Field\FieldFormatter` namespace:

   ```
   mkdir -p src/Plugin/Field/FieldFormatter
   ```

2. Create a `RealNameFormatter.php` file in the newly created directory so that we can define the `RealNameFormatter` class. This will provide a custom formatter to display the field's values.

3. The `RealNameFormatter` class will extend the `\Drupal\Core\Field\`
    `FormatterBase` class:

    ```php
    <?php

    namespace Drupal\mymodule\Plugin\Field\FieldFormatter;

    use Drupal\Core\Field\FormatterBase;
    use Drupal\Core\Field\FieldItemListInterface;

    class RealNameFormatter extends FormatterBase {
    }
    ```

    We extend the `FormatterBase` class, which satisfies methods defined by inherited interfaces
    for the `FieldFormatter` plugin type, except the `viewElements` method.

4. We will provide the field widget's identifier, label, and supported field types in the plugin's annotation:

    ```php
    <?php

    namespace Drupal\mymodule\Plugin\Field\FieldFormatter;

    use Drupal\Core\Field\FormatterBase;
    use Drupal\Core\Field\FieldItemListInterface;

    /**
     * Plugin implementation of the 'realname_one_line'
     *   formatter.
     *
     * @FieldFormatter(
     *   id = "realname_one_line",
     *   label = @Translation("Real name (one line)"),
     *   field_types = {
     *     "realname"
     *   }
     * )
     */
    class RealNameFormatter extends FormatterBase {
    }
    ```

@FieldFormatter tells Drupal that this is a field formatter plugin. It defines id to represent the machine name, the human-readable name as label, and the field types that the formatter interacts with as the field_types property.

5. We will need to implement the viewElements method to satisfy the \Drupal\Core\ Field\FormatterInferface interface. This is used to render the field data. Add the following method to your class:

```
/**
 * {@inheritdoc}
 */
public function viewElements(
  FieldItemListInterface $items,
  $langcode
) {
  $element = [];
  foreach ($items as $delta => $item) {
    $element[$delta] = [
      '#markup' => $this->t('@first @last', [
        '@first' => $item->first_name,
        '@last' => $item->last_name,
      ]),
    ];
  }
  return $element;
}
```

The field values are provided to the viewElements method as a FieldItemListInterface iterable that contains each field item. Fields in Drupal can contain a single value, or an unlimited number of values. We iterate over each value and create a templated string that displays the first name and last name values in one line as a full name.

6. Next, we will need to modify our original RealName field type's plugin class to use the default formatter that we created. Open the src/Plugin/FieldType/RealName.php file, and update the default_formatter annotation property as realname_one_line:

```
/**
 * Plugin implementation of the 'realname' field type.
 *
 * @FieldType(
 *   id = "realname",
```

```
 *      label = @Translation("Real name"),
 *      description = @Translation("This field stores a
          first and last name."),
 *      category = @Translation("General"),
 *      default_widget = "realname_default",
 *      default_formatter = "realname_one_line"
 *  )
 */
class RealName extends FieldItemBase {
```

7. Rebuild your Drupal site's cache to update the field type definition and discovery of the new field formatter plugin:

    ```
    php vendor/bin/drush cr
    ```

8. The field added to **Comment type** will now use the field formatter:

admin   2 min 11 sec ago

A sample comment

Matt Glaman

A comment message

Delete   Edit   Reply

Figure 8.5 – Output of the real name formatter

How it works...

The plugin manager for field types is the `plugin.manager.field.formatter` service. This plugin manager defines that field type plugins must be in the `Plugin\Field\FieldFormatter` namespace and implement `\Drupal\Core\Field\FormatterInterface`.

The entity view display system uses the plugin manager to load field definitions as options on the view display configuration form. When the entity is built using the view display configuration, the process iterates through each field on the entity and invokes the configured formatter's `viewElements` method. The final result is used to render the display of the entity.

There's more...

Field formatters have additional methods to provide more information; they are covered in the next section.

Formatter settings and summary

The `\Drupal\Core\Field\FormatterInterface` interface defines three methods that can be overridden to provide a settings form and a summary of the current settings:

- `defaultSettings`: This returns an array of the setting keys and default values
- `settingsForm`: This returns a Form API array that is used for the settings form
- `settingsSummary`: This allows an array of strings to be returned and displayed on the manage display form for the field

Settings can be used to alter how the formatter displays information. For example, these methods can be implemented to provide settings to hide or display the first or last name.

Creating a custom plugin type

The **plugin system** provides a means to create specialized objects in Drupal that do not require the data storage features of the entity system. As we have seen with the block and field plugins, each plugin type serves a specific purpose and allows for extensibility.

In this recipe, we will create a new plugin type called `GeoLocator`, which will return the country code for a given IP address. We will create a plugin manager, a default plugin interface, a plugin annotation definition, and plugin implementations. A **Content Delivery Network** (**CDN**) commonly provides HTTP headers with the visitor's country code. We will provide plugins for **Cloudflare** and **AWS CloudFront**.

How to do it...

1. All plugins need to have a service that acts as a plugin manager. Create a file in the `src` directory of your module called `GeoLocatorManager.php`. This will hold the `GeoLocatorManager` class.

2. Create the `GeoLocatorManager` class by extending the `\Drupal\Core\Plugin\DefaultPluginManager` class provided by Drupal core:

```php
<?php

namespace Drupal\mymodule;
```

```php
use Drupal\Core\Plugin\DefaultPluginManager;
use Drupal\Core\Cache\CacheBackendInterface;
use Drupal\Core\Extension\ModuleHandlerInterface;

class GeoLocatorManager extends DefaultPluginManager {
}
```

DefaultPluginManager provides the essential functionality for a plugin manager, requiring implementors to only override its constructor.

3. Next, we will need to override the __construct method from the DefaultPluginManager class to define information about our plugin type. Note, it will reference code created in the following steps:

```php
<?php

namespace Drupal\mymodule;

use Drupal\Core\Plugin\DefaultPluginManager;
use Drupal\Core\Cache\CacheBackendInterface;
use Drupal\Core\Extension\ModuleHandlerInterface;

class GeoLocatorManager extends DefaultPluginManager {

  public function __construct(
    \Traversable $namespaces,
    CacheBackendInterface $cache_backend,
    ModuleHandlerInterface
    $module_handler
  ) {
    parent::__construct(
      'Plugin/GeoLocator',
      $namespaces,
      $module_handler,
      'Drupal\mymodule\Plugin\GeoLocator
        \GeoLocatorInterface',
      'Drupal\mymodule\Annotation\GeoLocator'
    );
```

```
    }
  }
```

The first argument to the parent construct call of `Plugin/GeoLocator` specifies that the namespace `GeoLocator` plugins must reside in a module. The fourth argument, `Drupal\mymodule\Plugin\GeoLocator\GeoLocatorInterface`, identifies the interface that `GeoLocator` plugins must implement. The fifth argument, `Drupal\mymodule\Annotation\GeoLocator`, specifies the annotation class, so that plugins may register themselves with `@GeoLocator` annotations.

4. Before we create the `GeoLocator` plugin interface and annotation, we will create the service definition to register our plugin manager. Create a `mymodule.services.yml` file and add the following:

```
services:
  plugin.manager.geolocator:
    class: Drupal\mymodule\GeoLocatorManager
    parent: default_plugin_manager
```

While not required, it is a pattern to name plugin manager services with `plugin.manager.` and then the plugin type name. We can use the parent definition to tell the service container to use the same arguments as the `default_plugin_manager` definition when constructing our class.

5. All annotation-based plugins must provide an annotation class. Create `GeoLocator.php` in `src/Annotation` to provide the `GeoLocator` annotation class, as we specified in our plugin manager:

```php
<?php

namespace Drupal\mymodule\Annotation;

use Drupal\Component\Annotation\Plugin;

/**
 * @Annotation
 */
class GeoLocator extends Plugin
{
  /**
   * The human-readable name.
   *
```

```
    * @var \Drupal\Core\Annotation\Translation
    *
    * @ingroup plugin_translatable
    */
   public $label;


}
```

Each property is an item that can be defined in the plugin's annotation. The annotated definition will be @GeoLocator for our plugins, as the annotation's class name is GeoLocator.

6. Next, we will define the plugin interface that we defined in the plugin manager. The discovery process for plugins validates that GeoLocator plugins implement this interface. Create a GeoLocatorInterface.php file in our module's src/Plugin/GeoLocator directory to hold the interface:

```php
<?php

namespace Drupal\mymodule\Plugin\GeoLocator;

use Symfony\Component\HttpFoundation\Request;

interface GeoLocatorInterface {

  /**
   * Get the plugin's label.
   *
   * @return string
   *    The geolocator label
   */
  public function label();

  /**
   * Performs geolocation on an address.
   *
   * @param Request $request
   *    The request.
   *
   * @return string|NULL
```

```
 *     The geolocated country code, or NULL if not
 *        found.
 */
public function geolocate(Request $request):
  ?string;
}
```

We provide an interface so that we can guarantee that we have these expected methods when working with a GeoLocator plugin. The geolocate method receives a request object and returns a country code, or null if one could not be found.

7. Now that we have our plugin type set up, we will create our first plugin to support the Cloudflare country code header. Create the src/Plugin/GeoLocator/Cloudflare.php file for the Cloudflare plugin class:

```php
<?php

namespace Drupal\mymodule\Plugin\GeoLocator;

use Drupal\Core\Plugin\PluginBase;
use Symfony\Component\HttpFoundation\Request;

/**
 * @GeoLocator(
 *   id = "cloudflare",
 *   label = "Cloudflare"
 * )
 */
class Cloudflare extends PluginBase implements
    GeoLocatorInterface {

  public function label() {
    return $this->pluginDefinition['label'];
  }

  public function geolocate(Request $request): ?string {
    return $request->headers->get('CF-IPCountry');
```

```
    }

}
```

Cloudflare provides the visitor's country code in an HTTP header named CF-IPCountry. This plugin returns the value from that header, or null if it is missing.

8.   Next, we create a plugin for AWS CloudFront's country code header. Create the src/Plugin/ GeoLocator/CloudFront.php file for the CloudFront plugin class:

```php
<?php

namespace Drupal\mymodule\Plugin\GeoLocator;

use Drupal\Core\Plugin\PluginBase;
use Symfony\Component\HttpFoundation\Request;

/**
 * @GeoLocator(
 *   id = "cloudfront",
 *   label = "CloudFront"
 * )
 */
class CloudFront extends PluginBase implements
    GeoLocatorInterface {

  public function label() {
    return $this->pluginDefinition['label'];
  }

  public function geolocate(Request $request): ?string {
    return $request->headers->get('CloudFront-Viewer-
        Country');
  }

}
```

AWS CloudFront provides the visitor's country code in an HTTP header named CloudFront-Viewer-Country. This plugin returns the value from that header, or null if it is missing.

9. Finally, we will create a demonstration plugin that reads the country code from a query parameter. Create the `src/Plugin/GeoLocator/RequestQuery.php` file for the `RequestQuery` plugin class:

```php
<?php

namespace Drupal\mymodule\Plugin\GeoLocator;

use Drupal\Core\Plugin\PluginBase;
use Symfony\Component\HttpFoundation\Request;

/**
 * @GeoLocator(
 *   id = "request_query",
 *   label = "Request query"
 * )
 */
class RequestQuery extends PluginBase implements
    GeoLocatorInterface {

  public function label() {
    return $this->pluginDefinition['label'];
  }

  public function geolocate(Request $request): ?string {
    return $request->query->get('countryCode');
  }

}
```

Unlike the other plugins, this plugin returns the value of the `countryCode` query parameter in a URL.

10. The following is an example that will set a message of the country code, if one can be detected by a plugin, on each page:

```php
<?php

/**
```

```
 * Implements hook_page_top().
 */
function mymodule_page_top() {
  $request = \Drupal::request();
  /** @var \Drupal\mymodule\GeoLocatorManager $manager
    */
  $manager = \Drupal::service
    ('plugin.manager.geolocator');
  foreach ($manager->getDefinitions() as $plugin_id =>
    $definition) {
    /** @var \Drupal\mymodule\Plugin\GeoLocator
        \GeoLocatorInterface */
    $instance = $manager->createInstance($plugin_id);
    $country_code = $instance->geolocate($request);
    if ($country_code) {
      \Drupal::messenger()->addStatus("Country:
        $country_code");
      break;
    }
  }
}
```

We fetch the definitions from the plugin manager and create an instance of each plugin. We then check whether the plugin returns a result. If the plugin returns a country code, the country code is added as a message and then the loop is stopped.

How it works...

Plugins and plugin types are a way of grouping classes that operate with specific functionality. The plugin manager provides a way of discovering these classes and instantiating them. In the last step of this recipe, we used the plugin manager to find each definition, create an instance of the plugin, and then call the `geolocate` method to find a country code from the request object.

Plugin managers utilize discovery methods to find plugin classes. By default, the `\Drupal\Core\Plugin\Discovery\AnnotatedClassDiscovery` discovery method is used. The subdirectory is used to look for plugins, which we specified as `Plugin/GeoLocator` in our plugin manager's `__construct` method. The annotated class discovery then iterates through the mapping of namespaces to their directories. It discovers PHP files in the desired directory. These classes are then inspected for the proper `@GeoLocator` annotation and to make sure that they implement the `GeoLocatorInterface` interface. Discovered classes are then registered as plugin definitions.

There's more...

There are many additional items for creating a custom plugin type; we will discuss some of them in the following sections.

Specifying an alter hook

Plugin managers have the ability to define an alter hook. The following line of code will be added to the GeoLocatorManager class's constructor to provide the hook_geolocator_plugins_alter alter hook. This is passed to the module handler service for invocations:

```
public function __construct(
  \Traversable $namespaces,
  CacheBackendInterface $cache_backend,
  ModuleHandlerInterface
  $module_handler
) {
  parent::__construct(
    'Plugin/GeoLocator',
    $namespaces,
    $module_handler,
    'Drupal\mymodule\Plugin\GeoLocator
      \GeoLocatorInterface',
    'Drupal\mymodule\Annotation\GeoLocator'
  );
  // Specify the alter hook.
  $this->alterInfo('geolocator_info');
}
```

Modules implementing hook_geolocator_plugins_alter in their .module file have the ability to modify all the discovered plugin definitions. They also have the ability to remove defined plugin entries or alter any information provided for the annotation definition.

Using a cache backend

Plugins can use a cache backend to improve performance. This can be done by specifying a cache backend with the setCacheBackend method in the plugin manager's constructor. The following line of code will allow the GeoLocator plugin definitions to be cached and only discovered on a cache rebuild:

```
$this->setCacheBackend($cache_backend,
    'geolocator_plugins');
```

Without specifying a cache backend, Drupal will scan the filesystem for any annotated `GeoLocator` plugins provided by modules. The `$cache_backend` variable is passed to the constructor. The second parameter provides the cache key. The cache key will have the current language code added as a suffix.

There is an optional third parameter that takes an array of strings to represent cache tags that will cause the plugin definitions to be cleared. This is an advanced feature, and plugin definitions should normally be cleared through the manager's `clearCachedDefinitions` method. The cache tags allow the plugin definitions to be cleared when a relevant cache is cleared as well.

Accessing plugins through the manager

Plugins are loaded through the manager service. Plugin managers have various methods for retrieving plugin definitions, which are as follows:

- `getDefinitions`: This method will return an array of plugin definitions. It first makes an attempt to retrieve cached definitions, if any, and sets the cache of discovered definitions before returning them.
- `getDefinition`: This takes an expected plugin ID and returns its definition.
- `createInstance`: This takes an expected plugin ID and returns an initiated class for the plugin.
- `getInstance`: This takes an array that acts as a plugin definition and returns an initiated class from the definition.

9

Creating Custom Entity Types

In *Chapter 6*, *Accessing and Working with Entities*, we explored manipulating individual entities. This chapter covers creating custom entity types for custom data models. **Entities** in Drupal are made up of different entity types. **Entity types** are defined as annotated plugins. Each entity is an instance of its entity type class. Entity types can also be enhanced to have different classes based on their bundle. You will learn how to implement your own custom entity in this chapter.

In this chapter, we will go through the following recipes:

- Using custom classes for entity bundles
- Creating a configuration entity type
- Creating a content entity type
- Creating a bundle for a content entity type
- Implementing access control for an entity
- Providing a custom storage handler

Technical requirements

This chapter will require a custom module that is not installed. Drupal will not register a new entity type or update entity types automatically for already-installed modules. The *There's more...* section of the recipes will explain how to install or update entity types for already-installed modules.

In the following recipes, the module name is `mymodule`. Replace instances of `mymodule` with your module name as appropriate in your code. You can find the full code used in this chapter on GitHub: `https://github.com/PacktPublishing/Drupal-10-Development-Cookbook/tree/main/chp09`.

Using custom classes for entity bundles

Each entity is instantiated with its entity type class. A **Node** entity will be an instance of \Drupal\node\Entity\Node and a **Taxonomy Term** entity will be an instance of \Drupal\taxonomy\Entity\Term regardless of the entity's bundle. Drupal allows altering entity information to provide alternative classes when an entity of a specific bundle is instantiated. Entity bundles are often used for different specific business logic. This feature allows the creation of classes with specific business logic associated with fields on the bundle.

In this recipe, we will create an entity bundle class to be used when there is a **Recipe** node.

Getting started

In this recipe, we will be using the **Recipe** content type provided by the Umami demo installation.

How to do it...

1. First, we need to create the src/Entity directory in the module's directory. This will translate to the \Drupal\mymodule\Entity namespace, which is where we will create our bundle class:

   ```
   mkdir -p src/Entity
   ```

2. Create a file named Recipe.php in the newly created directory so that we can define the Recipe class to use for our **Recipe** nodes.

3. The Recipe class will extend \Drupal\node\Entity\Node. Bundle classes must extend the class for its entity type:

   ```php
   <?php

   namespace Drupal\mymodule\Entity;

   use Drupal\node\Entity\Node;

   class Recipe extends Node {

   }
   ```

   If a bundle class does not extend the class for an entity type, Drupal will throw a BundleClassInheritanceException exception when processing entity type definitions.

4. By default, the **Recipe** content type comes with various fields, including a **Tags** field for referencing multiple taxonomy terms. We will create a method named `getTags` to return those referenced term entities:

```
class Recipe extends Node {

  public function getTags(): array {
    /** @var \Drupal\Core\Field\EntityReferenceField
        ItemListInterface $field_tags */
    $field_tags = $this->get('field_tags');
    return $field_tags->referencedEntities();
  }

}
```

Entity reference fields implement `EntityReferenceFieldItemListInterface`, which defines the `referencedEntities` method. This loads and returns all referenced entity objects.

5. With the bundle class defined, we must implement hook_entity_bundle_info_alter to register our bundle class for the **Recipe** content type:

```
<?php

/**
 * Implements hook_entity_bundle_info_alter().
 */
function mymodule_entity_bundle_info_alter(&$bundles) {
  $bundles ['node']['recipe']['label'] = t('Recipe');
  $bundles['node']['recipe']['class'] = Drupal\
    mymodule\Entity\Recipe::class;
}
```

The `$bundles` argument is an array of entity type bundles, keyed by entity type. To register an entity bundle, you set the `class` key for that bundle as your bundle class's class name.

6. The `getTags` method can then be used in a **Twig** template for **Recipe** content:

```
{% for tag in node.getTags %}
  <div>Tag: {{ tag.label }}</div>
{% endfor %}
```

How it works...

When an entity record is loaded from the database, the values are passed to its entity class. Content entity types support bundles and thus allow defining classes for each bundle, which extend the entity type class.

This is handled in the entity storage `\Drupal\Core\Entity\ContentEntityStorageBase` base class and its `getEntityClass` method. This method returns the class that should be used when mapping the database records into an instantiated entity object. This logic is contained in the `\Drupal\Core\Entity\EntityStorageBase::mapFromStorageRecords` method:

```
foreach ($records as $record) {
  $entity_class = $this->getEntityClass();
  /** @var \Drupal\Core\Entity\EntityInterface $entity */
  $entity = new $entity_class($record, $this->
    entityTypeId);
  $entities[$entity->id()] = $entity;
}
```

Whenever an entity entity is loaded, assertions can be made to check the instance of an entity object to verify its bundle and access specific methods for that bundle class. These methods are also allowed in Twig template markup. Twig templates are covered in *Chapter 10, Theming and Frontend Development*.

See also

- The change record for Drupal 9.3.0 introducing the bundle class feature: https://www.drupal.org/node/3191609

Creating a configuration entity type

In this recipe, we will create a configuration entity type called Announcement. This will provide a **configuration entity** that allows you to create, edit, and delete messages that can be displayed on the site for important announcements.

Configuration entities do not interact with Drupal's Field API and do not have a user interface to add fields. They have properties defined on their class like models in other frameworks. However, configuration entities do not have dedicated tables in the database. They are stored in the config table as serialized data. The purpose of a configuration entity is for configuration. Examples of configuration entities are view displays, form displays, and contact forms.

How to do it...

1. First, we need to create the `src/Entity` directory in the module's directory. This will translate to the `\Drupal\mymodule\Entity` namespace and allow for entity type discovery:

    ```
    mkdir -p src/Entity
    ```

2. Create a file named `Announcement.php` in the newly created directory so that we can define the `Announcement` class for our entity type.

3. The `Announcement` class will extend the `\Drupal\Core\Config\Entity\ConfigEntityBase` class and define our entity type's properties:

    ```php
    <?php

    namespace Drupal\mymodule\Entity;

    use Drupal\Core\Config\Entity\ConfigEntityBase;

    class Announcement extends ConfigEntityBase {

      public string $label = '';

      public string $message = '';

    }
    ```

    We extend the `ConfigEntityBase` class, which implements `\Drupal\Core\Config\Entity\ConfigEntityInterface` and satisfies all required method implementations so that we only need to define our properties. The `label` property will contain the description of the announcement, and the `message` property will contain the announcement's text.

    > **Note**
    >
    > Typically, properties of an entity type are protected and use methods to set and get values. To simplify the code in this recipe, we are using public properties.

4. Next, we will write the plugin annotation in a class documentation block for our entity type:

    ```
    /**
     * @ConfigEntityType(
     *   id = "announcement",
     *   label = "Announcement",
    ```

```
 *     entity_keys = {
 *       "id" = "id",
 *       "label" = "label"
 *     },
 *     config_export = {
 *       "id",
 *       "label",
 *       "message",
 *     },
 *     admin_permission = "administer announcement",
 * )
 */
  class Announcement extends ConfigEntityBase {
```

The @ConfigEntityType symbol specifies that this is a ConfigEntityType annotation. id is the entity type ID, used to retrieve the entity type's storage and other handlers. label is the human-readable name of the entity type. The values in entity_keys instruct Drupal what the id and label properties are.

When specifying config_export, we are telling the configuration management system what properties are exportable when our entity type is exported. admin_permission specifies the permission name required to manage the entity type.

5. Next, we will add the handlers key to our annotation:

```
/**
 * @ConfigEntityType(
 *     id = "announcement",
 *     label = "Announcement",
 *     entity_keys = {
 *       "id" = "id",
 *       "label" = "label"
 *     },
 *     config_export = {
 *       "id",
 *       "label",
 *       "message",
 *     },
 *     admin_permission = "administer announcement",
 *     handlers = {
```

```
 *         "list_builder" = "Drupal\mymodule
 *             \AnnouncementListBuilder",
 *         "form" = {
 *           "default" = "Drupal\mymodule
 *               \AnnouncementForm",
 *           "delete" = "Drupal\Core\Entity
 *               \EntityDeleteForm"
 *         },
 *         "route_provider" = {
 *           "html" = "Drupal\Core\Entity\Routing
 *               \AdminHtmlRouteProvider",
 *         },
 *       },
 *   )
 */
class Announcement extends ConfigEntityBase {
```

The handlers array specifies classes that provide the functionality for Drupal to interact with our entity type. The `list_builder` class, which we will create, is used to show a table of entities for our entity type. The `form` handlers specify the form classes to be used when creating, editing, or deleting an entity. The `route_provider` handler is an array of handlers that will generate routes for our entity type.

6. Lastly, for our entity type's annotation, we will provide link templates that `route_provider` will use to build routes for our entity type:

```
/**
 * @ConfigEntityType(
 *   id = "announcement",
 *   label = "Announcement",
 *   entity_keys = {
 *     "id" = "id",
 *     "label" = "label"
 *   },
 *   config_export = {
 *     "id",
 *     "label",
 *     "message",
```

```
 *     },
 *     admin_permission = "administer announcement",
 *     handlers = {
 *       "list_builder" = "Drupal\mymodule
 *             \AnnouncementListBuilder",
 *       "form" = {
 *         "default" = "Drupal\mymodule
 *             \AnnouncementForm",
 *         "delete" = "Drupal\Core\Entity\
 *             EntityDeleteForm"
 *       },
 *       "route_provider" = {
 *         "html" = "Drupal\Core\Entity\Routing\
 *             AdminHtmlRouteProvider",
 *       },
 *     },
 *     links = {
 *       "collection" = "/admin/config/system/
 *             announcements",
 *       "add-form" = "/admin/config/system/
 *             announcements/add",
 *       "delete-form" = "/admin/config/system/
 *             announcements/manage/{announcement}/delete",
 *       "edit-form" = "/admin/config/system/
 *             announcements/manage/{announcement}",
 *     },
 * )
 */
class Announcement extends ConfigEntityBase {
```

The links array defines keys expected from the html route provider, such as collection (list), add-form, delete-form, and edit-form. The route provider will generate routes for the given paths.

7. Create the `AnnouncementListBuilder` class defined in our `list_builder` handler by creating an `AnnouncementListBuilder.php` file in the `src` directory:

```php
<?php

namespace Drupal\mymodule;

use Drupal\Core\Config\Entity\ConfigEntityListBuilder;
use Drupal\Core\Entity\EntityInterface;

class AnnouncementListBuilder extends
    ConfigEntityListBuilder {

/**
 * Builds the header row for the entity listing.
 *
 * @return array
 *    A render array structure of header strings.
 *
 * @see \Drupal\Core\Entity
 *        \EntityListBuilder::render()
 */
    public function buildHeader()
  {
      $header['label'] = $this->t('Label');
      return $header + parent::buildHeader();
    }

/**
 * Builds a row for an entity in the entity listing.
 *
 * @param \Drupal\Core\Entity\EntityInterface $entity
 *    The entity for this row of the list.
 *
 * @return array
 *    A render array structure of fields for this
 *        entity.
```

```
 *
 * @see \Drupal\Core\Entity\
     EntityListBuilder::render()
 */
  public function buildRow(EntityInterface $entity) {
    $row['label'] = $entity->label();
    return $row + parent::buildRow($entity);
  }

}
```

Our `AnnouncementListBuilder` class extends `\Drupal\Core\Config\Entity\` `ConfigEntityListBuilder`, which provides all the required methods to build our table of entities. We override the `buildHeader` and `buildRow` methods to ensure entity labels are displayed.

8. Now, we will create the entity form that is used for creating and editing our entity type. Create the `AnnouncementForm` class, defined as the `default` form handler, by creating an `AnnouncementForm.php` file in the `src` directory:

```
<?php

namespace Drupal\mymodule;

use Drupal\Core\Entity\EntityForm;
use Drupal\Core\Form\FormStateInterface;
use Drupal\mymodule\Entity\Announcement;

class AnnouncementForm extends EntityForm {

/**
 * Gets the actual form array to be built.
 *
 * @see \Drupal\Core\Entity\EntityForm::processForm()
 * @see \Drupal\Core\Entity\EntityForm::afterBuild()
 */
  public function form(array $form, FormStateInterface
    $form_state) {
    $form = parent::form($form, $form_state);
```

```
    /** @var \Drupal\mymodule\Entity\Announcement
        $entity */
    $entity = $this->entity;

    $form['label'] = [
      '#type' => 'textfield',
      '#title' => $this->t('Label'),
      '#required' => TRUE,
      '#default_value' => $entity->label,
    ];
    $form['id'] = [
      '#type' => 'machine_name',
      '#default_value' => $entity->id(),
      '#disabled' => !$entity->isNew(),
      '#machine_name' => [
        'exists' => [Announcement::class, 'load'],
      ],
    ];
    $form['message'] = [
      '#type' => 'textarea',
      '#title' => $this->t('Message'),
      '#required' => TRUE,
      '#default_value' => $entity->message,
    ];
    return $form;
  }


/**
 * Form submission handler for the 'save' action.
 *
 * Normally this method should be overridden to
   provide specific messages to
 * the user and redirect the form after the entity has
     been saved.
 *
```

```
 * @param array $form
 *   An associative array containing the structure of
        the form.
 * @param \Drupal\Core\Form\FormStateInterface
        $form_state
 *   The current state of the form.
 *
 * @return int
 *   Either SAVED_NEW or SAVED_UPDATED, depending on
        the operation performed.
 */
 public function save(array $form, FormStateInterface
    $form_state) {
    $result = parent::save($form, $form_state);

    if ($result === SAVED_NEW) {
      $this->messenger()->addMessage('The announcement
        has been created.');
    }
    else {
      $this->messenger()->addMessage('The announcement
        has been updated.');
    }

    $form_state->setRedirectUrl($this->entity->
        toUrl('collection'));

    return $result;
  }

}
```

We override the `form` method to add our form elements. We define a text field for our `label` property followed by a `machine_name` element for `id`. This element will transliterate and convert the `label` value into a storage-friendly value to serve as the entity's identifier. The `message` property uses a normal text area element.

We also override the `save` method to provide messages about the changes that have been made. We also ensure the user is redirected back to the collection page for the entity.

9. To make our announcements accessible from the administrative pages, we need to define a menu link. Create a `mymodule.links.menu.yml` file and add the following code:

```yaml
mymodule.announcements:
  title: 'Announcements'
  parent: system.admin_config_system
  description: 'Manage announcements.'
  route_name: entity.announcement.collection
```

This registers a menu link for the specified `route_name` under the specified `parent`.

10. Next, we will define an action link. In Drupal, action links are buttons on pages generally used to bring the user to a form. Our action link will add an **Add announcement** link from the collection route. Create a `mymodule.links.action.yml` file and add the following:

```yaml
announcement.add:
  route_name: entity.announcement.add_form
  title: 'Add announcement'
  appears_on:
    - entity.announcement.collection
```

`route_name` matches the route name generated by our route provider for the add-form link. The `appears_on` array specifies what routes the action link should render on.

11. Now that we have provided our entity type and its handlers, we need to create a schema file that describes our configuration entity's properties. We must create the `config/schema` directory, which is where the schema file will reside:

```
mkdir -p config/schema
```

12. Create a file named `mymodule.schema.yml` to contain the schema definition for our configuration entity's properties:

```yaml
mymodule.announcement.*:
  type: config_entity
  label: 'Announcement'
  mapping:
    id:
      type: string
      label: 'ID'
    label:
      type: label
      label: 'Label'
```

```
message:
  type: text
  label: 'Text'
```

The `mymodule.announcement.*` key instructs Drupal that all of the `announcement` configuration entities apply to this schema. The key is built by taking the module name, which provides the entity type and the entity type's ID.

13. Before installing the module, we must define the permission specified in `admin_permission`. Create a `mymodule.permissions.yml` file and add the following:

```
administer announcement:
  title: 'Administer announcements'
```

Defining the permission in the entity type's annotation does not register it as a permission with Drupal automatically.

14. Install the module. On the **Configuration** page, you will now see **Announcements**, which allows you to create announcement configuration entities.

System

> **Basic site settings**

Change site name, email address, slogan, default front page, and error pages.

> **Announcements**

Manage announcements.

> **Cron**

Manage automatic site maintenance tasks.

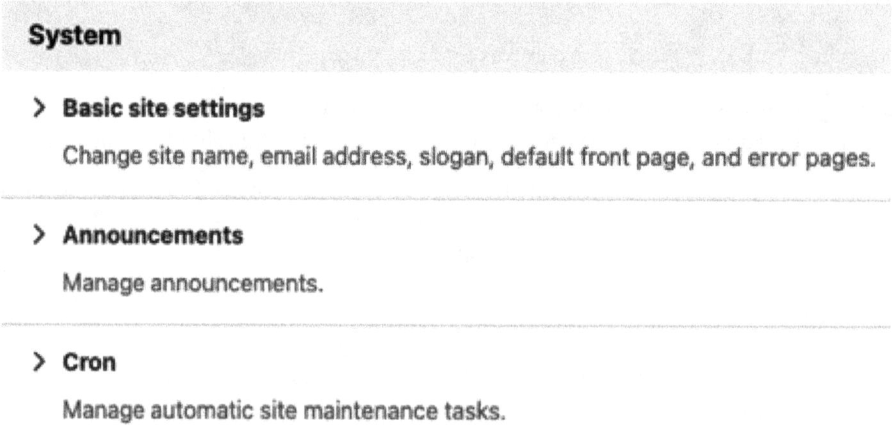

Figure 9.1 – The Announcements link on the configuration page

How it works...

Entity types are plugins in Drupal. The entity type manager provides discovery of entity types and accesses their handlers. The `ConfigEntityType` plugin type's class is `\Drupal\Core\Config\Entity\ConfigEntityType`. This class sets up the default `storage` handler to `\Drupal\Core\Config\Entity\ConfigEntityStorage` and the `entity_keys` entries for the `uuid` and `langcode` properties, which are defined in the `ConfigEntityBase` class.

Entity types are expected to define permission for administration, via the admin_permission annotation value. The de facto pattern is to use the word administer and then the entity type ID. That is why our permission name is administered announcement and not administer announcements. More about entity type permissions and access is covered in the *Implementing access control for an entity* recipe.

The entity system is integrated with the routing system to invoke registered route_provider handlers. Our entity type uses the AdminHtmlRouteProvider class, which extends the DefaultHtmlRouteProvider class and ensures each route is rendered with the administrative theme.

There's more...

In the following sections, we'll cover more information about defining configuration entity types.

Registering a configuration entity for an installed module

When a module is first installed, Drupal also installs the entity type. If a module is already installed, we need to use the entity definition update manager to do so. This is accomplished by writing an update hook in the module's .install file.

The following update hook would install the announcement entity type on a Drupal site that already has the providing module installed:

```
function mymodule_update_10001() {
  /** @var \Drupal\Core\Entity\EntityDefinition
    UpdateManager $edum */
  $edum = \Drupal::service
      ('entity.definition_update_manager');
  $definition = $edum->getEntityType('announcement');
  $edum->installEntityType($definition);
}
```

The entity definition update manager allows retrieving entity type definitions that have not yet been installed with its getEntityType method. This definition must then be passed to installEntityType to properly install the new entity type.

Generating configuration entity types with Drush

Drush provides code-generation tools to automate the steps taken in this chapter. The following command will begin the code-generation process:

```
php vendor/bin/drush generate entity:configuration
```

The command will prompt for a module name that should provide the entity type, the entity types label, and its ID. The code generated will differ from that described in this recipe as the code generation is improved. For instance, at the time of writing, it generates `routing.yml` overusing `route_provider`.

```
Welcome to config-entity generator!
------------------------------------------

Module machine name [web]:
‣ drush_generated

Entity type label [Drush generated]:
‣ Config Generated

Entity type ID [config_generated]:
‣

The following directories and files have been created or updated:
------------------------------------------
• /var/www/html/web/modules/custom/drush_generated/drush_generated.info.yml
• /var/www/html/web/modules/custom/drush_generated/drush_generated.links.action.yml
• /var/www/html/web/modules/custom/drush_generated/drush_generated.links.menu.yml
• /var/www/html/web/modules/custom/drush_generated/drush_generated.permissions.yml
• /var/www/html/web/modules/custom/drush_generated/drush_generated.routing.yml
• /var/www/html/web/modules/custom/drush_generated/config/schema/drush_generated.schema.yml
• /var/www/html/web/modules/custom/drush_generated/src/ConfigGeneratedInterface.php
• /var/www/html/web/modules/custom/drush_generated/src/ConfigGeneratedListBuilder.php
• /var/www/html/web/modules/custom/drush_generated/src/Entity/ConfigGenerated.php
• /var/www/html/web/modules/custom/drush_generated/src/Form/ConfigGeneratedForm.php
```

Figure 9.2 – Output from Drush code generation

Available data types for schema definitions

Drupal core provides its own configuration information. There is a `core.data_types.schema.yml` file located at `core/config/schema`. These are the base types of data that the core provides and can be used when making configuration schema. The file contains YAML definitions of data types and the class that represents them:

```
boolean:
  label: 'Boolean'
  class: '\Drupal\Core\TypedData\Plugin\DataType
    \BooleanData'
email:
  label: 'Email'
  class: '\Drupal\Core\TypedData\Plugin\DataType\Email'
string:
  label: 'String'
  class: '\Drupal\Core\TypedData\Plugin\DataType
    \StringData'
```

When a configuration schema definition specifies an attribute that has email for its type, that value is then handled by the `\Drupal\Core\TypedData\Plugin\DataType\Email` class. Data types are a form of plugins, and each plugin's annotation specifies constraints for validation. This is built around the Symfony **Validator** component.

See also

- *Chapter 4, Extending Drupal with Custom Code*
- *Chapter 8, Plug and Play with Plugins*
- *Chapter 7, Creating forms with the Form API*
- Refer to configuration schema/metadata at `https://www.drupal.org/node/1905070`

Creating a content entity type

Content entities provide base field definitions and configurable fields with the **Field UI** module. There is also support for revisions and translations with content entities. Display modes, both form and view, are available for content entities to control how the fields are edited and displayed. When an entity does not specify bundles, there is automatically one bundle instance with the same name as the entity.

In this recipe, we will create a custom content entity that does not specify a bundle. We will create a **Message** entity that can serve as a content entity for generic messages.

How to do it...

1. First, we need to create the `src/Entity` directory in the module's directory. This will translate to the `\Drupal\mymodule\Entity` namespace and allow for entity type discovery:

   ```
   mkdir -p src/Entity
   ```

2. Create a file named `Message.php` in the newly created directory so that we can define the Message class for our entity type.

3. The Message class will extend the `\Drupal\Core\Entity\ContentEntityBase` class:

   ```php
   <?php

   namespace Drupal\mymodule\Entity;

   use Drupal\Core\Entity\ContentEntityBase;
   use Drupal\Core\Entity\EntityTypeInterface;
   ```

```
use Drupal\Core\Field\BaseFieldDefinition;

class Message extends ContentEntityBase {
}
```

We extend `ContentEntityBase`, which implements `\Drupal\Core\Entity\`
`ContentEntityInterface` and satisfies all required methods.

4. Content entities do not define class properties for their values but instead rely on field definitions.
We must define the base fields for our content entity type:

```
class Message extends ContentEntityBase {

  public static function baseFieldDefinitions
     (EntityTypeInterface $entity_type) {
    $fields = parent::baseFieldDefinitions
       ($entity_type);

    $fields['title'] = BaseFieldDefinition
        ::create('string')
      ->setLabel(t('Title'))
      ->setRequired(TRUE)
      ->setDisplayOptions('form', [
        'type' => 'string_textfield',
      ])
      ->setDisplayConfigurable('form', TRUE)
      ->setDisplayOptions('view', [
        'label' => 'hidden',
        'type' => 'string',
      ])
      ->setDisplayConfigurable('view', TRUE);
    $fields['content'] = BaseFieldDefinition
        ::create('text_long')
      ->setLabel(t('Content'))
      ->setRequired(TRUE)
      ->setDescription(t('Content of the message'))
      ->setDisplayOptions('form', [
        'type' => 'text_textarea',
```

```
        ])
        ->setDisplayConfigurable('form', TRUE)
        ->setDisplayOptions('view', [
          'label' => 'hidden',
          'type' => 'text_default',
        ])
        ->setDisplayConfigurable('view', TRUE);

      return $fields;
    }

  }
```

The `baseFieldDefinitions` method defines the fields the content entity has. It must return an array of field definitions, generated with `BaseFieldDefinition`.

5. Next, we will write the plugin annotation in a class documentation block for our content entity type:

```
  /**
   * Defines the message entity class.
   *
   * @ContentEntityType(
   *   id = "message",
   *   label = @Translation("Message"),
   *   base_table = "message",
   *   entity_keys = {
   *     "id" = "message_id",
   *     "label" = "title",
   *     "uuid" = "uuid"
   *   },
   *   admin_permission = "administer message",
   *   field_ui_base_route =
   *       "entity.message.collection",
   * )
   */
  class Message extends ContentEntityBase {
```

The @ContentEntityType symbol specifies that this is a ContentEntityType annotation. id is the entity type ID, used to retrieve the entity type's storage and other handlers. label is the human-readable name of the entity type. base_table is the database table name to be used for the entity type. The values in entity_keys instruct Drupal what the id, label, and uuid properties are.

admin_permission specifies the permission name required to manage the entity type. field_ui_base_route contains a route name that the **Field UI** will use to provide field management interfaces.

6. Next, we will add the handlers key to our annotation:

```
/**
 * Defines the message entity class.
 *
 * @ContentEntityType(
 *   id = "message",
 *   label = @Translation("Message"),
 *   base_table = "message",
 *   entity_keys = {
 *     "id" = "message_id",
 *     "label" = "title",
 *     "uuid" = "uuid"
 *   },
 *   admin_permission = "administer message",
 *   field_ui_base_route =
 *       "entity.message.collection",
 *   handlers = {
 *     "list_builder" = "Drupal\mymodule\
 *           MessageListBuilder",
 *     "form" = {
 *       "default" = "Drupal\mymodule\MessageForm",
 *       "delete" = "Drupal\Core\Entity\
 *           ContentEntityDeleteForm",
 *     },
 *     "route_provider" = {
 *       "html" = "Drupal\Core\Entity\
 *           Routing\DefaultHtmlRouteProvider",
 *     },
```

```
 *    },
 * )
 */
class Message extends ContentEntityBase {
```

The handlers array specifies classes that provide the functionality for Drupal to interact with our entity type. The `list_builder` class, which we will create, is used to show a table of entities for our entity type. The `form` handlers specify the form classes to be used when creating, editing, or deleting an entity. The `route_provider` handler is an array of handlers that will generate routes for our entity type.

7. For our entity type's annotation, we will provide link templates that `route_provider` will use to build routes for our entity type:

```
/**
 * Defines the message entity class.
 *
 * @ContentEntityType(
 *   id = "message",
 *   label = @Translation("Message"),
 *   base_table = "message",
 *   entity_keys = {
 *     "id" = "message_id",
 *     "label" = "title",
 *     "uuid" = "uuid"
 *   },
 *   admin_permission = "administer message",
 *   field_ui_base_route =
 *       "entity.message.collection",
 *   handlers = {
 *     "list_builder" = "Drupal\mymodule
 *           \MessageListBuilder",
 *     "form" = {
 *       "default" = "Drupal\mymodule\MessageForm",
 *       "delete" = "Drupal\Core\Entity\
 *           ContentEntityDeleteForm",
 *     },
 *     "route_provider" = {
 *       "html" = "Drupal\Core\Entity\Routing
```

```
 *             \DefaultHtmlRouteProvider",
 *         },
 *       },
 *     links = {
 *       "canonical" = "/messages/{message}",
 *       "add-form" = "/messages/add",
 *       "edit-form" = "/messages/{message}/edit",
 *       "delete-form" = "/messages/{message}/delete",
 *       "collection" = "/admin/structure/messages"
 *     },
 *   )
 */
class Message extends ContentEntityBase {
```

The links array defines keys expected from the html route provider, such as collection (list), add-form, delete-form, and edit-form. The route provider will generate routes for the given paths.

8. Create the MessageListBuilder class defined in our list_builder handler by creating a MessageListBuilder.php file in the src directory:

```php
<?php

namespace Drupal\mymodule;

use Drupal\Core\Entity\EntityInterface;
use Drupal\Core\Entity\EntityListBuilder;

class MessageListBuilder extends EntityListBuilder {

  public function buildHeader() {
    $header['title'] = $this->t('Title');
    return $header + parent::buildHeader();
  }

  public function buildRow(EntityInterface $entity) {
    $row['title'] = $entity->toLink();
    return $row + parent::buildRow($entity);
```

```
      }

  }
```

Our `MessageListBuilder` class extends `\Drupal\Core\Entity\`
`EntityListBuilder`, which provides all the required methods to build our table of
entities. We override the `builderHeader` and `buildRow` methods to ensure entity
labels are displayed and linked to view the entity.

9. Now, we will create the entity form that is used for creating and editing our entity type. Create
   the `MessageForm` class defined as the default form handler by creating a `MessageForm.`
   `php` file in the `src` directory:

```php
<?php

namespace Drupal\mymodule;

use Drupal\Core\Entity\ContentEntityForm;
use Drupal\Core\Form\FormStateInterface;

class MessageForm extends ContentEntityForm {

  public function save(array $form, FormStateInterface
    $form_state) {
    $result = parent::save($form, $form_state);

    if ($result === SAVED_NEW) {
      $this->messenger()->addMessage('The message has
        been created.');
    }
    else {
      $this->messenger()->addMessage('The message has
        been updated.');
    }

    $form_state->setRedirectUrl($this->entity->
        toUrl('collection'));

    return $result;
```

```
      }

  }
```

We override the `save` method to provide messages about the changes that have been made. We ensure the user is redirected back to the collection page for the entity. All other processing of field values is handled in the base form class.

10. To make our messages accessible from the administrative area on the **Structure** page, we need to define a menu link. Create a `mymodule.links.menu.yml` file and add the following:

```
mymodule.messages:
  title: 'Messages'
  parent: system.admin_structure
  description: 'Manage messages.'
  route_name: entity.message.collection
```

This registers a menu link for the specified `route_name` under the specified `parent`.

11. Next, we will define an action link. In Drupal, action links are buttons on pages generally used to bring the user to a form. Our action link will add an **Add message** link from the collection route. Create a `mymodule.links.action.yml` file and add the following:

```
message.add:
  route_name: entity.message.add_form
  title: 'Add message'
  appears_on:
    - entity.message.collection
```

`route_name` matches the route name generated by our route provider for the `add-form` link. The `appears_on` array specifies what routes the action link should render on.

12. To display the field management tabs from the **Field UI**, we must create `mymodule.links.task.yml` to register our route entity collection route as the root task:

```
entity.message.collection_tab:
  route_name: entity.message.collection
  base_route: system.admin_content
  title: 'Messages'
```

13. Before installing the module, we must define the permission specified in `admin_permission`. Create a `mymodule.permissions.yml` file and add the following:

```
administer message:
  title: 'Administer messages'
```

Defining the permission in the entity type's annotation does not register it as a permission with Drupal automatically.

14. Install the module. On the `Structure` page, you will now see `Messages`, which allows you to create message content entities.

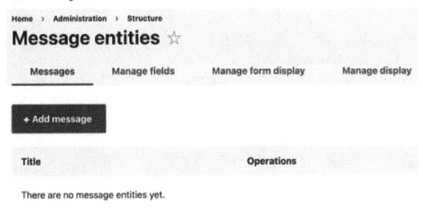

Figure 9.3 – Messages collection, with field management tabs

How it works...

The `ContentEntityType` plugin type's class is `\Drupal\Core\Entity\ContentEntityType`. This class sets up the `storage` handler to be `\Drupal\Core\Entity\Sql\SqlContentEntityStorage`, which controls storing the entity in the database. It also specifies a `view_builder` handler, which is used to render entities, to the `\Drupal\Core\Entity\EntityViewBuilder` class.

Entity types are expected to define permission for administration, via the `admin_permission` annotation value. The de facto pattern is to use the word `administer` and then the entity type ID. That is why our permission name is `administer announcement` and not `administer announcements`. More about entity type permissions and access is covered in the *Implementing access control for an entity* recipe.

When defining base field definitions, their view and form display mode configuration is defined in code. The `setDisplayOptions` method provides the default display options that should be used for the field. Calling `setDisplayConfigurable` with `TRUE` allows controlling the field with the **Field UI** interface for managing view and form display modes.

There's more...

We will discuss how to add additional functionality to our content entity.

Registering a content entity for an installed module

When a module is first installed, Drupal will also install the entity type. If a module is already installed, we need to use the entity definition update manager to do so. This is accomplished by writing an update hook in the module's `.install` file.

The following update hook would install the message entity type on a Drupal site that already has the providing module installed:

```
function mymodule_update_10001() {
  /** @var \Drupal\Core\Entity\
        EntityDefinitionUpdateManager $edum */
  $edum = \Drupal::service
      ('entity.definition_update_manager');
  $definition = $edum->getEntityType('message');
  $edum->installEntityType($definition);
}
```

The entity definition update manager allows retrieving entity type definitions that have not yet been installed with its `getEntityType` method. This definition must then be passed to `installEntityType` to properly install the new entity type.

Generating configuration entity types with Drush

Drush provides code-generation tools to automate the steps taken in this chapter. The following command will begin the code-generation process:

```
php vendor/bin/drush generate entity:content
```

The command will prompt for a module name that should provide the entity type, the entity types label, and its ID. It allows configuring the entity type to be translatable and support revisions, discussed in the following sections. The code generated will differ from what's described in this recipe as the code generation is improved.

Tabs for View, Edit, and Delete

When editing content, you may have used the **View, Edit,** or **Delete** tabs. These are defined in a module's `links.task.yml`, like the one defined to enable the **Field UI** in this recipe. The following definitions will add the same tabs to the content entity type defined in this recipe:

```
entity.message.canonical:
  route_name: entity.message.canonical
  base_route: entity.message.canonical
  title: 'View'
entity.message.edit_form:
  route_name: entity.message.edit_form
  base_route: entity.message.canonical
  title: Edit
entity.message.delete_form:
  route_name: entity.message.delete_form
  base_route: entity.message.canonical
  title: Delete
  weight: 10
```

Allowing a content entity type to be translatable

One of Drupal's major features is its ability to handle multilingual content, as we'll cover in *Chapter 11, Multilingual and Internationalization*. For a content entity to be translatable, it must provide a `langcode` entity key and mark its base fields as being translatable.

The `Message` entity's updated `entity_keys` annotation would look like the following:

```
*    entity_keys = {
*      "id" = "message_id",
*      "label" = "title",
*      "uuid" = "uuid",
*      "langcode" = "langcode",
*    },
```

The `ContentEntityBase` class will check whether this `langcode` entity key exists and automatically generate a language field.

By default, fields are not translatable. To mark a field as being translatable, the `setTranslatable` method on the field definition object must be called. The following code makes the `title` field translatable:

```
$fields['title'] = BaseFieldDefinition::create('string')
  ->setLabel(t('Title'))
  ->setRequired(TRUE)
  ->setTranslatable(TRUE)
```

Allowing a content entity type to support revisions

Drupal has the `Content Moderation and Workspaces` module to provide advanced content management workflows using revisions, as we covered in *Chapter 3, Displaying Content through Views*. For a content entity to support revisions, it must provide additional information in its entity type annotation and mark base fields as supporting revisions.

Content entity types that support revisions must define `revision_table` and `revision_metadata_keys`. These are similar to `base_table` and `entity_keys`, respectively:

```
*    revision_table = "message_revision",
*    show_revision_ui = TRUE,
*    revision_metadata_keys = {
*      "revision_user" = "revision_uid",
*      "revision_created" = "revision_timestamp",
*      "revision_log_message" = "revision_log"
*    },
```

The `show_revision_ui` key controls whether the entity form displays the revision log whenever modifying an entity.

The content entity type must implement `\Drupal\Core\Entity\RevisionLogInterface` and can use the `\Drupal\Core\Entity\RevisionLogEntityTrait` trait to automatically create the required base fields and methods for revision support:

```
class Message extends ContentEntityBase {

  use RevisionLogEntityTrait;

  public static function baseFieldDefinitions
      (EntityTypeInterface $entity_type) {
    $fields = parent::baseFieldDefinitions($entity_type);
```

```
    // Add the revision metadata fields.
    $fields += static::revisionLogBaseFieldDefinitions
        ($entity_type);
```

Finally, fields must be flagged as supporting revisions:

```
$fields['title'] = BaseFieldDefinition::create('string')
  ->setLabel(t('Title'))
  ->setRequired(TRUE)
  ->setRevisionable(TRUE)
```

Creating a bundle for a content entity type

Bundles allow you to have different variations of a content entity. All bundles share the same base field definitions but not configured fields. This allows each bundle to have its own custom fields. Display modes are also dependent on a specific bundle. This allows each bundle to have its own configuration for the form mode and view mode.

Using the custom entity from the preceding recipe, we will add a configuration entity to act as the bundle. This will allow you to have different message types for multiple custom field configurations.

How to do it...

1. Create a file named MessageType.php in the src/Entity directory so that we can define the MessageType class for our configuration entity type that will provide bundles for our Message entity.

2. The MessageType class will extend the \Drupal\Core\Config\Entity\ ConfigEntityBundleBase class and define our entity type's properties:

```php
<?php

namespace Drupal\mymodule\Entity;

use Drupal\Core\Config\Entity\ConfigEntityBundleBase;

class MessageType extends ConfigEntityBundleBase {

  public string $label = '';

}
```

We extend the `ConfigEntityBundleBase` class. This is a class that extends `ConfigEntityBase` and provides various enhancements for configuration entity types that are used to provide bundles for a content entity type. The `label` property will contain the label of the message type.

3. Next, we will write the plugin annotation in a class documentation block for our entity type:

```
/**
 * @ConfigEntityType(
 *   id = "message_type",
 *   label = "Message type",
 *   config_prefix = "message_type",
 *   bundle_of = "message",
 *   entity_keys = {
 *     "id" = "id",
 *     "label" = "label"
 *   },
 *   config_export = {
 *     "id",
 *     "label",
 *   },
 *   admin_permission = "administer message_type",
 */
class MessageType extends ConfigEntityBundleBase {
```

The annotation definition is just like other configuration entities, except for the `bundle_of` key. The `bundle_of` key defines the entity type that this configuration entity type provides bundles for and denotes this as a bundle configuration entity type.

4. Next, we will add the `handlers` key to our annotation:

```
/**
 * @ConfigEntityType(
 *   id = "message_type",
 *   label = @Translation("Message type"),
 *   config_prefix = "message_type",
 *   bundle_of = "message",
 *   entity_keys = {
 *     "id" = "id",
 *     "label" = "label"
```

```
 *    },
 *    config_export = {
 *      "id",
 *      "label",
 *    },
 *    admin_permission = "administer message_type",
 *    handlers = {
 *      "list_builder" = "Drupal\mymodule\
 *        MessageTypeListBuilder",
 *      "form" = {
 *        "default" = "Drupal\mymodule
 *          \MessageTypeForm",
 *        "delete" = "Drupal\Core\Entity
 *          \EntityDeleteForm"
 *      },
 *      "route_provider" = {
 *        "html" = "Drupal\Core\Entity\Routing
 *          \AdminHtmlRouteProvider",
 *      },
 *    },
 *  )
 */
 class MessageType extends ConfigEntityBundleBase {
```

We define the entity type's handlers just as we did in the *Creating a configuration entity type* recipe, but with our specific `form` and `list_builder` handlers.

5. Lastly, for our entity type's annotation, we will provide link templates that `route_provider` will use to build routes for the entity type:

```
/**
 * @ConfigEntityType(
 *   id = "message_type",
 *   label = @Translation("Message type"),
 *   config_prefix = "message_type",
 *   bundle_of = "message",
 *   entity_keys = {
 *     "id" = "id",
```

```
 *      "label" = "label"
 *    },
 *    config_export = {
 *      "id",
 *      "label",
 *    },
 *    admin_permission = "administer message_type",
 *    handlers = {
 *      "list_builder" = "Drupal\mymodule\
 *        MessageTypeListBuilder",
 *      "form" = {
 *        "default" = "Drupal\mymodule\
 *           MessageTypeForm",
 *        "delete" = "Drupal\Core\Entity\
 *           EntityDeleteForm"
 *      },
 *      "route_provider" = {
 *        "html" = "Drupal\Core\Entity\Routing
 *           \AdminHtmlRouteProvider",
 *      },
 *    },
 *    links = {
 *      "collection" = "/admin/structure/message-
 *        types",
 *      "add-form" = "/admin/structure/message-
 *          types/add",
 *      "delete-form" = "/admin/structure/message-
 *          types/{message_type}/delete",
 *      "edit-form" = "/admin/structure/message-
 *          types/{message_type}/edit",
 *    },
 *  )
 */
 class MessageType extends ConfigEntityBundleBase {
```

This defines routes for our entity at /admin/structure/message-types.

6. Create the `MessageTypeListBuilder` class defined in our `list_builder` handler by creating a `MessageTypeListBuilder.php` file in the `src` directory:

```php
<?php

namespace Drupal\mymodule;

use Drupal\Core\Config\Entity\ConfigEntityListBuilder;
use Drupal\Core\Entity\EntityInterface;

class MessageTypeListBuilder extends
    ConfigEntityListBuilder {

/**
 * Builds the header row for the entity listing.
 *
 * @return array
 *   A render array structure of header strings.
 *
 * @see \Drupal\Core\Entity\EntityListBuilder
 *   ::render()
 */
  public function buildHeader() {
    $header['label'] = $this->t('Label');
    return $header + parent::buildHeader();
  }

/**
 * Builds a row for an entity in the entity listing.
 *
 * @param \Drupal\Core\Entity\EntityInterface $entity
 *   The entity for this row of the list.
 *
 * @return array
 *   A render array structure of fields for this
 *       entity.
 *
```

```
   * @see \Drupal\Core\Entity\EntityListBuilder
     ::render()
 */
  public function buildRow(EntityInterface $entity) {
    $row['label'] = $entity->label();
    return $row + parent::buildRow($entity);
  }

}
```

7. Next, we will create the entity form that is used for creating and editing the entity type. Create the MessageTypeForm class defined as the default form handler by creating MessageTypeForm. php file in the src directory:

```php
<?php

namespace Drupal\mymodule;

use Drupal\Core\Entity\BundleEntityFormBase;
use Drupal\Core\Form\FormStateInterface;
use Drupal\mymodule\Entity\MessageType;

class MessageTypeForm extends BundleEntityFormBase {

/**
 * Gets the actual form array to be built.
 *
 * @see \Drupal\Core\Entity\EntityForm::processForm()
 * @see \Drupal\Core\Entity\EntityForm::afterBuild()
 */
  public function form(array $form, FormStateInterface
    $form_state) {
    $form = parent::form($form, $form_state);

    /** @var \Drupal\mymodule\Entity\MessageType
        $entity */
    $entity = $this->entity;
```

```php
    $form['label'] = [
      '#type' => 'textfield',
      '#title' => $this->t('Label'),
      '#required' => TRUE,
      '#default_value' => $entity->label,
    ];

    $form['id'] = [
      '#type' => 'machine_name',
      '#default_value' => $entity->id(),
      '#machine_name' => [
        'exists' => [MessageType::class, 'load'],
      ],
    ];

    return $this->protectBundleIdElement($form);
  }

/**
 * Form submission handler for the 'save' action.
 *
 * Normally this method should be overridden to provide
specific messages to
 * the user and redirect the form after the entity has
     been saved.
 *
 * @param array $form
 *   An associative array containing the structure of
       the form.
 * @param \Drupal\Core\Form\FormStateInterface
     $form_state
 *   The current state of the form.
 *
 * @return int
 *   Either SAVED_NEW or SAVED_UPDATED, depending on
```

```
            the operation performed.
  */
  public function save (array $form, FormStateInterface
    $form_state) {
    $result = parent::save ($form, $form_state);

    if ($result === SAVED_NEW) {
      $this->messenger ()->addMessage ('The message type
        has been created.');
    }
    else {
      $this->messenger ()->addMessage ('The message type
        has been updated.');
    }

    $form_state->setRedirectUrl ($this->entity->
      toUrl ('collection'));

    return $result;
  }

}
```

We extend the `BundleEntityFormBase` form class, which is a special base class for configuration entity types that are used as bundles. It provides the `protectBundleIdElement` method, which prevents changes to the entity ID.

8. To make the message types accessible from the administrative pages, we need to define a menu link. Add the following to `mymodule.links.menu.yml`:

```
mymodule.message_types:
  title: 'Message types'
  parent: system.admin_structure
  description: 'Manage message types.'
  route_name: entity.message_type.collection
```

This registers a menu link for the specified `route_name` under the specified `parent`.

9. Next, we need to update the `mymodule.links.action.yml` file:

```yaml
message.add:
  route_name: entity.message.add_page
  title: 'Add message'
  appears_on:
    - entity.message.collection
message_type.add:
  route_name: entity.message_type.add_form
  title: 'Add message type'
  appears_on:
    - entity.message_type.collection
```

Now that the `Message` entity type has bundles, we must use the `add_page` route for the `message.add` task so that a message type can be chosen when creating a message. We add `message_type.add` to display an **Add message type** button on the message type collection page.

10. We must add a task link for the message type's edit form route so that the **Field UI** tabs appear correctly. Add the following to the `mymodule.links.task.yml` file:

```yaml
entity.message_type.edit_form:
  route_name: entity.message_type.edit_form
  base_route: entity.message_type.edit_form
  title: Edit
```

11. We must define the permission defined in the `admin_permission` annotation key. Add the following to the `mymodule.permissions.yml` file:

```yaml
administer message_types:
  title: 'Administer message types'
```

12. We must define the configuration schema for our configuration entity type. Create the `mymodule.schema.yml` file in the `config/schema` directory to contain the schema definition:

```yaml
mymodule.message_type.*:
  type: config_entity
  label: 'Message type settings'
  mapping:
    id:
      type: string
      label: 'Machine-readable name'
```

```
    label:
      type: label
      label: 'Label'
```

13. Next, we need to update the `Message` entity type's annotation to use our bundled entity type:

```
/**
 * Defines the message entity class.
 *
 * @ContentEntityType(
 *   id = "message",
 *   label = @Translation("Message"),
 *   base_table = "message",
 *   entity_keys = {
 *     "id" = "message_id",
 *     "label" = "title",
 *     "uuid" = "uuid",
 *     "bundle" = "type",
 *   },
 *   admin_permission = "administer message",
 *   bundle_entity_type = "message_type",
 *   field_ui_base_route =
 *       "entity.message_type.edit_form",
 *   handlers = {
 *     "list_builder" = "Drupal\mymodule\
 *           MessageListBuilder",
 *     "form" = {
 *       "default" = "Drupal\mymodule\MessageForm",
 *       "delete" = "Drupal\Core\Entity\
 *           ContentEntityDeleteForm",
 *     },
 *     "route_provider" = {
 *       "html" = "Drupal\Core\Entity\Routing\
 *           DefaultHtmlRouteProvider",
 *     },
 *   },
 *   links = {
```

```
 *        "canonical" = "/messages/{message}",
 *        "add-page" = "/messages/add",
 *        "add-form" = "/messages/add/{message_type}",
 *        "edit-form" = "/messages/{message}/edit",
 *        "delete-form" = "/messages/{message}/delete",
 *        "collection" = "/admin/structure/messages"
 *      },
 *  )
 */
```

We add the `bundle_entity_type` key and give it the identifier of our configuration entity type, `message_type`. We then move the **Field UI** base route to the message type edit form route by changing `field_ui_base_route`.

The links are also modified to support bundles. The `add-page` link has been added, which is a landing page to select a bundle when creating a message. The `add-form` link has been updated to contain a `message_type` parameter.

14. Install the module. On the **Structure** page, you will now see **Message Types** alongside **Messages**, allowing you to manage the message types and their field configuration.

Home > Administration > Structure > Message type entities

Edit *Alert* ☆

| Edit | Manage fields | Manage form display | Manage display |

Label *

| Alert | Machine name: alert |

Save   🗑 Delete

Figure 9.4 – Message type form and tabs overview

How it works...

Content entity types have bundles as a way to segment the entity type into specific types. Bundles can merely be a string value on a content entity or, more commonly, a reference to a configuration entity, like in this recipe. When a content entity type does not define bundles, it is considered to have a single bundle with the same name as the entity type.

The **Field UI** module is designed to allow managing custom fields on a bundle. When a content entity type uses bundles, `field_ui_base_route` must point to the edit form route of the configuration entity type.

Internally, Drupal uses the `bundle_entity_type` and `bundle_of` keys to automatically get information about the related entity types, such as building the Field UI forms.

When using the code generation commands in Drush, generating a content entity type provides an option to generate a configuration entity type for bundles.

Implementing access control for an entity

All entity types have an `access` handler used to control whether a user has access to create, read, update, or delete an entity. Both configuration and content entity types default to the `\Drupal\Core\Entity\EntityAccessControlHandler` class as their access handler. This handler, however, only supports checking the `admin_permission` of the entity type.

The **Entity API** module is a contributed project used to build enhancements on the Entity system in Drupal core and improve the developer experience with creating and maintaining custom entity types. It provides a permission provider to generate create, read, update, and delete permissions for an entity type. To complement the permission provider, it also has an access handler that supports the generated permissions.

In this recipe, we will use the permission provider and access handlers from the `Entity API` module for the `Message` entity type created previously in this chapter.

Getting ready

This recipe uses entity handler classes provided by the **Entity API** module. You must add the `Entity API` module and install it to use the entity handler classes it provides:

```
composer require drupal/entity
php vendor/bin/drush en entity --yes
```

How to do it...

1. First, we need to update the `mymodule.info.yml` file to mark the `Entity API` module as a dependency:

    ```
    name: My Module
    type: module
    description: This is an example module from the Drupal
      Development Cookbook!
    ```

```
core_version_requirement: '>=10'
dependencies:
  - entity:entity
```

The dependencies array contains namespaced module names. Drupal utilizes this pattern to support projects that contain submodules and act as a mono-repository.

2. We must update the Message entity type's annotation to specify that permissions for the entity type should be granular per bundle:

```
 *    admin_permission = "administer message",
 *    permission_granularity = "bundle",
 *    bundle_entity_type = "message_type",
 *    field_ui_base_route =
 *        "entity.message_type.edit_form",
```

The permission_granularity key tells the system what permissions should be generated and whether access should be checked by just the entity type or also take into consideration the bundle. This way, there could be permissions for Announcement messages but not Bulletin messages for a specific user role.

3. Next, we add the permission_provider handler, which will generate our permissions. Note that { . . . } indicates the same code from the previous section, removed for readability for what we are adding here:

```
 *    handlers = {
 *      "list_builder" = "Drupal\mymodule\
 *        MessageListBuilder",
 *      "form" = {...},
 *      "route_provider" = {...},
 *      "permission_provider" = "\Drupal\entity\
 *        EntityPermissionProvider",
 *    },
```

4. Then, we provide the access handler, which supports our generated permissions:

```
 *    handlers = {
 *      "list_builder" = "Drupal\mymodule\
 *        MessageListBuilder",
 *      "form" = {...},
 *      "route_provider" = {...},
 *      "permission_provider" = "\Drupal\entity\
```

```
                 EntityPermissionProvider",
 *        "access" = "\Drupal\entity\
          EntityAccessControlHandler",
 *    },
```

5. We will add one more handler, a `query_access` handler to implement our access controls when querying for entities:

```
 *    handlers = {
 *      "list_builder" = "Drupal\mymodule\
          MessageListBuilder",
 *      "form" = {
 *        "default" = "Drupal\mymodule\MessageForm",
 *        "delete" = "Drupal\Core\Entity\
            ContentEntityDeleteForm",
 *      },
 *      "route_provider" = {
 *        "html" = "Drupal\Core\Entity\Routing\
            DefaultHtmlRouteProvider",
 *      },
 *      "permission_provider" = "\Drupal\entity\
          EntityPermissionProvider",
 *      "access" = "\Drupal\entity\
            EntityAccessControlHandler",
 *      "query_access" = "\Drupal\entity\QueryAccess\
          QueryAccessHandler",
 *    },
```

The `query_access` handler ensures that entities returned from an entity query are accessible to the user.

6. The permission provider also generates the `admin_permission` specified on the entity type. You may remove the `administer message` permission from `mymodule.permissions. yml`.

7. Rebuild Drupal's caches, or install the module if it is not yet installed. You will see the generated permissions on the **Permissions** form.

Permission	Anonymous user	Authenticated user	Content editor	Administrator
My Module				
Access the message entities overview page	☐	☐	☐	☑
Administer message entities *Warning: Give to trusted roles only; this permission has security implications.*	☐	☐	☐	☑
Administer message types	☐	☐	☐	☑
Announcement: Create message entities	☐	☐	☐	☑
Announcement: Delete message entities	☐	☐	☐	☑
Announcement: Update message entities	☐	☐	☐	☑
Announcement: View message entities	☐	☐	☐	☑
View message entities	☐	☐	☐	☑

Figure 9.5 – Permissions form for a message type

How it works...

The **Entity API** module dynamically generates permissions by finding all entity types that use its `permission_provider` handler. The permission provider then inspects the entity type and creates the correct permissions that may be needed. For instance, if the entity type implements \ `Drupal\Core\Entity\EntityPublishedInterface`, it will generate permission to allow viewing unpublished entities of that entity type. The permissions are based on the `permission_granularity` value in the entity type annotation. The default value is `entity_type`. When using `entity_type`, there is one set of permissions for working with the entity type.

The correlating `access` handler has logic to match the create, read, update, and delete permissions provided by the permission provider. The `query_access` handler adds access checks when querying for entities based on the current user's permissions. When using `EntityPublishedInterface`, this ensures unpublished entities are not exposed to users without permission to view them.

This allows you to implement robust access control for your custom entity type without having to write your own access logic.

There's more...

This recipe showed how to provide permission-based access to entities. The next section will show how you can control access to specific fields as well.

Controlling access to entity fields

The `checkFieldAccess` method in the core's entity access control handler can be overridden to control access to specific entity fields when modifying an entity. Without being overridden by a child class, the default `\Drupal\Core\Entity\EntityAccessControlHandler` class will always return an allowed access result. The method receives the following parameters:

- The view and edit operations
- The current field's definition
- The user session to check against
- A possible list of field item values

Entity types can implement their own access control handlers and override this method to provide granular control over the modification of their base fields. A good example would be the `User` module and its `\Drupal\user\UserAccessControlHandler`.

User entities have a `pass` field that is used for the user's current password. There is also a `created` field that records when the user was added to the site.

For the `pass` field, it returns `denied` if the operation is a view, but allows access if the `$operation` argument passed to `checkFieldAccess` is `edit`:

```
case 'pass':
  // Allow editing the password, but not viewing it.
  return ($operation == 'edit') ? AccessResult::
      allowed() : AccessResult::forbidden();
```

The `created` field uses the opposite logic. When a user logs in, the site can be viewed but cannot be edited:

```
case 'created':
  // Allow viewing the created date, but not editing it.
  return ($operation == 'view') ? AccessResult
      ::allowed() : AccessResult::neutral();
```

Providing a custom storage handler

Storage handlers control the loading, saving, and deleting of an entity. Content entity types have the default storage handler of \Drupal\Core\Entity\Sql\SqlContentEntityStorage. Configuration entity types have the default storage handler of \Drupal\Core\Config\Entity\ ConfigEntityStorage. These classes can be extended to implement alternative methods and set as the entity type's storage handler.

In this recipe, we will create a method for the Message entity type created previously in this chapter to load all messages of a specific type.

How to do it...

1. Create a MessageStorage class in the module's src directory. This class will extend the SqlContentEntityStorage class:

    ```php
    <?php

    namespace Drupal\mymodule;

    use Drupal\Core\Entity\Sql\SqlContentEntityStorage;

    class MessageStorage extends SqlContentEntityStorage {

    }
    ```

    The default storage for content entity types is the SqlContentEntityStorage class, which is why we extend that class.

2. Create a loadMultipleByType method; using this method, we will provide a simple way to load all messages of a specific bundle:

    ```php
    public function loadMultipleByType(string $type): array {
      $message_ids = $this->getQuery()
        ->accessCheck(TRUE)
        ->condition('type', $type)
        ->execute();
      return $this->loadMultiple($message_ids);
    }
    ```

    The method performs an entity query with access checks. It performs a condition on the type field for the bundle value and then passes any returned entity IDs to be loaded and returned.

3. Update the `Message` entity type's annotation to specify the customized `storage` handler:

```
 *    handlers = {
 *       "list_builder" = "Drupal\mymodule\
          MessageListBuilder",
 *       "form" = {
 *          "default" = "Drupal\mymodule\MessageForm",
 *          "delete" = "Drupal\Core\Entity\
             ContentEntityDeleteForm",
 *       },
 *       "route_provider" = {
 *          "html" = "Drupal\Core\Entity\Routing\
             DefaultHtmlRouteProvider",
 *       },
 *       "storage" = "\Drupal\mymodule\MessageStorage",
 *    },
```

4. You can now programmatically interact with your message entities using the following code:

```
$messages = \Drupal::entityTypeManager()
  ->getStorage('message')
  ->loadMultipleByType('alert');
```

How it works...

Extending `SqlContentEntityStorage` ensures that our entity type's storage matches the requirements for content entity storage in the database and allows adding custom methods for loading entities.

When the entity type storage is retrieved from the entity type manager, the methods may be used.

10

Theming and Frontend Development

Theming is the process through which we can affect the output of entities (nodes, users, taxonomy terms, media, and so on) with CSS, JavaScript, Twig templates, and HTML. Drupal comes with a handful of out-of-the-box themes to provide a basic look and feel after you install it. Olivero is the default site theme in Drupal 10 and Claro provides the administration theme.

There are numerous options available on `Drupal.org` that either provide a starting point for your own theme (Bootstrap, ZURB Foundation, or Barrio, for example) or a full ready-to-use solution. It is also possible to create your own custom theme from scratch.

Everything you see on the screen after a page has loaded in Drupal has gone through the theming and rendering pipeline. This means that you can customize the theme that you see and control its markup and styling. Understanding how Drupal theming works will make you a more effective developer and this chapter will help you do so.

In this chapter, we will cover the following recipes:

- Creating a custom theme to style your Drupal site
- Adding CSS and JavaScript to your theme
- Using Twig templates in your theme
- Delivering responsive images
- Compiling CSS and JavaScript pre- and post-processors with Laravel Mix
- Using Laravel Mix to theme your Drupal site with live reloading

Technical requirements

You can find the full code used in this chapter on GitHub: `https://github.com/PacktPublishing/Drupal-10-Development-Cookbook/tree/main/chp10`

Creating a custom theme to style your Drupal site

Drupal provides a theme generator to create custom themes for Drupal sites based on the Starterkit theme. This provides all of the base CSS stylesheets, JavaScript files, and Twig templates to begin customizing the look and feel of your Drupal site. The theme generator is bundled with a developer command-line tool provided by Drupal core in `core/scripts/drupal`.

How to do it...

1. The script for generating a theme needs to be executed in the web directory, so navigate there in your terminal:

   ```
   cd web
   ```

2. Run the `generate-theme` command from the `core/scripts/drupal` script:

   ```
   php core/scripts/drupal generate-theme mytheme --name
     "My theme"
   ```

   The `generate-theme` command accepts one argument – the machine name for the theme. You can also pass the `name` option to give it a human-readable name.

3. After the theme has been generated, it will be available in the `web/themes` directory. The command will output something similar to the following:

   ```
   Theme generated successfully to themes/mytheme
   ```

4. You can now visit `/admin/appearance` and install your new theme:

Uninstalled themes

Figure 10.1 – Appearance management screen to install the new custom theme

How it works...

The theme generator uses a *copy-and-forget* model, also known as *fork-and-forget*, with the Starterkit theme. This means your theme is a copy of the Starterkit theme as it was when you created your theme and cannot be broken if the Starterkit theme changes in later versions of Drupal.

This differs from other systems that need to be built upon child themes, such as WordPress, or built from scratch, such as *Laravel* and *Symfony*. This allows you to create a theme from a starting point and begin working without worrying about backward incompatibility due to changes to a base theme.

Other themes may act as a starterkit. They are contributed themes and can be specified using the `--starterkit` option.

The next recipe will cover how to add new CSS stylesheets and JavaScript files to your Drupal site.

There's more

Next, we will dive into additional information on themes and the theme generator.

Creating your starter kit theme

Very often, organizations have a shared starting base for their themes. You can define your own starterkit for creating new themes and leveraging existing setups. This is done by adding the `starterkit` key to your theme's `info.yml` file:

```
starterkit: true
```

When this value is set to `true`, the theme generation command allows you to generate new themes using it. This flag is required since some themes are not intended to be starterkits with a generic base of features.

Theme screenshots

Themes can provide a screenshot that shows up on the **Appearance** page. A theme's screenshot can be provided by placing a `screenshot.png` image file into the theme folder or a file specified in the `info.yml` file under the `screenshot` key.

Themes, logos, and favicons

Drupal controls the site's favicon and logo settings as a theme setting. These settings are active on a theme-by-theme basis and are not global. A `favicon.ico` placed in the theme's directory will also be the default value of the `favicon` for the website. Themes can provide a default logo by providing `logo.svg` in the theme's directory. An alternative logo file can be specified by using a `logo` key in the `info.yml` file with a path to the file.

You can change the site's logo and favicon by navigating to **Appearance** and then clicking on **Settings** for your current theme. Unchecking the default checkboxes for the favicon and logo settings allows you to provide custom files:

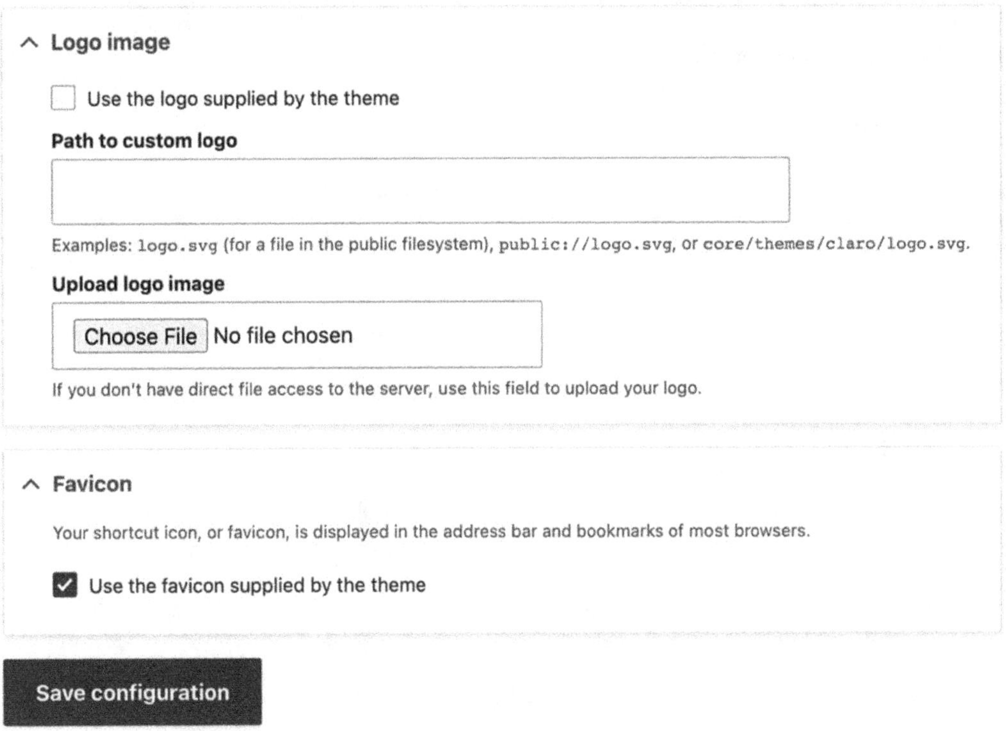

Figure 10.2 – Overview of the theme settings for logos and favicons

See also

- Documentation for the Starterkit theme: `https://www.drupal.org/docs/core-modules-and-themes/core-themes`

- Documentation for theme generation: `https://www.drupal.org/docs/theming-drupal`

- Documentation on the properties of a theme's `info.yml` file: `https://www.drupal.org/node/2349827`

Adding CSS and JavaScript to your theme

In Drupal, CSS stylesheets and JavaScript files are associated with libraries, and specific libraries are added to a page. This allows CSS style sheets and JavaScript files to be attached only when they are needed. Themes can be associated with libraries that must always be attached for global styling.

In this recipe, we will update a theme's `libraries.yml` file to register a CSS stylesheet and JavaScript file provided by the custom theme.

Getting ready

This recipe uses a theme created by the theme generator as done in the *Creating a custom theme to style your Drupal site* recipe.

How to do it...

1. First, create `css` and `js` directories in your theme's directory that will contain the CSS stylesheets and JavaScript files, respectively:

   ```
   mkdir -p css js
   ```

2. In the `css` directory, add a `styles.css` file that will hold your theme's CSS declarations. For the purpose of demonstration, add the following CSS declaration to `styles.css`:

   ```
   body {
       background: cornflowerblue;
   }
   ```

3. In the `js` directory, add a `scripts.js` file that will hold the theme's JavaScript items. For the purpose of demonstration, add the following JavaScript code to `scripts.js`:

   ```
   (function(Drupal) {
     Drupal.behaviors.myTheme = {
       attach() {
         console.log('Hello world!')
       }
     }
   })(Drupal);
   ```

   This script will print a message in the console when the script is loaded.

4. Modify the `mytheme.libraries.yml` file and add a `global-styling` library definition for your theme:

   ```
   global-styling:
     version: VERSION
     css:
       theme:
   ```

```
      css/styles.css: {}
  js:
    js/scripts.js: {}
  dependencies:
    - core/drupal
```

The library's name is `global-styling`. Libraries can define a `version` key and use `VERSION` as a default, which defaults to the most recent version of Drupal core. The `css/styles.css` file is added to the `theme` group for the `css` key. `js/script.js` is added to the `js` key.

The `dependencies` key specifies other libraries that must be present for JavaScript to work.

5. Edit `mytheme.info.yml` to add the `global-styling` library to the `libraries` key:

```
name: 'My theme'
type: theme
'base theme': stable9
libraries:
    - mytheme/global-styling
    - mytheme/base
    - mytheme/messages
    - core/normalize
```

6. Rebuild your Drupal site's cache to rebuild the library definitions cache, triggering a rediscovery of the library definitions and theme information:

```
php vendor/bin/drush cr
```

7. View your Drupal site to verify that the background color has changed and that `Hello world!` has been printed to the browser's console:

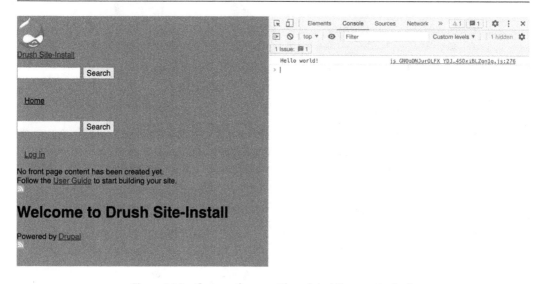

Figure 10.3 – Custom theme with a global library attached

How it works...

Drupal uses libraries to attach CSS stylesheets and JavaScript files to a page. This allows libraries to have dependencies on other libraries, such as base CSS stylesheets or JavaScript functionality. In this recipe, the `core/drupal` dependency ensures that `core/misc/drupal.js` is attached to the page. `core/misc/core.js` adds the global `Drupal` object, which allows you to define `behaviors`. Each entry in `Drupal.behaviors` has its `attach` function invoked whenever the page is loaded or AJAX events are triggered.

> **Asset aggregation**
>
> If Drupal is configured to aggregate assets, you will have to rebuild Drupal's caches after each file time so that a new aggregate is created. This is done by visiting `/admin/config/development/performance` and unchecking the checkboxes for aggregation.

Drupal's CSS architecture borrows concepts from the **Scalable and Modular Architecture for CSS (SMACSS)** system to organize CSS declarations. CSS styles are applied with cascading layers. Drupal libraries have different groups that a CSS stylesheet may be attached to, to control the ordering of when a stylesheet is loaded. The CSS groups are as follows:

- `base`: Intended for styles that target HTML elements
- `layout`: Intended for styles that lay out a page
- `component`: Intended for styles that apply to design components

- `state`: Intended for styles that apply states to components
- `theme`: Intended for styles to customize components

Themes may then specify libraries to be included on every page that the theme is used.

There's more

We will explore more options with libraries in more detail in the next section.

Library file options

Libraries files can have configuration data associated with them. If there are no additional configuration items provided, an empty YAML array ({   }) is used.

The following example, taken from `core.libraries.yml`, adds the `es6-promise` polyfill for the library:

```
es6-promise:
  version: "4.2.8"
  license:
    name: MIT
    url: https://raw.githubusercontent.com/stefanpenner
        /es6-promise/v4.2.8/LICENSE
    gpl-compatible: true
  js:
    assets/vendor/es6-promise/es6-promise.auto.min.js: {
        weight: -20, minified: true }
```

This library provides a compatibility layer for **ES6 Promise** in JavaScript, which means it must be added to the page early on. The `weight` property allows you to control the priority of the library among other libraries. The `minified` property specifies that the file has already been minified and does not need to be processed by Drupal.

The `preprocess` property supports a Boolean value. If a file has `preprocess: false`, it will not be aggregated with other files at the same time.

Overriding and extending other libraries

Themes can override libraries using the `libraries-override` and `libraries-extend` keys in their `info.yml` files. This allows themes to easily customize existing libraries without having to add the logic to conditionally remove or add their assets when a particular library is attached to a page.

The `libraries-override` key can be used to replace an entire library, replace selected files in a library, remove an asset from a library, or disable an entire library. The following code will allow a theme to provide a custom jQuery UI theme:

```
libraries-override:
  core/jquery.ui:
    css:
      component:
        assets/vendor/jquery.ui/themes/base/core.css: false
      theme:
        assets/vendor/jquery.ui/themes/base/theme.css:
          css/jqueryui.css
```

The `override` declaration mimics the original configuration. Specifying `false` will remove the asset; otherwise, a supplied path will replace that asset.

The `libraries-extend` key can be used to load additional libraries with an existing library. The following code will allow a theme to associate a CSS style sheet with selected jQuery UI declaration overrides without always including them in the rest of the theme's assets:

```
libraries-extend:
  core/jquery.ui:
    - mytheme/jqueryui-theme
```

The theme generated with the `starterkit` already has examples of `libraries-extend`.

Using a CDN or external resource as a library

Libraries also work with external resources, such as assets loaded over a CDN. This is done by providing a URL for the file location, along with selected file parameters.

Here is an example of adding the Font Awesome font icon library from the `BootstrapCDN` provided by `jsDeliver`:

```
mytheme.fontawesome:
  remote: http://fontawesome.io/
  version: 5.15.4
  license:
    name: SIL OFL 1.1
    url: https://github.com/FortAwesome/Font-
        Awesome/blob/5.x/LICENSE.txt
    gpl-compatible: true
```

```
css:
  base:
    https://cdn.jsdelivr.net/npm/@fortawesome
      /fontawesome-free@5.15.4/css/fontawesome.min.css: {
          type: external, minified: true }
```

Remote libraries require additional meta information to work properly. The `remote` key describes the library as using external resources. While this key is not validated beyond its existence, it is best to define it with the external resource's primary website:

```
remote: http://fontawesome.io/
```

Like all libraries, `version` information is required. This should match the version of the external resource being added:

```
version: 5.15.4
```

If a library defines the `remote` key, it also needs to define the `license` key. This defines the license name and the URL for the license, and checks whether it is GPL-compatible. If this key is not provided, `\Drupal\Core\Asset\Extension\LibraryDefinitionMissingLicenseException` will be thrown:

```
license:
  name: SIL OFL 1.1
  url: https://github.com/FortAwesome/Font-
      Awesome/blob/5.x/LICENSE.txt
  gpl-compatible: true
```

Finally, specific external resources are added as normal. Instead of providing a relative file path, the external URL is provided.

Manipulating libraries from hooks

Modules can provide dynamic library definitions and alter libraries. A module can use the `hook_library_info()` hook to provide a library definition dynamically. This is not the recommended way to define a library, but it is provided for edge use cases.

Modules cannot use `libraries-override` or `libraries-extend` and need to rely on the `hook_library_info_alter()` hook. You can read about this hook at `core/lib/Drupal/Core/Render/theme.api.php` or at `https://api.drupal.org/api/drupal/core!lib!Drupal!Core!Render!theme.api.php/function/hook_library_info_alter/10`.

Placing JavaScript in the header

By default, Drupal ensures that JavaScript is placed last on the page. This improves the page's load performance by allowing the critical portions of the page to load first. Placing JavaScript in the header is now an opt-in option.

To render a library in the header, you will need to add the `header:  true` key-value pair:

```
js-library:
  header: true
  js:
    js/myscripts.js: {}
```

This will load a custom JavaScript library and its dependencies into the header of a page.

See also

- Refer to the CSS architecture for Drupal: Separate concerns at `https://www.drupal.org/node/1887918#separate-concerns`

- SMACSS website: `http://smacss.com/`

Using Twig templates in your theme

Drupal's theming layer uses the **Twig templating system**, a component from the Symfony project. **Twig** is a template language that uses a syntax similar to Django and Jinja templates.

In this recipe, we will override the default Twig template used for text inputs to provide customizations for the email form element. We will use the **Twig syntax** to add a new class to the input element and provide a placeholder attribute.

Getting ready

This recipe uses a theme created by the theme generator as done in the *Creating a custom theme to style your Drupal site* recipe.

How to do it...

1. To begin, in the `template/form` directory, copy the `input.html.twig` file as `input--email.html.twig`. The template will look like the following:

    ```
    {#
    /**
     * @file
    ```

```
 * Theme override for an 'input' #type form element.
 *
 * Available variables:
 * - attributes: A list of HTML attributes for the
   input element.
 * - children: Optional additional rendered elements.
 *
 * @see template_preprocess_input()
 */
#}
<input{{ attributes }} />{{ children }}
```

The attributes variable is an instance of `\Drupal\Core\Template\Attribute`, a value object for storing HTML element attributes.

2. The `Attribute` class has an `addClass` method for adding new `class` attribute values. We will use `addClass` to add a new class to the input element:

```
<input{{ attributes.addClass('input--email') }} />{{
    children }}
```

3. Before the preceding line, we will create a Twig variable using ternary operators to provide a default placeholder using the `setAttribute` method:

```
{% set placeholder = attributes.placeholder ?
  attributes.placeholder :
  'email@example.com'
%}
<input{{ attributes.addClass('input--
    email').setAttribute('placeholder', placeholder)
        }} />{{ children }}
```

This creates a new variable called `placeholder` using the `set` operator. The question mark (?) operator checks whether the placeholder property is empty in the `attributes` object. If it is not empty, it uses the existing value. If the value is empty, it provides a default value.

4. Rebuild your Drupal site's cache to rebuild your Drupal site's Twig templates:

```
php vendor/bin/drush cr
```

5. Assuming that you have used the standard Drupal install, go to the **Feedback** contact form installed at /contact/feedback while logged out, and review the changes to the email field:

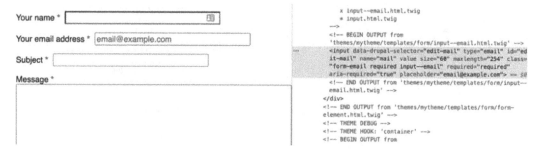

Figure 10.4 – HTML element source for email input

How it works...

Drupal's theme system is built around theme hooks and theme hook suggestions. When a theme hook has double underscores (__), Drupal's theme system understands this, and it can break apart the theme hook to find a more generic template.

The element definition of the email input element defines the input__email theme hook. If there is no input__email hook implemented through a Twig template or PHP function, it will step down to just the input theme hook and template.

> **Note**
>
> Drupal theme hooks are defined with underscores (_), but use hyphens (-) when used in Twig template files.

Given the email element definition provides input__email as its theme hook, Drupal understands this as follows:

- Look for a Twig template named input--email.html.twig provided by a theme or a theme hook in a module that defines input__email

- If the template is not found, look for a Twig template named input.html.twig or a theme hook in a module that defines the input

Drupal utilizes theme hook suggestions for ways to allow output variations based on different conditions. It allows site themes to provide a more specific template for certain instances. Theme hook suggestions can be provided by the hook_theme_suggestions() hook in a .module or .theme file.

A processor, such as Drupal's theme layer, passes variables to Twig. Variables or properties of objects can be printed by wrapping the variable name in curly brackets. All of Drupal core's default templates provide information in the file's document block that details the available Twig variables.

Twig has a simplistic syntax with basic logic and functions. The `addClass` method will take the `attributes` variable and add the class provided, in addition to the existing contents.

When providing a theme hook suggestion or altering an existing template, you will need to rebuild Drupal's cache. The compiled Twig template, as with PHP, is cached by Drupal so that Twig does not need to be compiled every time the template is invoked.

There's more

We will discuss more on using Twig in the following sections.

Debugging template file selection and hook suggestions

Debugging can be enabled to inspect the various template files that make up a page and their theme hook suggestions, and check which are active. This can be accomplished by editing the `sites/default/services.yml` file. If a `services.yml` file does not exist, copy `default.services.yml` to create one.

You need to change `debug: false` to `debug: true` under the `twig.config` section of the file. This will cause the Drupal theming layer to print out the source code comments that contain the template information. When `debug` is on, Drupal will not cache the compiled versions of Twig templates and render them on the fly.

There is another setting that prevents you from having to rebuild Drupal's cache on each template file change without leaving `debug` enabled. The `twig.config.auto_reload` Boolean can be set to `true`. If this is set to `true`, the Twig templates will be recompiled if the source code changes.

See also

- Refer to the Twig documentation at `https://twig.symfony.com/`
- Refer to the API documentation for `hook_theme_suggestions` at `https://api.drupal.org/api/drupal/core%21lib%21Drupal%21Core%21Render%21theme.api.php/function/hook_theme_suggestions_HOOK/10`

Delivering responsive images

The **Responsive Image** module provides a field formatter for image fields that use the HTML5 picture tag and source sets. Utilizing the **Breakpoint** module, mappings to breakpoints are made to denote an image style to be used at each breakpoint. The responsive image field formatter works by using a defined responsive image style. Responsive image styles are configurations that map image formats to specific breakpoints and modifiers. First, you will need to define a responsive image style, and then you can apply it to an image field.

In this recipe, we will create a responsive image style set called **Article image** and apply it to the **Article** content type's image field.

How to do it...

1. First, you need to install the `responsive_image` module:

   ```
   php vendor/bin/drush en responsive_image -y
   ```

2. From the administrative toolbar, go to **Configuration** and then to **Responsive image styles** under the **MEDIA** section. Click on **Add responsive image style** to create a new style set.

3. Select **Olivero** from the **Breakpoint group** select list to use the breakpoints defined by the Olivero theme.

4. Each breakpoint will be grouped by a fieldset. Expand the fieldset, choose **Select a single image style.**, and then pick an appropriate **Image style** option:

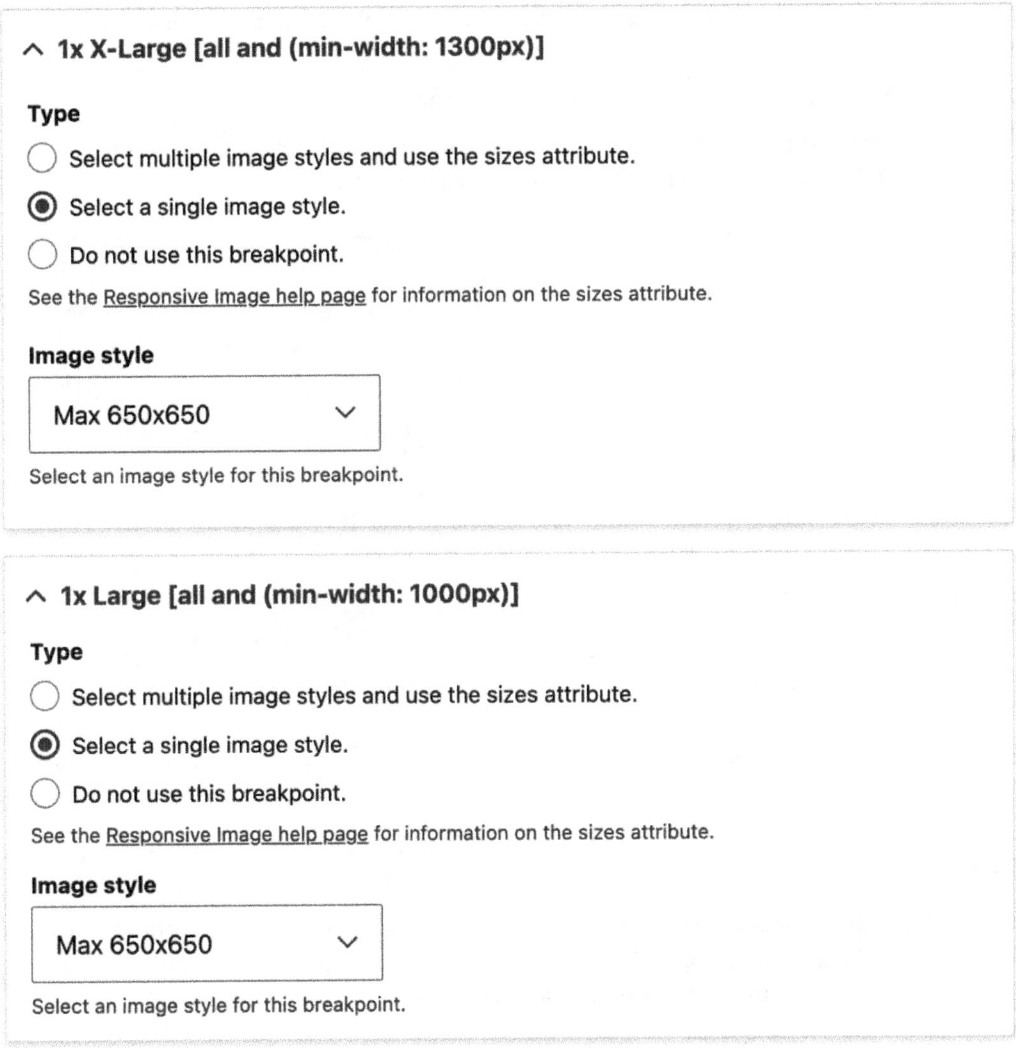

∧ **1x X-Large [all and (min-width: 1300px)]**

Type

◯ Select multiple image styles and use the sizes attribute.

◉ Select a single image style.

◯ Do not use this breakpoint.

See the Responsive Image help page for information on the sizes attribute.

Image style

Max 650x650 ⌄

Select an image style for this breakpoint.

∧ **1x Large [all and (min-width: 1000px)]**

Type

◯ Select multiple image styles and use the sizes attribute.

◉ Select a single image style.

◯ Do not use this breakpoint.

See the Responsive Image help page for information on the sizes attribute.

Image style

Max 650x650 ⌄

Select an image style for this breakpoint.

Figure 10.5 – Responsive image style form

5. Additionally, choose a **Fallback image style** option in the event of a browser that doesn't support source sets or an error occurring.

6. Click on **Save** to save the configuration, and add the new style set.

7. Go to **Structure** and **Content types** and select **Manage Display** from the **Article** content type's drop-down menu.

8. Change the **Image** field's formatter to **Responsive image**.

9. Click on the **Settings** cog of the field formatter to choose your new **Responsive image style** set. Select **Article image** from the **Responsive image style** dropdown:

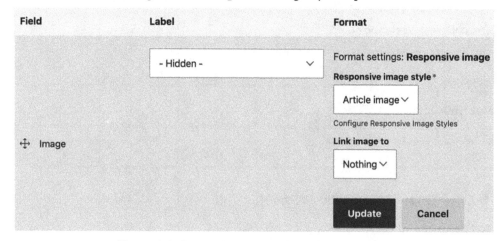

Figure 10.6 – Responsive image style configuration form

10. Click on **Update** to save the field formatter settings, and then click on **Save** to save the field display settings.

How it works...

A benefit of using the responsive image formatter is its performance. Browsers will only download the resources defined in the `srcset` of the appropriate `source` tag. This not only allows you to deliver a more appropriate image size but also carries a smaller payload on smaller devices.

The **Responsive image** style provides three components:

- A responsive image element
- The responsive image style configuration entity
- The responsive image field formatter

The configuration entity is consumed by the field formatter and displayed through the responsive image element.

The responsive image style entity contains an array of breakpoints to image style mappings. The available breakpoints are defined by the selected breakpoint groups. Breakpoint groups can be changed anytime; however, the previous mappings will be lost.

The responsive image element prints a picture element with each breakpoint, defining a new source element. The breakpoint's media query value is provided as the media attribute for the element.

See also

- Refer to the picture element on the **Mozilla Developer Network** (**MDN**) at `https://developer.mozilla.org/en-US/docs/Web/HTML/Element/picture`

Compiling CSS and JavaScript pre- and post-processors with Laravel Mix

Laravel Mix is a project that streamlines configuring Webpack, a bundler for frontend development. Laravel Mix was originally built to be used with Laravel projects but can be used for any project that bundles JavaScript or CSS pre- and post-processing.

In this recipe, we will add Laravel Mix to our theme for transpiling our ES6 JavaScript and PostCSS to post-process our CSS based on the desired browser support.

Getting ready

The *Adding CSS and JavaScript to your theme* recipe from this chapter covers how to create asset libraries for your theme. This section will use information from that recipe.

How to do it...

1. First, create a `src` directory in your theme to store source files for your CSS and JavaScript that will be processed by Webpack:

   ```
   mkdir src
   ```

2. Next, create a `styles.css` file in the `src` directory with the following:

   ```css
   :root {
     --text-color: rgb(43, 43, 43);
   }

   body {
     color: var(--text-color);
   }
   ```

   This CSS file uses CSS variables. While commonly supported now, `PostCSS` will ensure backward compatibility in the post-processed CSS stylesheet.

3. Then, create a `scripts.js` file in the `src` directory with the following:

```
(function(Drupal) {
  Drupal.behaviors.myTheme = {
    attach() {
      console.log('Hello world!')
    }
  }
})(Drupal);
```

4. Now, we will get ready to install Laravel Mix. In your theme's directory, use the `npm init` command to initialize a project:

```
npm init -y
```

This creates a `package.json` file, which stores dependency information for projects using npm.

5. Use `npm install` to install Laravel Mix:

```
npm install laravel-mix --save-dev
```

6. We also need to install `postcss-present-env` to ensure our CSS is post-processed to be compatible with all browsers:

```
npm install postcss-preset-env --save-dev
```

Laravel Mix comes bundled with `@babel/preset-env`, which ensures browser compatibility with JavaScript.

7. Now that we have Laravel Mix, we must configure it. Create a `webpack.mix.js` file in your theme's directory with the following configuration:

```
let mix = require('laravel-mix');

mix.js('src/scripts.js', 'dist/');
mix.css('src/styles.css', 'dist/', [
  require('postcss-preset-env')
]);
```

The `js` method on `mix` sets up JavaScript bundling and transpiling with Webpack. The first argument is the source file and the second argument is the destination. The `css` method on `mix` sets up PostCSS. The first argument is the source file and the second argument is the destination. The third argument passes additional plugins to PostCSS.

8. To compile our CSS and JavaScript files, run `npx mix`. This will create `dist/styles.css` and `dist/scripts.js`:

```
npx mix
```

9. Now, we need to create our theme's library, which registers our CSS and JavaScript files from the `dist` directory:

```
theme-styling:
  version: VERSION
  css:
    theme:
      dist/styles.css: {}
  js:
    dist/scripts.js: {}
  dependencies:
    - core/drupal
```

10. Edit `mytheme.info.yml` to add the `theme-styling` library to the `libraries` key:

```
name: 'My theme'
type: theme
'base theme': stable9
starterkit: true
libraries:
    - mytheme/theme-styling
    - mytheme/base
    - mytheme/messages
    - core/normalize
```

11. Rebuild your Drupal site's cache to rebuild the library definitions cache, triggering a rediscovery of the library definitions and theme information:

```
php vendor/bin/drush cr
```

12. Your CSS and JavaScript files are now registered and will allow you to write the latest in CSS and JavaScript while preserving browser compatibility.

How it works...

Laravel Mix is a package to simplify configuring Webpack. When running `npx mix`, this runs the scripts for Laravel Mix. Laravel Mix reads `webpack.mix.js`, builds a Webpack configuration, and executes Webpack on your behalf.

See also

- Laravel Mix documentation: `https://laravel-mix.com/docs`

Using Laravel Mix to theme your Drupal site with live reloading

In the previous recipe, *Compiling CSS and JavaScript pre and post processors with Laravel Mix*, we set up Laravel Mix for a theme. Laravel Mix supports `Browsersync`. `Browsersync` is a tool that monitors changes in your source files and injects the changes into the browser so that you do not need to refresh the page manually.

In this recipe, we will leverage the `BrowserSync` functionality to speed up the development of building your Drupal theme.

Getting started

Make sure that aggregation of CSS and JavaScript files is disabled by visiting the **Performance** configuration form at `/admin/config/development/performance`.

Alternatively, you can add the following configuration override to your `settings.php` to force-disable aggregation:

```
$config['system.performance']['css']['preprocess'] = FALSE;
$config['system.performance']['js']['preprocess'] = FALSE;
```

This is also set up by default with `example.settings.local.php` in `sites/default`.

How to do it...

1. To configure Browsersync with Laravel Mix, we call the `browserSync` method on `mix`:

```
let mix = require('laravel-mix');

mix.js('src/scripts.js', 'dist/');
mix.css('src/styles.css', 'dist/', [
```

```
    require('postcss-preset-env')
]);
mix.browserSync();
```

2. Before configuring Browsersync, we need Laravel Mix to download the additional Webpack dependencies for Browsersync. Laravel Mix does this automatically when run and first configured:

```
npx mix
```

You will see a message similar to the following: *Additional dependencies must be installed. This will only take a moment.*

3. We need to specify the URL of our Drupal site for Browsersync to proxy:

```
mix.browserSync({
    proxy: 'mysite.ddev.site:80'
});
```

Browsersync launches on localhost:3000 and will proxy content from the Drupal site at the URL provided. Replace mysite.ddev.site with the domain of your Drupal site.

4. Next, we need to specify which files should be watched by Browsersync to inject updates into the browser by providing a files option:

```
mix.browserSync({
    proxy: 'mysite.ddev.site:80',
    files: [
        'dist/styles.css',
        'dist/scripts.js',
    ]
});
```

This tells Browsersync to react to changes to our compiled assets, which are the ones added to the page.

5. Finally, we need to run Laravel Mix in development mode to watch for changes. This will open a browser that uses Browsersync and will update as files are changed:

```
npx mix watch
```

6. With your browser now open, modify src/styles.css or src/scripts.js and watch your Drupal site's theme update without having to refresh the page.

How it works...

It can be cumbersome to configure and gather all of the necessary plugins for Webpack. Laravel Mix provides a way to configure Webpack easily across any project. Laravel Mix supports bundling JavaScript for Vue, React, and Preact. It also has built-in support for Sass and Less, along with PostCSS. All of these options can be found in the API documentation for Laravel Mix at `https://laravel-mix.com/docs/6.0/api`.

There's more

Browsersync can be used for more than just watching changes to your CSS and JavaScript files.

Watching changes to Twig templates

Browsersync can also be configured to watch for changes in Twig files as well so that your browser updates when Twig templates are modified. To watch for changes to Twig templates, add `templates/**/*` to the `files` option:

```
mix.browserSync({
  proxy: 'mysite.ddev.site:80',
  files: [
    'dist/styles.css',
    'dist/scripts.js',
    'templates/**/*'
  ]
});
```

Whenever you modify a Twig template for your theme, Browsersync will refresh the page for you.

For the best results, you will want to turn on Twig debugging by ensuring you have a `sites/default/services.yml` file with the following:

```
twig.config:
  debug: true
  auto_reload: null
  cache: true
```

This will ensure your Twig templates are rebuilt whenever they are modified. This is covered in the *Using Twig templates in your theme* recipe and the *There's more* section under *Debugging template file selection and hook suggestions*.

You will also need to bypass Drupal's `render` cache, which could cause stale output. Ensure `settings.php` has the following lines, which can also be found in `example.settings.local.php`:

```
$settings['container_yamls'][] = DRUPAL_ROOT . '/sites/
development.services.yml';
$settings['cache']['bins']['render'] = 'cache.backend.null';
$settings['cache']['bins']['page'] = 'cache.backend.null';
$settings['cache']['bins']['dynamic_page_cache'] = 'cache.
backend.null';
```

This forces Drupal to use a cached backend that does not cache any data for its render output. Your Drupal site may operate slower, but it allows you to build your theme without rebuilding Drupal's cache.

See also

- Browsersync documentation: https://browsersync.io/docs/options/
- Laravel Mix documentation: https://laravel-mix.com/docs

11

Multilingual and Internationalization

One of the greatest strengths of Drupal has always been its ability to provide multilingual and internationalization capabilities. Not only can you empower content editors with the ability to add site content in multiple languages, but you can also translate the administrative interface.

This chapter will cover the multilingual and internationalization features of **Drupal 10**, which have been greatly enhanced in each release since **Drupal 6**. The previous version of Drupal required many extra modules to provide internationalization efforts, but now the majority is provided by Drupal core.

Drupal core provides the following multilingual modules:

- **Language**: This provides you with the ability to detect and support multiple languages
- **Interface translation**: This takes installed languages and translates strings that are presented through the user interface
- **Configuration translation**: This allows you to translate configuration entities, such as date formats and views
- **Content translation**: This brings the power of providing content in different languages and displaying in the current language of the user

Each module serves a specific purpose in creating a multilingual experience for your Drupal site. Under the hood, Drupal supports the language code for all entities and cache contexts. These modules expose the interfaces to implement and deliver internationalized experiences.

In this chapter, we will cover the following recipes to make your site multilingual and internationalized:

- Determining how the current language is selected
- Translating administrative interfaces
- Translating configurations
- Translating content
- Creating multilingual views

Determining how the current language is selected

Out of the box, Drupal is capable of determining which language it should show for both the content and user interface without much more than adding a few settings from the admin screen. This is a required step in making sure that, at all times, the appropriate language is used for each user when presenting content.

The following recipe will show you how to set the parameters for how Drupal decides which language to use to present content on a page to a user. There are a handful of ways you can detect the language to use.

Getting ready

First, log in to your Drupal site and go to the **Extend** section of the admin. Enable the **Language**, **Content Translation**, and **Interface Translation** modules.

How to do it...

1. Next, navigate to the **Administration | Configuration | Regional and Language | Languages** sections of the admin.

2. Click on the **Detection and selection** tab. There are two sections on this screen:

    - The top section, **Interface text language detection**, lets you dictate how the current language is selected for the interface text:

Detection and selection ☆

List   Detection and selection

Define how to decide which language is used to display page elements (primarily text provided by modules, such as field labels and help text). This decision is made by evaluating a series of detection as browser detection when page-caching is enabled and a user is not currently logged in. Define the order of evaluation of language detection methods on this page. The default language can be

Interface text language detection

Order of language detection methods for interface text. If a translation of interface text is available in the detected language, it will be displayed.

Detection method	Description
⊹ Account administration pages	Account administration pages language setting.
⊹ URL	Language from the URL (Path prefix or domain).
⊹ Session	Language from a request/session parameter.
⊹ User	Follow the user's language preference.
⊹ Browser	Language from the browser's language settings.
⊹ Selected language	Language based on a selected language.

Figure 11.1 – Language detection options in the admin screen

- As you can see, there are many language detection methods available: **Account administration pages**, **URL**, **Session**, **User**, **Browser**, and **Selected language**.

- The second section, **Content language detection**, lets you dictate how the current language is selected when displaying content to users (browsing the site):

Content language detection

Order of language detection methods for content. If a version of content is available in the detected language, it will be displayed.

☑ Customize Content language detection to differ from Interface text language detection settings

Figure 11.2 – Customize Content language detection to differ
from Interface text language detection settings

So, there are two options available – **content language** and **interface**.

How it works...

Drupal is capable of detecting and setting the current language in a variety of ways. How does it know how to do this?

Under the hood, Drupal evaluates these language detection settings through its `LanguageNegotiator` class when a response is being generated to serve the user. It chooses the detected language based on the order and configuration of the settings.

The `LanguageNegotiator` class evaluates the language detection settings in order, which are evaluated using their specific language negotiation plugin implementations, located in the `modules/language/src/Plugin/LanguageNegotiation` directory within Drupal.

There's more...

Let's look at the two sections of the **Detection and selection** tab.

Interface text language detection

As stated, Drupal is capable of providing translation and language detection capabilities for content and the interface itself, as shown in *Figure 11.1*. On top of that, Drupal is also capable of controlling these rules for both scenarios, allowing maximum flexibility for users and editors regarding what language they see in different areas of the site.

Let's look at the detection methods displayed in *Figure 11.1*:

- **Account administration pages**: This option allows users who have access to the administration area of Drupal to set the preferred language of the administration interface. When you enable this option, a new field appears on the **User** form that lets you select which language to use. This is useful for users who may want to have the Drupal admin in one language while reviewing the site/editing content in another language. In this example, a user is setting the administrative language to **Spanish**:

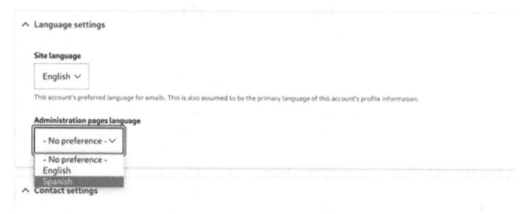

Figure 11.3 – Selecting Spanish as the Drupal admin language in the user account

- **URL**: As the name implies, the URL detection option will get the language setting from the language code in the URL. For example, if the current URL is `/es/admin/config/languages`, `es` is the language code, and Spanish would be used to translate the interface text for the user. The language code in the URL will always be set to **Spanish** in this case.

- **Session:** This option allows you to configure the language to use from either a request parameter in the URL as a query string (`/foo/bar?language=es`) or a session parameter:

Session language detection configuration ☆

Determine the language from a request/session parameter. Example: "http://example.com?language=de" sets language to German based on the use of "de" within the "language" parameter.

Request/session parameter

Language

Name of the request/session parameter used to determine the desired language.

Save configuration

Figure 11.4 – Setting the session parameter that will trigger the translation language to use

- **User:** This option will set the current language, based on the language preference in the Drupal user account under **Site language**. If a user edits their account, they will see this option and be able to set it to any of the listed languages.

- **Browser:** This option will set the current language based on the user's browser preferences (Chrome, Firefox, or Safari).

- **Selected language:** This option lets an admin set the default sitewide language. This is typically used as a final fallback setting if none of the preceding options are enabled or configured.

Content language detection

These options will determine how the current language is set when displaying content to a user. They will only appear if you enable the **Customize Content language detection to differ from Interface text language detection settings** checkbox just under its heading, as shown in *Figure 11.2*.

When enabled, you can set different criteria for language detection when viewing content. If not, the interface text settings are inherited. Most of the available options in this section are the same as the ones we already mentioned, except for two:

- **Content language:** Enabling this option will set the detected language to the language code passed in the `language_content_entity` request parameter in the URL

- **Interface:** Enabling this option will use whatever language was detected from the interface text detection configuration from the previous section

> **Important note**
>
> Take note that in both sections, the options are listed in a draggable table – you can set the language detection priority by moving them up or down the list. In most cases, however, the default settings are just fine and work for most scenarios.

Translating administrative interfaces

The interface translation module provides a method for translating strings found in the Drupal user interface. Harnessing the Language module, interface translations are automatically downloaded from the Drupal translation server. By default, the interface language is loaded through the language code as a path prefix. With the default Language configuration, paths will be prefixed with the default language.

Interface translations are based on strings provided in the code that are passed through the internal translation functions.

In this recipe, we will enable Spanish, import the language files, and review the translated interface strings to provide missing or custom translations.

Getting ready

Drupal provides an automated installation process for translation files. For this to work, your web server must be able to communicate with `https://localize.drupal.org/`. If your web server cannot automatically download the files from the translation server, you can refer to the manual installation instructions, which will be covered in the *There's more...* section.

How to do it...

1. Go to **Extend** and install the **Interface Translation** module. It will prompt you to enable the **Language**, **File**, and **Field** modules to also be installed if they are not already.

2. After the module is installed, click on **Configuration**. Go to the **Languages** page under the **Regional and Language** section.

3. Click on **Add language** in the languages overview table:

Figure 11.5 – The language overview section in the admin

4. The **Add language** page provides a select list of all available languages that the interface can be translated to. Select **Spanish**, and then click on **Add language**.

5. A batch process will run; install the translation language files, and import them.

6. The **INTERFACE TRANSLATION** column specifies the percentage of active translatable interface strings that have a matching translation. Clicking on the link allows you to view the **User interface translation** form:

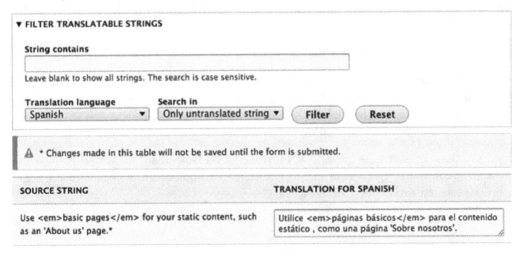

Figure 11.6 – The language overview screen with a newly added language, Spanish

7. The **Filter Translatable Strings** form allows you to search for translated strings or untranslated strings. Select **Only untranslated strings** from the **Search in** drop-down list and click on **Filter**.

8. Using the textbox on the right-hand side of the screen, a custom translation can be added to **Only untranslated strings**. Type in a translation for the item.

▼ FILTER TRANSLATABLE STRINGS

String contains

Leave blank to show all strings. The search is case sensitive.

Translation language   **Search in**
Spanish ▼   Only untranslated string ▼   Filter   Reset

⚠ * Changes made in this table will not be saved until the form is submitted.

SOURCE STRING	TRANSLATION FOR SPANISH
Use \basic pages\ for your static content, such as an 'About us' page.*	Utilice \páginas básicos\ para el contenido estático , como una página 'Sobre nosotros'.

Figure 11.7 – Translating raw strings for Spanish in the admin

9. Click on **Save translations** to save the modification.

10. Go to /es/node/add, and you will notice that the Basic page content type description will now match your translation.

How it works...

The interface translation module provides `\Drupal\locale\LocaleTranslation`, which implements `\Drupal\Core\StringTranslation\Translator\TranslatorInterface`. This class is registered under the `string_translation` service as an available lookup method.

When the `t` function or the `\Drupal\Core\StringTranslation\` `StringTranslationTrait::t` method is invoked, the `string_translation` service is called to provide a translated string. The `string_translation` service will iterate through the available translators and return a translated string, if possible.

> **Important note**
> Developers need to note that this is a key reason to ensure that module strings are passed through translation functions. It allows you to identify strings that need to be translated.

The translator provided in the interface translation will then attempt to resolve the provided string against known translations for the current language. If a translation has been saved, it will be returned.

There's more...

We will explore ways to install other languages, check translation statuses, and many more in the following sections.

Manually installing language files

Translation files can be manually installed by downloading them from the `Drupal.org` translation server and uploading them through the language interface. You can also use the `import` interface to upload custom **Gettext Portable Object** (`.po`) files.

Drupal core and most contributed projects have `.po` files available at the Drupal translations site, `https://localize.drupal.org`. On the site, click on **Download**, and you will be able to download a `.po` file for Drupal core in all available languages. Additionally, clicking on a language will provide more translations for a specific language across projects.

Spanish overview

Overview Board   Translate

Spanish translation team – Grupo de traducción al Español

Nuevo!: Ayuda a probar la nueva versión de localize.drupal.org en Drupal 7!

- Diccionario – Libro de estilo Wiki para crear un glosario de términos, manuales para traductores y libro de estilo en Español.
- Traducción de Drupal core Paquete de archivos .po que componen la traducción de Drupal, y los módulos del Core, al español neutro.
- Interfaz de traducción: Aportar sugerencias de traducción para cadenas de texto pendientes de traducir. Los moderadores validarán las sugerencias y seleccionarán la que será finalmente utilizada por la comunidad. Permite importar nuevas cadenas de texto (actualizaciones de módulos) y exportarlas para ser utilizadas en producción.
- Foro de traducciones: Iniciar y seguir debates sobre palabras o cadenas de texto concretas. Las discusiones sobre palabras establecen una base sólida sobre la que luego construir las sugerencias que serán posteadas en localize.drupal.org
- Glosario de términos: Establece una relación de traducción "automática" para los términos más comunes.
- Directrices para la traducción: Ofrece ideas sobre cómo realizar la traducción al español, de modo que los traductores tengamos un criterio homogéneo. Son ideas abiertas a discusión y por tanto no son realmente un "Libro de Estilo".
- Moderadores de la traducción: Cómo convertirse en moderador y líneas guía para moderar las traducciones.

Top downloads

Drupal core

Project	Version	Downloads	Date created	Up to date as of
Drupal core	5.23	Download (414.14 KB)	2011-Jun-23	2011-Jul-14
Drupal core	6.37	Download (529.03 KB)	2015-Oct-01	2015-Dec-06
Drupal core	7.41	Download (679.04 KB)	2015-Nov-03	2015-Dec-06
Drupal core	8.0.1	Download (1.04 MB)	2015-Dec-04	2015-Dec-06

Figure 11.8 – Language files available on Drupal.org

You can import a .po file by going to the **User interface translation** form and selecting the **Import** tab. You need to select the .po file and then the appropriate language. You can treat the uploaded files as custom-created translations. This is recommended if you are providing a custom translation file that was not provided by Drupal.org. If you are updating Drupal.org translations manually, make sure that you check the box that overwrites existing noncustom translations. The final option allows you to replace customized translations if the .po file provides them. This can be useful if you have translated missing strings that might now be provided by the official translation file.

Checking translation status

As you add new modules, the available translations will grow. The `Interface translation` module provides a translation status report that is accessible from the `Reports` page. This will check the default translation server for the project and check whether there is a `.po` file available or whether it has changed. In the event of a custom module, you can provide a custom translation server, which is covered in the *Providing translations for a custom module* section.

If an update is available, you will be alerted. You can then import the translation file updates automatically or download and manually import them.

Exporting translations

In the **User interface translation** form, there is an **Export** tab. This form will provide a `.po` file. You can export all the available source text that is discovered in your current Drupal site without translations. This will provide a base `.po` for translators to work on.

Additionally, you can download a specific language. Specific language downloads can include non-customized translations, customized translations, and missing translations. Downloading customized translations can be used to help make contributions to the multilingual and internationalization efforts of the Drupal community!

Interface translation permissions

The interface translation module provides a single permission called **Translate interface text**. This permission permits users to interact with all the module's capabilities. It is flagged with a security warning, as it allows users with this permission to customize all the output text presented to users.

However, it does allow you to provide a role for translators and limits their access to just translation interfaces.

Providing translations for a custom module

Modules can provide custom translations in their directories or point to a remote file. These definitions are added to the module's `info.yml` file. First, you need to specify the `interface translation project` key if it differs from the project's machine name.

You need to then specify a server pattern through the `interface translation server pattern` key. This can be a relative path to Drupal's root, such as `modules/custom/mymodule/translation.po`, or a remote file URL at `http://example.com/files/translations/mymodule/translation.po`.

Distributions (or other modules) can implement `hook_locale_translation_projects_alter` to provide this information on behalf of modules or alter defaults.

The server pattern accepts the following different tokens:

- `%core` for the version of a course (for example, *10.x*)
- `%project` for the project's name
- `%version` for the current version string
- `%language` for the language code

More information on the interface translation keys and variables can be found in the `local.api.php` document file, located in the interface translation module's base folder.

See also

- Refer to the Drupal translation server at `https://localize.drupal.org/translate/drupal8`
- You can contribute using the localization server at `https://www.drupal.org/node/302194`
- Refer to the `locale.api.php` documentation at `https://api.drupal.org/api/drupal/core%21modules%21locale%21locale.api.php/8`
- Refer to PO and POT files at `https://www.drupal.org/node/1814954`

Translating configuration

The `Configuration translation` module provides an interface for translating configurations with Interface translation and Language as dependencies. This module allows you to translate configuration entities. The ability to translate configuration entities adds an extra level of internationalization.

Interface translation allows you to translate strings provided in your Drupal site's code base. Configuration translation allows you to translate importable and exportable configuration items that you have created, such as your site title or date formats.

In this recipe, we will translate date format configuration entities. We will provide localized date formats for Danish to provide a more internationalized experience.

Getting ready

Your Drupal site needs to have two languages enabled in order to use **Configuration Translation**. Install **Danish** from the **Languages** interface.

How to do it...

1. Go to **Extend** and install the **Configuration Translation** module. It will prompt you to enable the **Interface Translation**, **Language**, **File**, and **Field** modules to also be installed if they are not already.

2. After the module is installed, go to **Configuration**. Then, go to the **Configuration translation** page under the **Regional and Language** section.

3. Click on the list for the **Date format** option in the configuration entity option table:

Figure 11.9 – Selecting a configuration entity type to translate

4. We will translate the default long date format to represent the **Danish** format. Click on the **Translate for the Default long date format** row.

5. Click on **Add** to create a **Danish** translation:

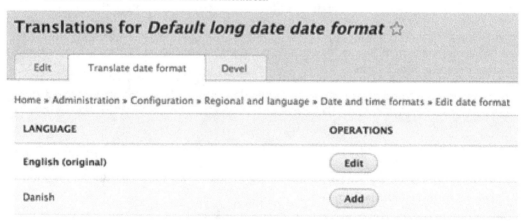

Figure 11.10 – Adding different date formats for different languages

For **Danish**, we will provide the following PHP date format in the translation form – l j . F, Y – H . i. This will display the day of the week, the day of the month, the month, the full year, and the 24-hour notation for time.

6. Click on **Save translation**.

7. Now, whenever a user is browsing your Drupal site with **Danish** as their language, the date format will be localized for their experience.

How it works...

The Configuration translation module requires interface translation; however, it does not work in the same fashion. The module modifies all entity types that extend the \Drupal\Core\ Config\Entity\ConfigEntityInterface interface. It adds a new handler under the config_translation_list key. This is used to build a list of available configuration entities and their bundles.

The module alters the configuration schema in Drupal and updates the default configuration element definitions to use a specified class under \Drupal\config_translation\Form. This allows \Drupal\config_translation\Form\ConfigTranslationFormBase and its child classes properly saved translated configuration data that can be modified through the configuration translation screens.

When the configuration is saved, it is identified as being part of a collection. The collection is identified as language.LANGCODE and all translated configuration entities are saved and loaded by this identifier. Here is an example of how the configuration items are stored in a database:

```
+-------------------------------------+---------------+
| name                                | collection    |
+-------------------------------------+---------------+
| block.block.bartik_account_menu     |               |
| block.block.bartik_account_menu     | language.es   |
+-------------------------------------+---------------+
2 rows in set (0.00 sec)
```

Figure 11.11 – The configuration export containing language-specific configuration files

When browsing the site in the es language code, the appropriate block.block.bartik_ account_menu configuration entity will be loaded. If you are using the default site, or no language code, the configuration entity with an empty collection will be used.

There's more...

Configuration entities and the ability to translate them are a big part of Drupal 8's multilingual capabilities. We'll explore them in detail in the next recipe.

Altering configuration translation info definitions

Modules can invoke the `hook_config_translation_info_alter` hook to alter discovered configuration mappers. For instance, the `Node` module does this to modify the `node_type` configuration entity:

```
/**
 * Implements hook_config_translation_info_alter().
 */
function node_config_translation_info_alter(&$info) {
  $info['node_type']['class'] = 'Drupal\node\
    ConfigTranslation\NodeTypeMapper';
}
```

This updates the `node_type` definition to use the `\Drupal\node\ConfigTranslation\NodeTypeMapper` custom mapper class. This class adds the node type's title as a configurable translation item.

Translating views

Views are configuration entities. When the `Configuration translation` module is enabled, it is possible to translate views. This will allow you to translate displayed titles, exposed form labels, and other items. Refer to the *Creating multilingual views* recipe in this chapter for more information.

Translating content

The content translation module provides a method for translating content entities, such as nodes and blocks. Each content entity needs to have translation enabled, which allows you to granularly decide what properties and fields are translated.

Content translations are duplications of the existing entity but flagged with a proper language code. When a visitor uses a language code, Drupal attempts to load content entities using that language code. If a translation is not present, Drupal will render the default untranslated entity.

Getting ready

Your Drupal site needs to have two languages enabled to use content translation. Install **Spanish** from the **Languages** interface.

How to do it...

1. Go to **Extend**, and install the **Content translation** module. It will prompt you to enable the **Language** modules to also be installed if they are not already.

2. After the module is installed, go to **Configuration**. Go to the **Content language and translation** page under the **Regional and Language** section.

3. Check the checkbox next to the **Content to expose** settings for the current content types.

4. Enable the content translation for the **Basic** page, and keep the provided default settings that enable translation for each field. Click on **Save configuration**:

Figure 11.12 – Selecting which properties and fields are translatable for a specific content type

5. First, create a new **Basic page** node. We will create this in the site's default language.

6. When viewing the new node, click on the **Translate** tab. From the **Spanish** language row, click on **Add** to create a translated version of the node:

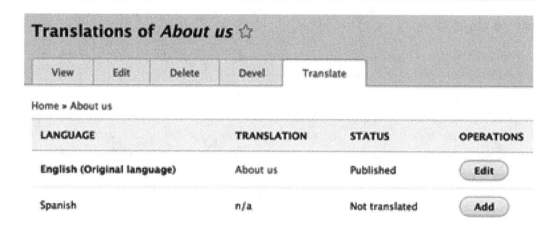

Figure 11.13 – Translating content for a node into other languages

7. The content will be prepopulated with the default language's content. Replace the title and body with the translated text:

Figure 11.14 – Adding a Spanish translation for the About us page

8. Click on **Save and keep published (this translation)** to save the new translation.

How it works...

The Content translation module works by utilizing language code flags. All content entities and field definitions have a language code key. A content entity has a language code column, which specifies what language the content entity is for. Field definitions also have a language code column, which is used to identify the translation for the content entity. Content entities can provide handler definitions for handling translations; otherwise, the Content translation module will provide its own.

Each entity and field record is saved with the proper language code to use. When an entity is loaded, the current language code is taken into consideration to ensure that the proper entity is loaded.

There's more...

Content translation is more than just providing content in different languages. Drupal has additional features on top to make managing and displaying translated content more flexible and robust as well.

Flagging translations as outdated

The Content translation module provides a mechanism to flag translated entities as possibly being outdated. The **Flag other translations as outdated** flag provides a way to make a note of entities that will need updated translations:

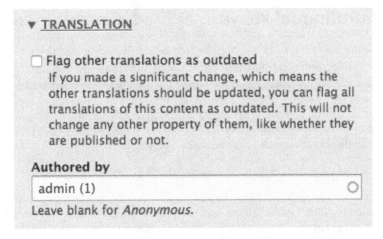

Figure 11.15 – You can flag other translations as outdated if the one being edited changes

This flag does not change any data but instead provides a moderation tool. This makes it easy for translators to identify content that has been changed and requires updating.

The **TRANSLATION** tab for the content entity will highlight all translations that are still marked as outdated. As they are changed, the editor can uncheck the flag.

Translating content links

Mostly, Drupal menus contain links to nodes. Menu links are not translated by default, and the **Custom menu links** option must be enabled under **Content translation**. You will need to translate node links manually from the menu administration interface.

Enabling a menu link from the node create and edit form will not work with translations. If you edit the menu settings from a translation, it will edit the untranslated menu link.

Defining translation handlers for entities

The Content translation module requires entity definitions to provide information about translation handlers. If this information is missing, it will provide its own defaults.

Content entity definitions can provide a `translation` handler. If not provided, they will default to `\Drupal\content_translation\ContentTranslationHandler`. A node provides this definition and uses it to place the content translation information into the vertical tabs.

The `content_translation_metadata` key defines how to interact with translation metadata information, such as flagging other entities as outdated. The `content_translation_deletion` key provides a form class to handle entity translation deletion.

Creating multilingual views

Views, being configuration entities, are available for translation. However, the power of multilingual views does not lie just in configuration translation. Views allow you to build filters that react to the current language code. This ensures that the content, which has been translated into the user's language, is displayed.

In this recipe, we will create a multilingual view that provides a block showing recent articles. If there is no content, we will display a translated `no results` message.

Getting ready

Your Drupal site needs to have two languages enabled in order to use **Content Translation**. Install **Spanish** from the **Languages** interface. Enable content translation for **Articles**. You will also need to have some translated content as well.

How to do it...

1. Go to **Views** from **Structure**, and click on **Add new view**.
2. Provide a view name, such as `Recent articles`, and change the type of content to `Article`. Mark that you would like to **Create a block**, and then click on **Save** and **edit**.

3. Add new **Filter criteria**. Search for **Translation language** and add the filter for **Content**. Set the filter to check **Interface text language selected for page**. This will only display that the content has been translated or the base language is the current language:

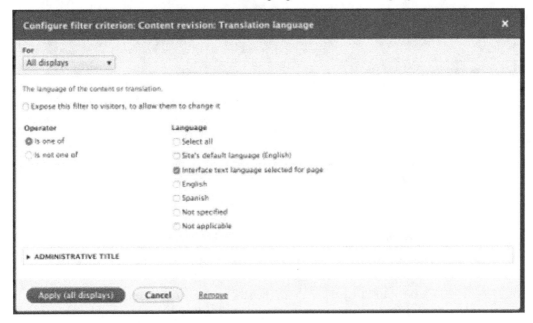

Figure 11.16 – Changing a view to return results in the language of the selected page

4. Add No results behavior to the **Text area** option. Provide some sample text, such as Currently no recent articles.

5. Save the view.

6. Click on the **Translate** tab. Click on **Add** for the **Spanish** row to translate the view for the language.

7. Expand the **Master display** settings and then the **Recent articles** display options' fieldsets. Modify the **Display title** option to provide a translated title:

Figure 11.17 - Translating the View display title property

8. Expand **No results behavior** to modify the text on the right-hand side of the screen, using the textbox on the left-hand side of the screen as the source for the original text:

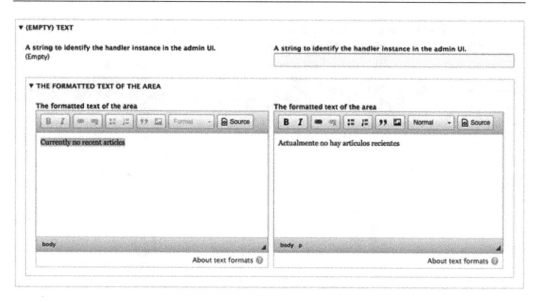

Figure 11.18 – Translating the No results behavior text

9. Click on **Save translation**.

10. Place the block on your Drupal site. Visit the site through /es and note the translated Views block:

Figure 11.19 – The home page translated to Spanish

How it works...

Views provide the translation language filter that builds off this element. The views plugin system provides a mechanism for gathering and displaying all available languages. These will be saved as a token internally and then substituted with the actual language code when a query is executed. If a language code is no longer available, you will see the **Content language for selected** page, and views will fall back to the current language when viewed.

> **Important note**
>
> You will come across the translation language filter option when editing views provided by Drupal core or contributed modules. While this is not an option in the user interface, it is a default practice to add a language filter defined as `***LANGUAGE_language_content***`, which will force the view to be multilingual.

The filter tells **Views** to query, based on the language code of the entity and its fields.

Views are configuration entities. The Configuration translation module allows you to translate views. Views can be translated from the main Configuration translation screens from the **Configuration** area or by editing individual views.

Most translation items will be under the **Master display settings** tab unless overridden in specific displays. Each display type will also have its own specific settings.

There's more...

Translating interface items in Drupal goes quite deep. This extends well into views, where you can translate exposed filters, display formats, and menu items stemming from views displays.

Translating exposed form items and filters

Each view can translate the exposed form from the **Exposed Form** section. This does not translate the labels on the form but the form elements. You can translate the **submit** button text, **reset** button label, **sort** label, and how **ascending** or **descending** should be translated.

You can translate the labels for exposed filters from the **Filters** section. Each exposed filter will show up as a collapsible fieldset, allowing you to configure the administrative label and front-facing label:

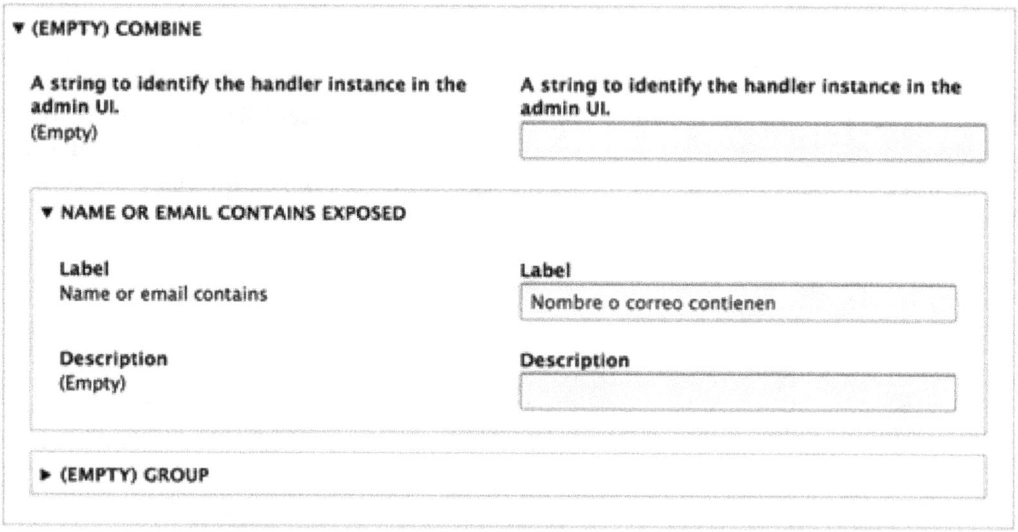

Figure 11.20 – Translating exposed filter labels in a view

By default, available translations need to be imported through the global interface translation context.

Translating display and row format items

Some display formats have translatable items. These can be translated in each display mode's section. For example, the following items can be translated with their display format:

- The `Table` format allows you to translate the table summary
- The `RSS feed` format allows you to translate the feed description
- The `Page` format allows you to translate the page's title
- The `Block` format allows you to translate the block's title

Translating page display menu items

Custom menu links can be translated through the Content translation module. Views use a page display; however, they do not create custom menu link entities. The `Views` module takes all views with a page display and registers their paths into the routing system directly, as if defined in a module's `routing.yml` file:

Figure 11.21 – Translating menu tabs provided by a view

For example, the **People** view that lists all users can be translated to have an updated tab name and link description.

12

Building APIs with Drupal

Drupal 10 comes with several awesome features to help facilitate building out RESTful APIs using the core Serialization and JSON:API modules. These enable you to build headless and/or decoupled solutions that can still interact with and query for data in Drupal.

In this chapter, we will look at how to do the following:

- Fetching data from Drupal using JSON:API (https://jsonapi.org/)
- Using POST to create data with JSON:API
- Using PATCH to update data with JSON:API
- Using DELETE to remove data with JSON:API
- Using Views to provide custom data sources
- Using OAuth methods

The Serialization module provides a means of serializing data to or deserializing from formats such as JSON and XML. The RESTful Web Services module then exposes entities and other resource types through web APIs. Operations done over RESTful resource endpoints use the same create, edit, delete, and view permissions that would be used in a non-API context. The JSON:API module exposes your data entities (nodes, taxonomy, media, and users) in JSON representation on API routes. We will also cover how to handle custom authentication for your API.

Technical requirements

All of the APIs in this chapter operate over HTTP. An HTTP response code is returned, regardless of whether the request was successful or not. If you are not familiar with HTTP response codes or just need to brush up on them, you can review them here: https://developer.mozilla.org/en-US/docs/Web/HTTP/Status. You will see plenty of HTTP response codes when working with the APIs in Drupal, so it is a good idea to review them. You can find the full code used in this chapter on GitHub: https://github.com/PacktPublishing/Drupal-10-Development-Cookbook/tree/main/chp12

Fetching data from Drupal using JSON:API

With just a few clicks, we can open up and expose data from Drupal to consume from external services. This will enable us to ask Drupal for data and return it to us in JSON, making it easy to consume.

Getting ready

First, we need to enable some core modules. Head to **Admin | Extend** and enable the following:

- **HTTP Basic Authentication**
- **JSON:API**
- **RESTful Web Services**
- **Serialization**:

	Web services	
☑	**HTTP Basic Authentication**	⌄ Supplies an HTTP Basic authentication provider.
☑	**JSON:API**	⌄ Exposes entities as a JSON:API-specification-compliant web API.
☑	**RESTful Web Services**	⌄ Exposes entities and other resources as RESTful web API
☑	**Serialization**	⌄ Provides a service for (de)serializing data to/from formats such as JSON and XML.

Figure 12.1 – Enabling the necessary modules in Drupal

The JSON:API module users the Serialization module to handle the normalization of a response and denormalization of data from requests. Endpoints support specific formats (JSON, XML, and so on), and authentication providers support passing authentication in the headers of requests.

> **Important note**
>
> Note that at the time of writing, multilingual support is still being finalized under JSON:API. You can track the status of this issue here: `https://www.drupal.org/project/drupal/issues/2794431`.

How to do it...

You will have a new area in the **Configuration** section of the Drupal admin area called **JSON:API**:

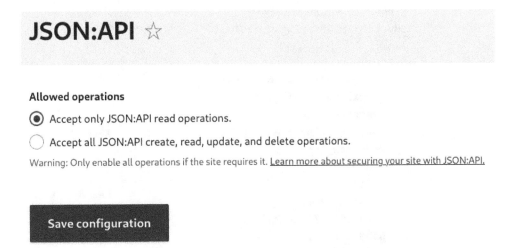

Figure 12.2 – JSON:API adds a new configuration section of the Drupal admin area

JSON:API does not provide many settings out of the box beyond two security settings. One allows only read endpoints, while the other allows **create, read, update, delete (CRUD)** operations on endpoints:

JSON:API ☆

Allowed operations

◉ Accept only JSON:API read operations.

◯ Accept all JSON:API create, read, update, and delete operations.

Warning: Only enable all operations if the site requires it. Learn more about securing your site with JSON:API.

Save configuration

Figure 12.3 – Configuration options for JSON:API

Leave the default as-is for now. Create a new Basic Page node and save it.

Then, go to this URL (replace localhost with your local site domain):

```
https://localhost/jsonapi/node/page
```

Drupal will respond with a JSON:API representation of all `Basic Page` nodes in your site:

```
{
  - jsonapi: {
      version: "1.0",
    - meta: {
      - links: {
        - self: {
            href: "http://jsonapi.org/format/1.0/"
          }
        }
      }
  },
  - data: [
    - {
        type: "node--page",
        id: "77d91b00-ada6-44b5-a4b0-22fcc812b5dd",
      + links: { … },
      - attributes: {
          drupal_internal__nid: 1,
          drupal_internal__vid: 1,
          langcode: "en",
          revision_timestamp: "2022-12-16T15:58:09+00:00",
          revision_log: null,
          status: true,
          title: "Test 1",
          created: "2022-12-16T15:57:59+00:00",
          changed: "2022-12-16T15:58:09+00:00",
          promote: false,
          sticky: false,
          default_langcode: true,
          revision_translation_affected: true,
        - path: {
            alias: null,
            pid: null,
            langcode: "en"
          },
          body: null
```

Figure 12.4 – A sample JSON:API response from Drupal

If you wanted to fetch a specific node by ID, you can use the `filter` keyword in the request URL as a query parameter.

The format for `filter` is `filter[attribute]`. Following that, we can fetch a node with an ID of 1 by requesting this URL in the browser:

```
https://localhost/jsonapi/node/page?filter[
    drupal_internal__nid]=1
```

You will get the same response you got in the first example, but now, the `data` array in the response will contain `only` the node matching ID 1. This works for any attribute you want to filter by. If you know an entity's UUID, you can also request it directly by using it as a parameter:

```
https://localhost/jsonapi/node/page/{ENTITY UUID}
```

By passing the UUID as a URL parameter, you would get that specific `Basic Page` node type's node information. Create a few more `Basic Page` nodes using the word `Test` in the title. Suppose you wanted to filter by nodes containing the word `Test` in the title; you could request this like so:

```
https://localhost/jsonapi/node/page?filter[title][operator]
  =CONTAINS&filter[title][value]=Test&fields[node--page]
    =title
```

Drupal will only return nodes with the word "Test" in the title. Here, we also added `&fields[node–page]=title` to the request to make the response easier to see:

```
{
 - jsonapi: {
      version: "1.0",
    - meta: {
      - links: {
        - self: {
            href: "http://jsonapi.org/format/1.0/"
          }
        }
      }
    },
 - data: [
    - {
        type: "node--page",
        id: "77d91b00-ada6-44b5-a4b0-22fcc812b5dd",
      - links: {
        - self: {
            href: "http://d10.docker.localhost/jsonapi/node/page/77d91b00-ada6-44b5-a4b0-22fcc812b5dd?resourceVersion=id%3A1"
          }
        },
      - attributes: {
          title: "Test 1"
        }
      },
    - {
        type: "node--page",
        id: "5107045b-6aa7-42b0-a65c-59065715702d",
      - links: {
        - self: {
            href: "http://d10.docker.localhost/jsonapi/node/page/5107045b-6aa7-42b0-a65c-59065715702d?resourceVersion=id%3A2"
          }
        },
      - attributes: {
          title: "Test 2"
        }
      },
    - {
        type: "node--page",
        id: "a4dfe010-db49-42e4-8797-7d66b3c8608e",
      - links: {
        - self: {
            href: "http://d10.docker.localhost/jsonapi/node/page/a4dfe010-db49-42e4-8797-7d66b3c8608e?resourceVersion=id%3A3"
          }
        },
      - attributes: {
          title: "Test 3"
        }
      }
    ],
```

Figure 12.5 – A filtered JSON:API response from Drupal

If you prefer to use cURL instead, you can do the following:

```
curl \
  --header 'Accept: application/vnd.api+json' \
  --url "https://localhost/jsonapi/node/page?filter
    [title] [operator] =CONTAINS&filter[title] [value] =
      Test&fields[node--page] =title" \
--globoff
```

You can request this from any HTTP API in any language or command-line tool such as cURL, so long as your parameters and options are correct. Consult the appropriate documentation on using fetch (https://developer.mozilla.org/en-US/docs/Web/API/Fetch_API) in JavaScript, for example, to integrate this with a decoupled JavaScript application.

> **curl: (60) SSL certificate problem**
>
> If you get an error about an SSL certificate problem with cURL, it is likely your SSL certificate could not be verified. This is common with local self-signed certificates. To get around this error in development, you can pass the --insecure flag with the cURL request mentioned previously. In production, make sure you have a valid working SSL certificate – do not use this flag for real-world applications.

JSON:API can also include related data in the response by asking for it with include. If we add include to the query parameter plus any relationship name under the relationships section of a JSON item, we receive them back with the JSON:API response.

If you want the node author information, for example, you can request it like so:

```
https://localhost/jsonapi/node/page?filter[title]
[operator] =CONTAINS&filter[title] [value] =Test&fields[node—
page] =title&include=uid
```

We will receive that information in the response:

```
- included: [
  - {
        type: "user--user",
        id: "cf2637c1-6f35-40ae-90aa-29d453dddfaa",
      - links: {
        - self: {
              href: "http://d10.docker.localhost/jsonapi/user/use
          }
        },
      - attributes: {
            display_name: "admin",
            drupal_internal__uid: 1,
            langcode: "en",
            preferred_langcode: "en",
            preferred_admin_langcode: null,
            name: "admin",
            mail: "admin@example.com",
            timezone: "UTC",
            status: true,
            created: "2022-12-16T15:17:47+00:00",
            changed: "2022-12-16T15:17:47+00:00",
            access: "2022-12-17T01:16:51+00:00",
            login: "2022-12-16T15:18:23+00:00",
            init: "admin@example.com",
            default_langcode: true
        },
```

Figure 12.6 – A sample JSON:API response with the author data attached

Note that to view user data, the requesting user needs the View user information permission. You will get an **access denied** error otherwise.

Any item listed under **relationships** can be requested – for example, author data, taxonomy attached to returned entities, media attached to returned entities, or other types of related data.

Paginating, filtering, and sorting requests

Pagination is done by appending a page query parameter. To limit the request to 10 nodes, we must use append ?page[limit]=10. To access the next set of results, we must also pass page[offset]=10.

The following is an example of returning the first and second pages of results:

```
https://localhost/jsonapi/node/article?page[limit]=10
https://localhost/jsonapi/node/article?page[offset]=10&page
    [limit]=10
```

Each request contains a link property; this will also contain the next and previous links when using a paginated result.

Filtering is done by appending a filter query parameter. The following is an example of requesting all nodes that have been promoted to the front page:

```
https://localhost/jsonapi/node/article?filter[promoted]
    [path]=promote&filter[promoted][value]=1&filter[promoted]
        [operator]==
```

Each filter is defined by a name – in the preceding example, it is promoted. The filter then takes path, which is the field to filter on. The value and operator decide how to filter.

Sorting is the simplest operation to perform. Here, a sort query parameter is added. The field name value is the field to sort by; to sort in descending order, you must add a minus symbol in front of the field name. The following examples show how to sort by nid in ascending and descending order, respectively:

```
https://localhost/jsonapi/node/article?sort=nid
https://localhost/jsonapi/node/article?sort=-nid
```

How it works...

The Serialization module in Drupal provides the necessary plumbing to normalize and denormalize data structures to and from formats such as JSON and XML. When requests are made to Drupal, the responsible route gets the resource and normalizes it to an array; then, a registered **encoder** (in this case, **JsonEncoder**) returns the data in the requested format (JSON, XML, and so on):

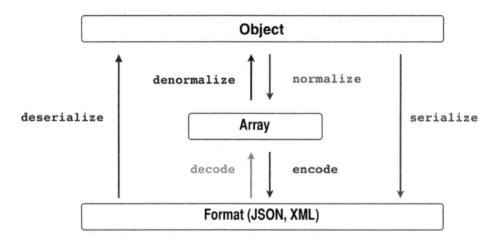

Figure 12.7 – A high-level look at how serialization works in Drupal

This is the backbone of the normalization and serialization of data in Drupal. When you enabled the JSON:API module, new routes were registered for resources under /jsonapi/. These dynamically generated routes automatically encode data and return it as JSON. Any time an entity is requested, the serializer and encoders are responsible for building the data for the response.

There's more...

Installing the JSON:API Extras module

The JSON:API Extras module provides a user interface for additional customization. The JSON:API Extras module should be added to your Drupal installation like all other modules – that is, using Composer:

```
composer require drupal/jsonapi_extras:^3.0
```

Once the module has been installed in Drupal, you will be able to enable or disable endpoints, change resource names, alter resource paths, disable fields, provide alias field names, and enhance field outputs of JSON:API routes.

Changing the JSON:API path prefix

The API path prefix can be changed from jsonapi to api or any other prefix using the Extras module.

From the administrative toolbar, navigate to **Configuration**. Under the **Web services** section, click on **JSON:API Overwrites** to customize the JSON:API implementation. The **Settings** tab allows you to modify the API path prefix:

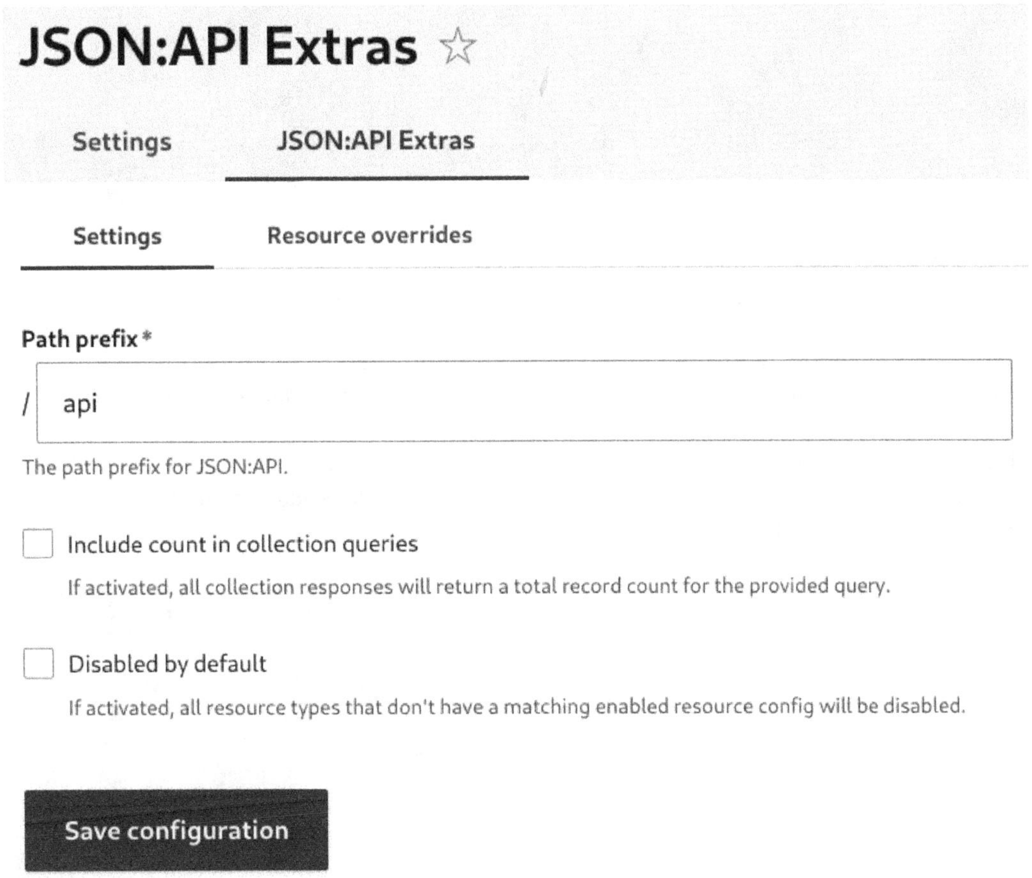

JSON:API Extras ☆

Settings	**JSON:API Extras**

Settings	Resource overrides

Path prefix *

/ api

The path prefix for JSON:API.

☐ Include count in collection queries

　　If activated, all collection responses will return a total record count for the provided query.

☐ Disabled by default

　　If activated, all resource types that don't have a matching enabled resource config will be disabled.

Save configuration

Figure 12.8 – Using JSON:API Extras to change the JSON path prefix

After changing **Path prefix**, clear the cache in Drupal to see the result and the new path.

Disabling and enhancing returned entity fields

The JSON:API Extras module allows you to overwrite endpoints automatically exposed by the JSON:API module. This allows you to disable fields from being returned. It also allows you to use enhancers to simplify the structure of a field property.

From the administrative toolbar, go to **Configuration**. Under the **Web services** section, click on **JSON:API Overwrites** to customize the JSON:API implementation.

To disable an endpoint, click on **Overwrite** on any endpoint. Check the **Disabled** checkbox to turn off that specific endpoint:

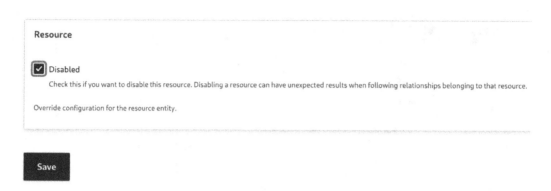

Figure 12.9 – You can disable resources with JSON:API Extras so that endpoints are not accessible

To disable, alias, or use an enhancer, click on **Overwrite** on any endpoint. This checkbox will allow you to prevent a field from being used in the API. The enhancers allow you to simplify fields when returned or used in POST/PATCH requests:

Disabled	Field name	Alias	
☐	nid	nid	► Advanced
☐	uuid	uuid	► Advanced
☐	vid	vid	► Advanced
☐	langcode	langcode	► Advanced
☐	type	type	► Advanced
☑	revision_timestamp		► Advanced
☑	revision_uid		► Advanced
☑	revision_log		► Advanced

Figure 12.10 – You can change field aliases and disable fields in JSON:API endpoints

Here, we have disabled the revision fields from appearing in the JSON:API output. We can apply enhancers to the created and changed fields:

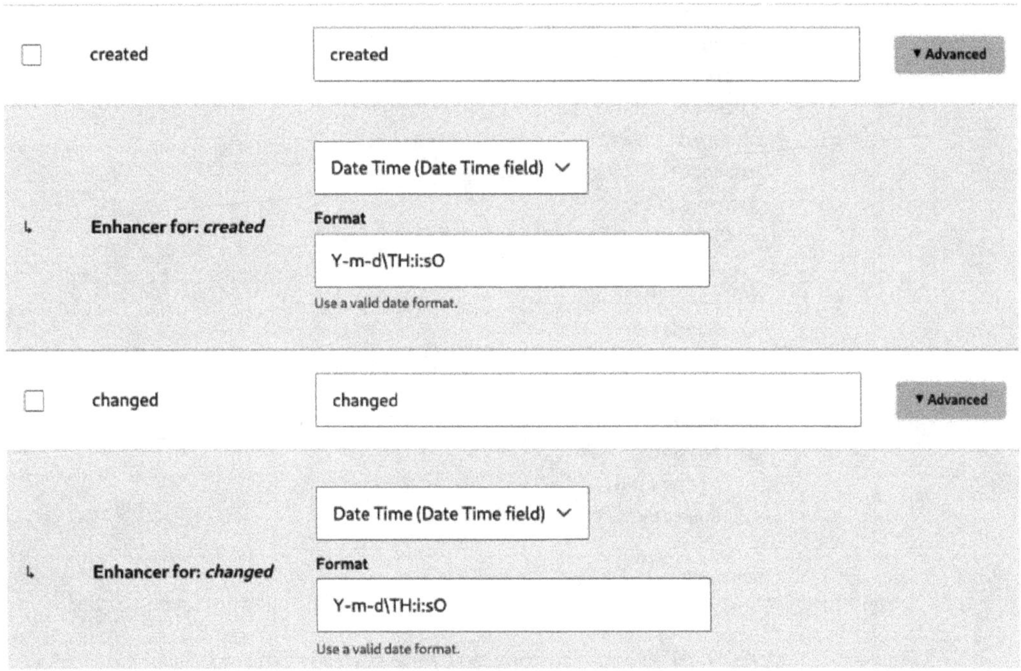

Figure 12.11 – Using enhancers to format data returned in JSON:API

In this example, the created and changed fields will no longer return Unix timestamps, but *RFC ISO 8601*-formatted timestamps.

Going back and viewing our JSON:API route now, we can see that revision fields were removed and that the created and changed fields are formatted:

```
- attributes: {
      drupal_internal__nid: 8,
      drupal_internal__vid: 14,
      langcode: "en",
      status: true,
      title: "Test Article",
      created: "2022-12-17T19:41:31+0000",
      changed: "2022-12-17T19:41:40+0000",
      promote: true,
      sticky: false,
    - path: {
          alias: null,
          pid: null,
          langcode: "en"
      },
    - body: {
          value: "<p>Test article content</p>",
          format: "basic_html",
          processed: "<p>Test article content</p>",
          summary: ""
      },
    + comment: { … }
  },
```

Figure 12.12 – A JSON:API response customized by the JSON:API Extras module

See also

JSON and XML are not the only formats Drupal can return data in as a response. There are contributed modules that provide other data formats as well, such as PDF, CSV, and XLS (Excel) serialization. Check out the source code of these modules if you are curious as to how they work:

- PDF serialization: `https://www.drupal.org/project/pdf_serialization`

- CSV serialization: `https://www.drupal.org/project/csv_serialization`

- Excel Serialization serialization: `https://www.drupal.org/project/xls_serialization`

Using POST to create data with JSON:API

An API that returns data is great, but to make a more functional decoupled app or integrate external services, we need to be able to send data into Drupal as well. After reading the following section, you will be able to create entities in a Drupal 10 application from remote sources.

Getting ready

We are going to use the `Article` content type that comes installed in the Drupal 10 standard profile. If you do not have an `Article` content type, create one and add a basic field such as `Body`.

How to do it...

First, we need to tell Drupal to allow CRUD operations for JSON:API. Head back to the JSON:API settings page in the **Configuration** section of the Drupal admin and enable **Accept all JSON:API create, read, update, and delete operations.**:

Allowed operations

◯ Accept only JSON:API read operations.

◉ Accept all JSON:API create, read, update, and delete operations.

Warning: Only enable all operations if the site requires it. Learn more about securing your site with JSON:API.

Save configuration

Figure 12.13 – Enabling JSON:API to allow more actions

If you do not enable this, you cannot do anything other than read data from a JSON:API endpoint.

Next, create a user account that has only the necessary permissions to create an `Article` node. This is the account we will use in our requests to create new nodes. You should not use an administrator account in your APIs for security reasons.

With each request to create an API in Drupal, we need to authenticate before our request will be accepted.

Open a terminal (command line). Unlike the previous section, we cannot perform these requests directly in the browser. For this, we are going to use `curl`, which comes pre-installed on many operating systems:

```
curl \
    --user chapter12:chapter12 \
```

```
    --header 'Accept: application/vnd.api+json' \
    --header 'Content-type: application/vnd.api+json' \
    --request POST https://localhost/jsonapi/node/article \
    --data-binary '{
  "data": {
    "type": "node--article",
    "attributes": {
      "title": "New article created by chapter12",
      "body": {
        "value": "This node was created using JSON:API!",
        "format": "plain_text"
      }
    }
  }
}'
```

Again, remember to replace `localhost` with the correct hostname for your development site. We created a user named `chapter12` with a password of `chapter12` and set them as the `Content Editor` role (included with the Standard install profile), which has basic permissions to create and edit nodes. This user is passed in the `--user` parameter.

The response will return either a successful or unsuccessful authorization response. If it succeeded, you will see a large JSON response reflecting the new node that was created, and you will see the new node in Drupal:

	Title		Content type		Author	Status		Updated	↑
☐	New article created by chapter12		Article		chapter12	Published		12/17/2022 - 15:51	

Figure 12.14 – The node created by a POST request

We can also see that it was correctly added to the body field, along with the text format we specified in the request:

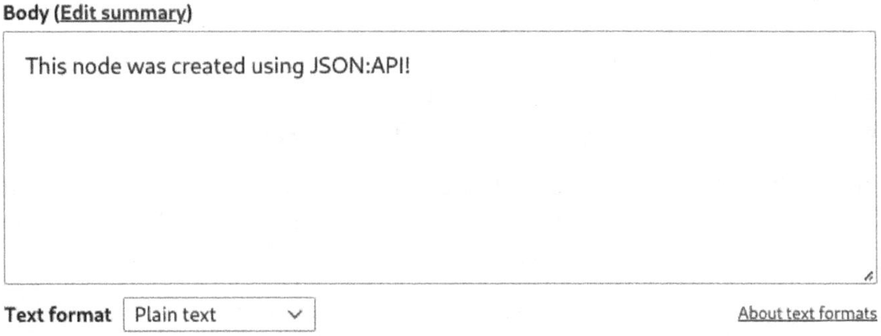

Body (Edit summary)

This node was created using JSON:API!

Text format | Plain text ⌄ | About text formats

Figure 12.15 – Verifying that the content we passed in a POST request was created correctly

If we look back at our JSON:API route in the browser, we will see this new node there as well:

```
- data: [
    - {
        type: "node--article",
        id: "1ddf244d-e8e6-40f5-be48-23bc8fa0fa3e",
      + links: { … },
        - attributes: {
            drupal_internal__nid: 5,
            drupal_internal__vid: 5,
            langcode: "en",
            revision_timestamp: "2022-12-17T15:51:23+00:00",
            revision_log: null,
            status: true,
            title: "New article created by chapter12",
            created: "2022-12-17T15:51:23+00:00",
            changed: "2022-12-17T15:51:23+00:00",
            promote: true,
            sticky: false,
            default_langcode: true,
            revision_translation_affected: true,
          + path: { … },
          - body: {
              value: "This node was created using JSON:API!",
              format: "plain_text",
              processed: "<p>This node was created using JSON:API!</p>
              ",
              summary: null
          },
```

Figure 12.16 – Accessing the newly created node with an HTTP request

How it works...

In this instance, the JSON:API module in this instance is not doing anything extra concerning authentication or entity access. The request is processed by Drupal no differently than if the chapter12 user came to the site, logged in, and created the node in the admin interface.

The type of request is a POST request. This is different from the GET request in the first section for reading data. A POST is required to send data to the server. You can read more about POST request(s) on MDN: https://developer.mozilla.org/en-US/docs/Web/HTTP/Methods/POST.

This is a powerful abstraction that can help you build out APIs and decoupled applications as it requires valid user authentication, but it cannot perform any actions outside of the scope of what that user/user role is permitted to do. This means that if we were to remove the permission to Create article nodes for the Content Editor role, this POST request would fail with a 403 Forbidden response. Therefore, it is a good idea to create an API User role with limited permissions in the real world that you can toggle on or off at a moment's notice.

Never use the superuser (user 1) or user with the administrator role for API requests. If the credentials leak, a bad actor could perform any request they desire. After reading this chapter, it would be a good idea to review the security considerations when using APIs in Drupal on Drupal.org: https://www.drupal.org/docs/core-modules-and-themes/core-modules/jsonapi-module/security-considerations.

In the curl request, when we pass the --user parameter, it automatically creates the Authorization header for the request. This header passes along a basic authentication, which the Basic Auth module in Drupal intercepts and uses to authenticate the request.

Alternatively, you can get the basic auth token manually with the command line; for example:

```
echo -n "chapter12:chapter12" | base64
```

This returns Y2hhcHRlcjEyOmNoYXB0ZXIxMg==. Then, you can pass that in a header instead of using the –user parameter:

```
curl \
    --header 'Accept: application/vnd.api+json' \
    --header 'Content-type: application/vnd.api+json' \
    --header 'Authorization:Basic Y2hhcHRlcjEyOmNoYXB0ZZX
    IxMg=='Y2hhcHRlcjEyOmNoYXB0ZXIxMg==' \
  … rest of request
```

See also

While powerful, **cURL** is a low-level tool that can be difficult to use from the command line for longer, larger requests. You can install Google's Postman tool to make working with APIs easier. You can download it from `https://www.postman.com/`.

Using PATCH to update data with JSON:API

Now that we know how to create some data in Drupal, let's learn how to update existing data.

How to do it...

Our request will look similar to the POST request from the previous sections but with a few changes.

First, to update an entity in Drupal, you need to pass the entity UUID in the request payload for it to work. This is different than the numeric entity ID. You can get the UUID from fetching data from JSON:API, as we saw in the *Fetching data from Drupal using JSON:API* section. For the node that we created in our POST request, the UUID value is 1ddf244d-e8e6-40f5-be48-23bc8fa0fa3e.

Let's go ahead and change the title and body of the article node we created previously. This time, we must pass the UUID in the URL as well as the request body:

```
curl \
  --user chapter12:chapter12 \
  --header 'Accept: application/vnd.api+json' \
  --header 'Content-type: application/vnd.api+json' \
  --request PATCH 'https://localhost/jsonapi/node/
    article/1ddf244d-e8e6-40f5-be48-23bc8fa0fa3e' \
  --data-binary '{
"data": {
  "type": "node--article",
  "id": "1ddf244d-e8e6-40f5-be48-23bc8fa0fa3e",
  "attributes": {
    "title": "Article updated by chapter12",
    "body": {
      "value": "This node was updated using JSON:API!",
      "format": "plain_text"
    }
  }
}
}'
```

Note that the id property is outside of the attributes data. If you try to pass it under attributes, you will get an HTTP 422 Unprocessable Content error. If you pass invalid attributes, you will receive a 500 error. What you are updating must match the data model to be successful.

After submitting this request, we get the updated node back in JSON format on the command line, and we will see in Drupal that our updates were applied:

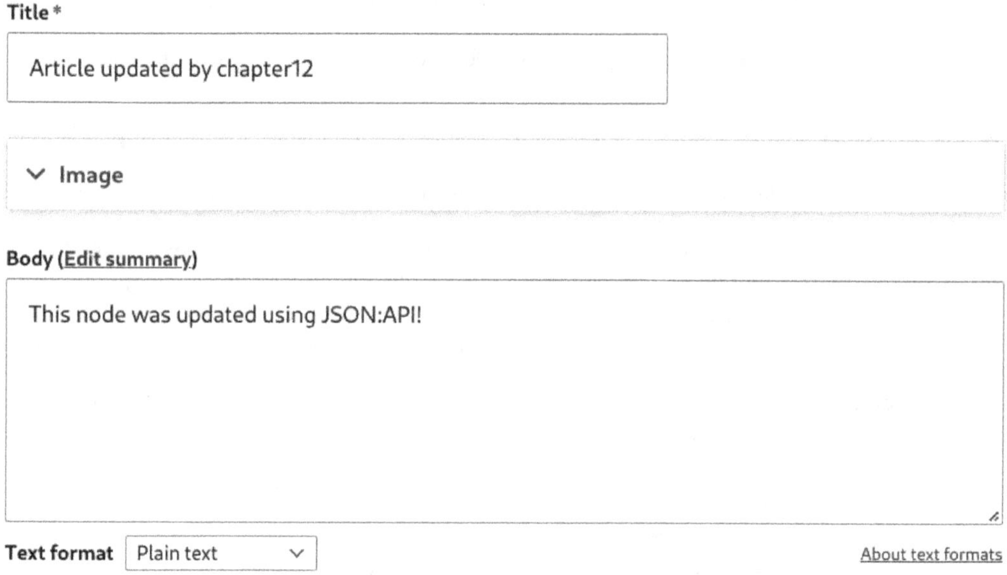

Title *

> Article updated by chapter12

> ∨ **Image**

Body (Edit summary)

> This node was updated using JSON:API!

Text format | Plain text   ∨ | About text formats

Figure 12.17 – Reviewing a node that was updated using a PATCH request

What if we wanted to attribute the node to another user? It is a good idea to use an account solely to handle API actions, but we certainly don't want all content attributed to that user.

For example, assume you have an external publishing platform where users are submitting content. When content is published, that system makes a POST request to Drupal so that the content is created. Let's attribute that content to a user in Drupal named Johnny Editor with a UUID of c1ce9fe6-4eea-4f69-92c2-883415019002. Like nodes, you can view user entity data at /jsonapi/user/user.

We can fix the existing content with a PATCH request and change the author from the chapter12 user to the Johnny Editor user by passing relationships data in the request body. Before we can do that, though, our API user role needs **Administer Content** and **Edit any article content** enabled; otherwise, they will not have access to PATCH the data. Go ahead and enable that permission.

This is because, in this example, we are requesting to change ownership of a node from one user to another, and this is explicitly checked by Drupal before the action is executed.

> **Review your permissions**
>
> Again, once you've read this chapter, it is a good idea to review the security considerations when using APIs in Drupal on Drupal.org: `https://www.drupal.org/docs/core-modules-and-themes/core-modules/jsonapi-module/security-considerations`.

Now, we can make our new PATCH request:

```
curl \
  --user chapter12:chapter12 \
  --header 'Accept: application/vnd.api+json' \
  --header 'Content-type: application/vnd.api+json' \
  --request PATCH 'https://localhost/jsonapi/node/
    article/1ddf244d-e8e6-40f5-be48-23bc8fa0fa3e' \
  --data-binary '{
"data": {
  "type": "node--article",
  "id": "1ddf244d-e8e6-40f5-be48-23bc8fa0fa3e",
  "attributes": {
    "title": "Using Drupal 10 PATCH & JSON:API by Johnny
      Editor",
    "body": {
      "value": "This is how you use Drupal 10 PATCH &
        JSON:API.",
      "format": "plain_text"
    }
  },
  "relationships": {
    "uid": {
      "data": {
        "type": "user--user",
        "id": "c1ce9fe6-4eea-4f69-92c2-883415019002"
      }
    }
  }
}'
```

Here, we receive a successful response from Drupal, along with the JSON representation of the node. We can see that the content was updated and that the node owner was re-assigned to **Johnny Editor**:

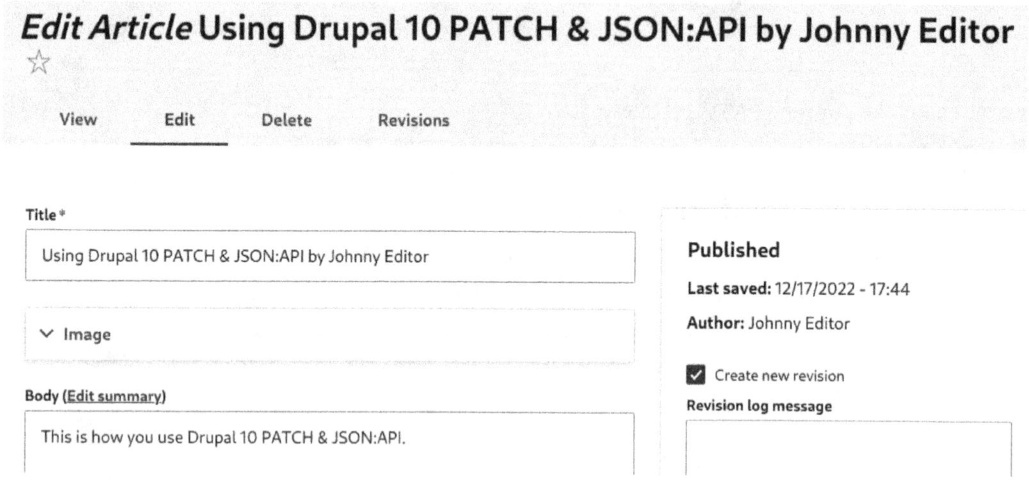

Figure 12.18 – Re-assigning node ownership using a PATCH request

You can use relationships to add any entity reference you want to add to entities. Using this same formula, we can add some taxonomy to this article. Let's assume there are two terms in the `taxonomy` tag called `Technology` and `News`. We want to tag them in this article.

Like nodes and users, you can see taxonomy term data by navigating to `/jsonapi/taxonomy_term/tags`:

```
- data: [
  - {
      type: "taxonomy_term--tags",
      id: "4ef201ed-7cb6-49e5-b125-4c2709be1a42",
    + links: { … },
    - attributes: {
        drupal_internal__tid: 2,
        drupal_internal__revision_id: 2,
        langcode: "en",
        revision_created: "2022-12-17T17:50:12+00:00",
        revision_log_message: null,
        status: true,
        name: "Technology",
        description: null,
        weight: 0,
        changed: "2022-12-17T17:50:12+00:00",
        default_langcode: true,
        revision_translation_affected: true,
      - path: {
          alias: null,
          pid: null,
          langcode: "en"
        }
```

Figure 12.19 – Reading taxonomy terms using its JSON:API endpoint

Using the UUIDs here, we can pass both of them in the relationships part of the request:

```
curl \
  --user chapter12:chapter12 \
  --header 'Accept: application/vnd.api+json' \
  --header 'Content-type: application/vnd.api+json' \
  --request PATCH 'https://localhost/jsonapi/node/
    article/1ddf244d-e8e6-40f5-be48-23bc8fa0fa3e' \
  --data-binary '{
"data": {
  "type": "node--article",
  "id": "1ddf244d-e8e6-40f5-be48-23bc8fa0fa3e",
  "attributes": {
```

```
      "title": "Using Drupal 10 PATCH & JSON:API by Johnny
        Editor",
      "body": {
        "value": "This is how you use Drupal 10 PATCH &
          JSON:API.",
        "format": "plain_text"
      }
    },
    "relationships": {
      "field_tags": {
        "data": [
          {
            "type": "taxonomy_term--tags",
            "id": "4ef201ed-7cb6-49e5-b125-4c2709be1a42"
          },
          {
            "type": "taxonomy_term--tags",
            "id": "09504010-8eff-4be0-8205-607f9e74ffa1"
          }
        ]
      }
    }
  }
}'
```

When submitted, we will see that the article node was successfully updated with the two taxonomy terms specified:

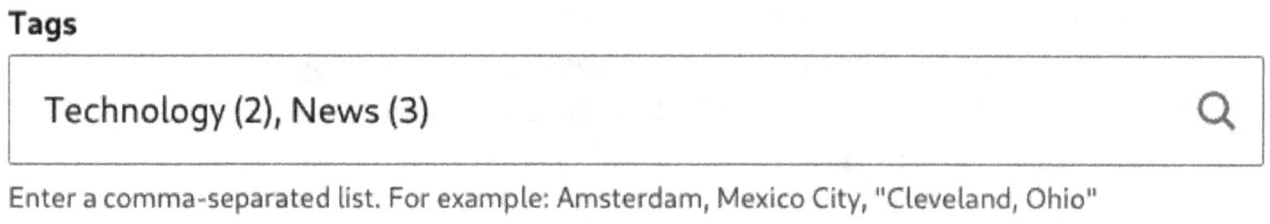

Tags

Technology (2), News (3)	Q

Enter a comma-separated list. For example: Amsterdam, Mexico City, "Cleveland, Ohio"

Figure 12.20 – Taxonomy tags added to a node via a PATCH request

Now, if we were to fetch the data from Drupal as we did in the first section, we will see the author and taxonomy relationships in the node data:

```
- relationships: {
    + node_type: { … },
    + revision_uid: { … },
    - uid: {
        - data: {
            type: "user--user",
            id: "c1ce9fe6-4eea-4f69-92c2-883415019002",
            - meta: {
                drupal_internal__target_id: 3
            }
        },
        + links: { … }
    },
    + field_image: { … },
    - field_tags: {
        - data: [
            - {
                type: "taxonomy_term--tags",
                id: "4ef201ed-7cb6-49e5-b125-4c2709be1a42",
                - meta: {
                    drupal_internal__target_id: 2
                }
            },
            - {
                type: "taxonomy_term--tags",
                id: "09504010-8eff-4be0-8205-607f9e74ffa1",
                - meta: {
                    drupal_internal__target_id: 3
                }
            }
        ]
```

Figure 12.21 – Taxonomy relationships in the response for a node

When you combine that this with `include` in the URL query string, you will get the author data, as well as the taxonomy data: `include=uid, field_tags`.

If you want to remove referenced items, you can submit a PATCH request without that item. If we wanted to remove one of the terms, we can just pass the term we want to keep:

```
"relationships": {
      "field_tags": {
        "data": [
          {
            "type": "taxonomy_term--tags",
            "id": "4ef201ed-7cb6-49e5-b125-4c2709be1a42"
          },
        ]
      }
    }
```

To completely empty the tags field, pass an empty value:

```
"relationships": {
      "field_tags": {
        "data": {}
      }
    }
```

You will see that the terms have been removed from the article node:

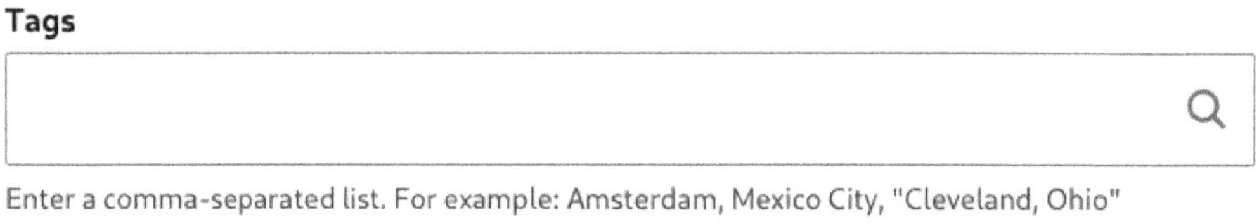

Tags

Enter a comma-separated list. For example: Amsterdam, Mexico City, "Cleveland, Ohio"

Figure 12.22 – Passing an empty value in a PATCH request will remove relationships

How it works...

Just like POST, PATCH provides a powerful way to update entity data in Drupal from a decoupled application or remote system. When you understand your entity data and schema, you can create and manipulate it in any way that you want via the API.

Also like POST, PATCH requests must abide by the permission system in Drupal. The same rules are respected as if this were a real user logging in to Drupal to update content.

With these two methods, you can create a decoupled site that can collect data from users and post it back to Drupal, such as a kiosk, survey, or commenting system. The possibilities are endless.

Using DELETE to remove data with JSON:API

Finally, we have come to the final action of the CRUD acronym: the delete method. This method removes requested data in Drupal, provided you have the UUID.

How to do it...

Like PATCH, issuing DELETE requires the appropriate permission in Drupal. In this case, the role assigned to our API user needs to be allowed to delete article nodes. Head back to the permissions section of the Drupal admin area and grant **Article: Delete any content** to the role.

We need to assign delete any instead of delete own since we assigned the node ownership to another user.

All the DELETE request needs is the UUID of the entity we wish to remove. Using the node we created, the UUID of it is 1ddf244d-e8e6-40f5-be48-23bc8fa0fa3e. The DELETE request looks like this:

```
curl \
  --user chapter12:chapter12 \
  --header 'Accept: application/vnd.api+json' \
  --header 'Content-type: application/vnd.api+json' \
  --request DELETE 'https://localhost/jsonapi/node/
    article/1ddf244d-e8e6-40f5-be48-23bc8fa0fa3e'
```

When you submit it this time, there will be no response output on the command line. When successful, the response will be an HTTP 204 empty response.

The JSON:API route now shows no nodes, which means DELETE was successful:

```
{
  - jsonapi: {
        version: "1.0",
      - meta: {
          - links: {
              - self: {
                    href: "http://jsonapi.org/format/1.0/"
                }
            }
        }
    },
    data: [ ],
  - links: {
      - self: {
            href: "http://localhost/jsonapi/node/article"
        }
    }
}
```

Figure 12.23 – After using a DELETE request, the node was successfully deleted

How it works...

Just like POST and PATCH, DELETE performs actions on behalf of the specified user. Since this user has permission to delete any article content, the request is permitted and Drupal removes the article node from the website.

For some use cases, DELETE may be too destructive of an action to either have an API perform or permission to grant. In this case, you could use PATCH and change the entity status to unpublished or archived (if using the Content Moderation module).

Using Views to provide custom data sources

The RESTful Web Services module provides Views plugins that allow you to expose data over Views for your RESTful API. This allows you to create a view that has a path and outputs data using a serializer plugin. You can use this to output entities in JSON or XML and it can be sent with appropriate headers.

In this recipe, we will create a view that outputs the users of the Drupal site, providing their username, email, and picture if provided.

Getting ready

Make sure you have the following core modules enabled:

- Views
- Views UI
- RESTful Web Services

How to do it...

1. Navigate to **Structure** and then **Views**.
2. Click on **Add new view**.
3. Name the view API Users and have it show **Users**. At the bottom of the View creation page, check off **Provide a REST export**. Give it a path of /api/users:

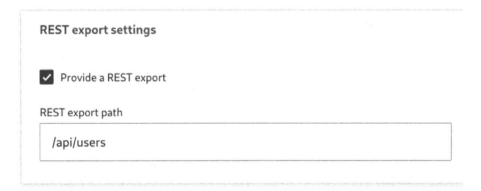

Figure 12.24 – Setting the path for Views for a custom REST endpoint

4. Save the view and continue.

With the view created, make the following changes:

- Change the format of the row plugin from **Entity** to **Fields** so that we can control the specific output.
- Under the **Settings** section of format, enable **json** under **Accepted request formats**.
- Ensure that your view has **Name**, **Email**, and **Picture** as user entity fields
- Change the **User: Name** field to the **Plain text** formatter. Do not link it to the user to ensure the response does not contain any HTML.
- Change the **User: Picture** field so that it uses the URL to image formatter so that only a URL is returned and not HTML.

- Save the updated View.

- Access your view by visiting /api/users. You will receive a JSON response containing the user information.

In your browser, you will see the output of the users in your system formatted in the way we set it in the View:

```
[
  {
    "name": "spuvest",
    "mail": "spuvest@example.com",
    "user_picture": "\/sites\/default\/files\/pictures\/
      2017-07\/generateImage_xIQkfx.jpg"
  },
  {
    "name": "crepathuslus",
    "mail": "crepathuslus@example.com",
    "user_picture": "\/sites\/default\/files\/pictures\/
      2017-07\/generateImage_eauTko.gif"
  },
  {
    "name": "veradabufrup",
    "mail": "veradabufrup@example.com",
    "user_picture": "\/sites\/default\/files\/pictures\/
      2017-07\/generateImage_HsEjKW.png"
  }
]
```

How it works...

The RESTful Web Services module provides a display, row, and format plugin that allows you to export content entities in a serialized format. The REST Export display plugin is what allows you to specify a path to access the RESTful endpoint, and properly assigns the Content-Type header for the requested format.

The Serializer style is provided as the only supported style plugin for the REST Export display. This style plugin only supports row plugins that identify themselves as data display types. It expects data from the row plugin to be raw so that it can be passed to the appropriate serializer.

You then have the option of using the Data entity or Data field row plugins. Instead of returning a render array from their render method, they return raw data that will be serialized into the proper format. With the row plugins returning raw format data and the data then serialized by the style plugin, the display plugin will return the response, converted into the proper format via the Serialization module, which we saw earlier in this chapter.

Using Views is an excellent way to provide API routes for reading. You get all the convenience of using the Views UI that you are used to in Drupal with the combined power of JSON or XML serialization. You can create as many of these as you need to satisfy different use cases.

There's more...

Views allow you to deliver specific RESTful endpoints. With Views, you can add displays with custom paths and add fields to them, creating a custom JSON response. This makes for a rapid way of developing custom read-only data APIs in Drupal.

Controlling the key name in the JSON output

The Data fields row plugin allows you to configure field aliases. When the data is returned to the view, it will contain Drupal's machine names. This means that custom fields will look something like `field_my_field`, which may not make sense to the consumer. By clicking on **Settings** next to **Fields**, you can set aliases in the modal form:

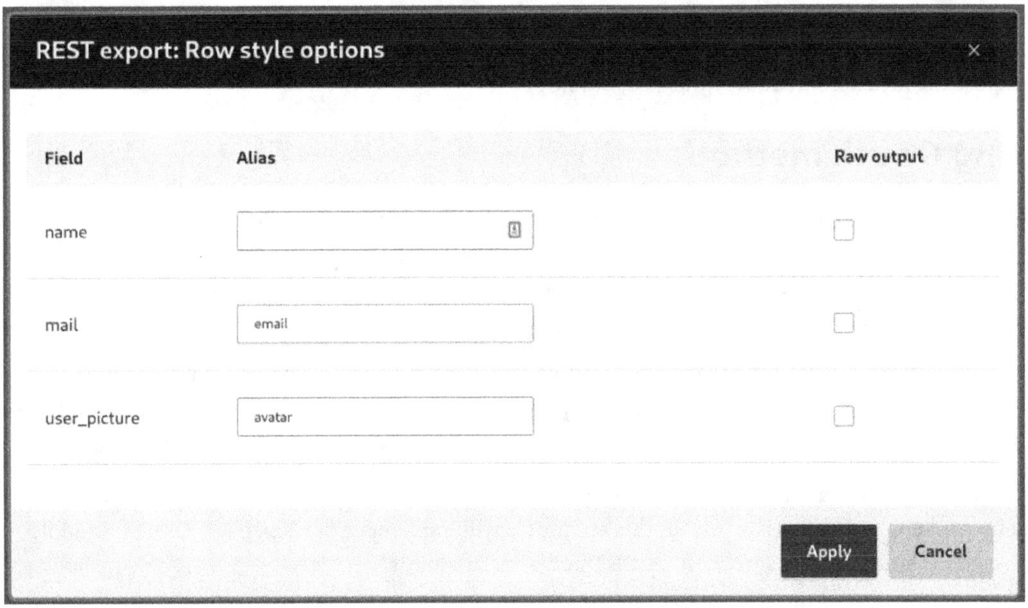

Figure 12.25 – You can alias field names in a Views REST display

When you provide an alias, the fields will match. For example, `user_picture` can be changed to `avatar` and the `mail` key can be changed to `email`:

```
[
  {
    "name": "spuvest",
    "email": "spuvest@example.com",
    "avatar": "\/sites\/default\/files\/pictures\/2017-07\/
      generateImage_xIQkfx.jpg"
  },
]
```

Controlling access to RESTful Views

When you create a RESTful endpoint with Views, you are not using the same permissions created by the RESTful Web Services module. You need to define the route permissions within the view, allowing you to specify specific roles or permissions for the request.

The default GET method provided by the `EntityResource` plugin does not provide a way to list entities and allows any entity to be retrieved by an ID. Using Views, you can provide a list of entities, limiting them to specific bundles and much more.

With Views, you can even provide a new endpoint to retrieve a specific entity. Using Contextual filters, you can add route parameters and filters to limit and validate entity IDs. For example, you may want to expose the article content over the API, but not pages.

Using OAuth methods

Using the RESTful Web Services module, we can define specific supported authentication providers for an endpoint. Drupal core provides a cookie provider, which authenticates through a valid cookie, such as your regular login experience. Then, there is the HTTP Basic Authentication module to support HTTP authentication headers.

Some alternatives provide more robust authentication methods. With cookie-based authentication, you need to use CSRF tokens to prevent unrequested page loads by an unauthorized party. When you use HTTP authentication, you are sending a password for each request in the request header.

A popular, and open, authorization framework is OAuth. OAuth is a proper authentication method that uses tokens and not passwords. In this recipe, we will implement the `Simple OAuth` module to provide OAuth 2.0 authentication for GET and POST requests.

Getting ready

If you are not familiar with OAuth or OAuth 2.0, it is a standard for authorization. The implementation of OAuth revolves around the usage of tokens sent in HTTP headers. Refer to the OAuth home page for more information: `http://oauth.net/`.

For the following sections, you will need the contributed **Rest UI** module. Rest UI will make it easier for you to see and control your REST-based routes in Drupal.

How to do it...

Go ahead and get the necessary module with Composer:

```
composer require drupal/restui:^1.0
```

Enable the **REST UI** module in the admin area under **Extend**.

Now, do the following:

1. First, we must add the `Simple OAuth` module to our Drupal site:

    ```
    composer require drupal/simple_oauth:^6.0@beta
    ```

2. Go to **Configuration** and click on **REST** under **Web Services** to configure the available endpoints:

Resource name	Path	Description	Operations
Content	/node/{node}: GET, PATCH, DELETE /node: POST	methods: GET, POST, PATCH, DELETE formats: json authentication: basic_auth	Edit ⌄

Figure 12.26 – With the REST UI module, you can manage RESTful endpoints in the admin

3. Now that the endpoint has been enabled, it must be configured. Check the **GET** and **POST** method checkboxes to allow `GET` and `POST` requests. Then, check the **JSON** checkbox so that data can be returned as JSON. Check the **oauth2** checkbox and then save it.

4. Before we can configure the `Simple OAuth` module, we have to generate a pair of keys to encrypt the `OAuth` tokens. We can do this in one of two ways:

    A. Create a directory outside of the webroot, then click **Generate keys**. In the dialog that appears, add the full path to this folder on the server and click **Generate**.

B.   If the admin UI does not work, we can use the following two commands to generate keys. Place them on the server outside of the webroot:

```
openssl genrsa -out private.key 2048
openssl rsa -in private.key -pubout > public.key
```

5.   With the keys generated, go to the **Configuration** page and then to **Simple OAuth**. Enter the paths to the private and public keys that were just generated and click on **Save configuration**:

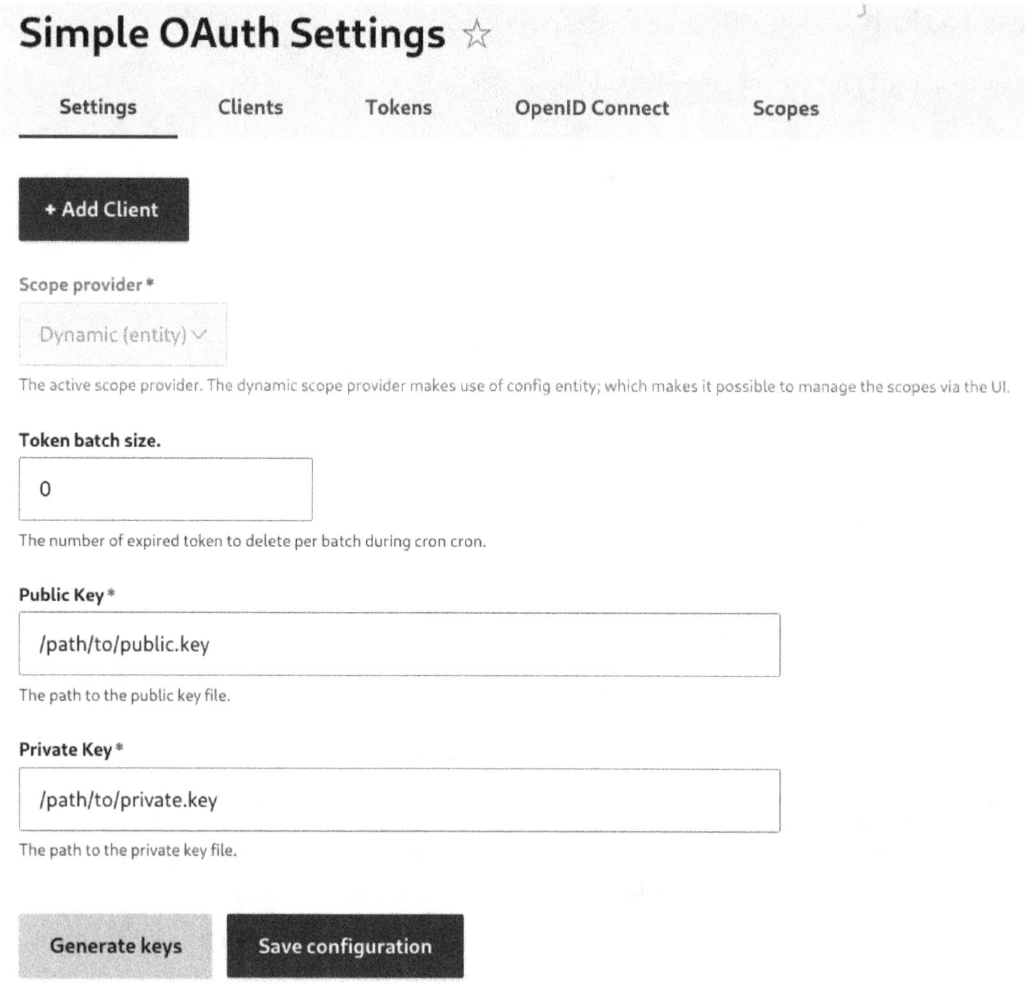

Simple OAuth Settings ☆

| Settings | Clients | Tokens | OpenID Connect | Scopes |

+ Add Client

Scope provider *

Dynamic (entity) ∨

The active scope provider. The dynamic scope provider makes use of config entity; which makes it possible to manage the scopes via the UI.

Token batch size.

```
0
```

The number of expired token to delete per batch during cron cron.

Public Key *

```
/path/to/public.key
```

The path to the public key file.

Private Key *

```
/path/to/private.key
```

The path to the private key file.

Generate keys   **Save configuration**

Figure 12.27 – Managing keys in Simple OAuth in the admin area

6.   From the **Simple OAuth Settings** configuration form, click on + **Add Client**. Provide a label for the client and select the **Administrator** scope. Then, click on **Save** to create the client.

7. Next, we will generate a token through the /oauth/ token endpoint. You will need the ID from the client you just created. We must pass grant_type, client_id, and the username and password. grant_type is the password, whereas client_id is the ID from the created client. The username and password will be of the account you wish to use:

```
curl -X POST https://localhost/oauth/token \
  -H 'content-type: application/x-www-form-
    urlencoded' \
  -d 'grant_type=client_credentials&client_id=
    CLIENT_ID&username=chapter12&client_secret=
      chapter12'
```

8. The response will contain an access_token property. This is to be used as your token when making API requests.

9. Request a node over REST with the **Authorization: Bearer [token]** header:

```
curl -X GET 'https://localhost/node/8?_format=json' \
  -H 'accept: application/json' \
  -H 'authorization: Bearer ACCESS_TOKEN'
```

That's it! You can now set authenticated routes using OAuth to various resources in Drupal and configure all the different REST endpoints with the methods and authentication types they accept.

How it works...

The Simple OAuth module is built using the League\OAuth2 PHP library, a community standard library for OAuth2 implementation.

In a typical authentication request, there is an authentication manager that uses the authentication_collector service to collect all the tagged authentication provider servers. Based on the provider's set priority, each service is invoked to check whether it applies to the current request. Each applied authentication provider then gets invoked to see whether the authentication is invalid.

For the RESTful Web Services module, this process is more explicit. The providers identified in the supported_auth definition for the endpoint are the only services that run through the applies and authenticates processes.

13
Writing Automated Tests in Drupal

In previous chapters, we reviewed how to add custom functionality to Drupal with controllers, routes, responses, custom modules, custom entity types, hooks, and more. With even just a little bit of code, you can add a lot of functionality to your Drupal application.

But how do you know that *it works*? Sure, you can click around and try things out – but it is not a 100% guarantee that things are working under the hood as intended. The more code and features you add, the harder it will be to verify that existing functionality is still intact without providing tests.

By implementing automated tests, you can ensure that the code and features you have added actually work the way you expect. Most importantly, automated tests help significantly reduce bugs and regressions making it to your production website, which in turn will help build your confidence as a developer.

Drupal provides several classes of tools to help provide tests for your application. This chapter covers the following:

- Installing the PHPUnit test suite
- Running PHPUnit
- Writing a unit test
- Writing a kernel test
- Writing a functional test
- Writing a functional JavaScript test
- Writing a NightwatchJS test

Types of tests

There are five types of tests you can run and write in Drupal – **unit tests**, **kernel tests**, **functional tests**, **functional JavaScript tests**, and **NightwatchJS tests**. Which ones you write will depend on the kind of feature(s) you are creating and the level of test coverage you are willing to accept to prove your code is working. Let's take a look at each of these types of tests. You can find the full code used in this chapter on GitHub: `https://github.com/PacktPublishing/Drupal-10-Development-Cookbook/tree/main/chp13`

Unit tests

Unit tests are tests that do not need a Drupal installation to evaluate because they test code that executes code only. They are the lowest-level test you can write. Unit tests are useful for testing plugins, services, or other code that do not require interaction with the database. If you need to write tests that require a database or Drupal environment in some way, you would write a kernel test.

Kernel tests

Kernel tests are the next step up from unit tests. A kernel test is a test that can execute and test functionality that requires some level of database interaction. If you want to test the functionality of features that act when saving entities, test field formatters, check user role access to routes, or test controllers and their responses, a kernel test is what you would write. When executing kernel tests, an instance of Drupal is installed where the tests are performed. This level of isolation is what permits you to test interactive functionality without interfering with your current working database. You are able to specify modules to install and configurations to include in a kernel test, making it an excellent way of testing your modules. These are the most common tests you will see in Drupal.

Functional tests

Functional tests are the highest-level test you can write. Like kernel tests, a functional test will install a working copy of Drupal to run the tests in. These tests are evaluated with a headless browser and are useful for testing functionality from the user perspective. These types of tests are good for testing user workflows, user permissions, and evaluating page content for what you expect to see. For example, if you have a feature where a user navigates to a site, logs in, navigates to the Drupal admin, and sees sections that other roles should not, you can evaluate this with a functional test.

Functional JavaScript tests

Functional JavaScript tests are executed using a real browser, such as Chrome or Firefox. Regular functional tests run in a headless PHP browser emulator called Mink under the hood. Since it is not a full-fledged browser, it cannot test any JavaScript-related features that real browsers such as Chrome have. If you want to test features related to AJAX, cookies, or DOM-related JavaScript events in the browser, you would write a functional JavaScript test. Functional JavaScript tests will require the presence of a browser such as Chrome and tools such as Selenium to orchestrate Chrome under test.

NightwatchJS tests

Similar to a functional JavaScript test, **NightwatchJS** uses Google Chrome and ChromeDriver (`https://chromedriver.chromium.org/`) to evaluate tests. However, instead of PHP files, the test files are written entirely in JavaScript and require **NodeJS** and `yarn` to run and interact with. If you are a developer who tends to write far more JavaScript than you do PHP, you may be interested in using NightwatchJS instead of **PHPUnit**. Another added benefit is that you can write unit tests for the custom JavaScript you write, which is something you cannot test with PHPUnit.

Functional JavaScript and NightwatchJS tests require the most effort to set up and implement, but they can be very valuable because they are running under the same setup, conditions, user role(s), and browser that your visitors are using. They also take the longest to execute but still run in a fraction of the time any human could perform the same tasks.

Installing the PHPUnit test suite

All of the preceding types of tests (with the exception of NightwatchJS tests) are executed from one test harness, PHPUnit. We can add any number of tests to our custom modules or custom themes and run them using PHPUnit – all we have to do is install it and configure it to point at our test files.

Getting ready

The first thing to do before proceeding is to install all the test dependencies so that you can actually run tests in Drupal. Drupal has a specific Composer package that brings in PHPUnit and the required dependencies for it.

To install, follow these steps:

Open up a Terminal (command line) at the root of your project.

Run the following Composer command:

```
composer require --dev drupal/core-dev:^10
```

The `drupal/core-dev` package will bring in PHPUnit and various dependencies to your project that are needed for writing and running tests in Drupal.

> **The --dev flag**
>
> Note that when installing, we are using the `--dev` flag. This tells Composer to list these packages under the `require-dev` section in `composer.json`. The `drupal/core-dev` package is not something you want to have in your production environment; it is for testing only.

How to do it...

Next, we need to configure PHPUnit so that it knows where our tests reside. Drupal core ships with an example `phpunit.xml.dist` file in the `core` directory. This is the file that PHPUnit reads when it executes. You don't have to understand it line for line, but there are a few areas we need to adjust so that it will execute within your custom module directory.

Copy the `phpunit.xml.dist` file out of the `core` directory and place this file in the root of your project. Rename the file `phpunit.xml` and make the following edits:

1. Edit the bootstrap attribute on the `<phpunit>` tag at the top of the document to point to the core tests' `bootstrap` file:

   ```
   bootstrap="./web/core/tests/bootstrap.php"
   ```

2. In order to run kernel or functional tests, edit the following environment settings in the `<php>` section:

   ```
   <env name="SIMPLETEST_BASE_URL"
       value="http://localhost"/>
   <env name="SIMPLETEST_DB" value="
       mysql://database:database@database/database"/>
   <env name="BROWSERTEST_OUTPUT_DIRECTORY" value=""/>
   <env name="SYMFONY_DEPRECATIONS_HELPER" value="weak"/>
   <env name="MINK_DRIVER_ARGS_WEBDRIVER" value="
       ["chrome", {"browserName":"chrome",
       "chromeOptions":{"args":["--disable-gpu","--
       headless"]}}, "http://chrome:9515"] "/>
   ```

   > **DDEV, Lando, Docksal, or Docker?**
   >
   > If you use DDEV, Lando, Docksal, or other readymade tools to run Drupal locally, check their documentation and what the service names are. Depending on which one you use, the preceding values can differ for `SIMPLETEST_BASE_URL`, `SIMPLETEST_DB`, and `MINK_DRIVER_ARGS_WEBDRIVER`.

3. Next, edit the `testsuites` section to point to your custom modules directory. You need to specify a `testsuite` entry per test type:

   ```
   <testsuites>
     <testsuite name="unit">
       <directory>
   ```

```
            web/modules/custom/*/tests/src/Unit
        </directory>
      </testsuite>
      <testsuite name="kernel">
        <directory>
          web/modules/custom/*/tests/src/Kernel
        </directory>
      </testsuite>
      <testsuite name="functional">
        <directory>
          web/modules/custom/*/tests/src/Functional
        </directory>
      </testsuite>
      <testsuite name="functional-javascript">
        <directory>
      web/modules/custom/*/tests/src/FunctionalJavascript
        </directory>
      </testsuite>
    </testsuites>
```

These changes will tell PHPUnit where to locate the tests that we write for our custom modules, located in web/modules/custom. Tests live in the tests/src directory of a module.

Each type of test lives in its own directory within that:

Unit tests go into tests/src/Unit

Kernel tests go into tests/src/Kernel

Functional tests go into tests/src/Functional

Function JavaScript tests go into tests/src/FunctionalJavascript

By defining each type of test as its own test suite in phpunit.xml, we can choose which kind of test type to execute using PHPUnit, which we will look at in the next section. You can also set several testsuite entries, or several directories within a testsuite entry. For example, if you wanted to include all unit tests from contributed modules when you run PHPUnit, you can add another directory entry:

```
<testsuite name="unit">
    <directory>
        web/modules/contrib/*/tests/src/Unit
```

```
    </directory>
    <directory>
        web/modules/custom/*/tests/src/Unit
    </directory>
  </testsuite>
```

The reason we have created a `phpunit.xml` file and placed it at the root of the project is that the file prevents the project from being overwritten or removed the next time you update Drupal. This way, you can commit the configuration to your repository and share it with a team, as well as be able to run tests in continuous integration services provided by GitHub, GitLab, or CircleCI.

It is important to know that this is just one possible way to set your PHPUnit configuration. There are more settings that you can configure here once you are more comfortable with PHPUnit.

There are other settings that can output test coverage results, where to save screenshots of test failures, additional test listeners, logging output, and so on. Be sure to check the online documentation (`https://phpunit.readthedocs.io/en/9.5/configuration.html`) for configuring PHPUnit for more information.

How it works...

When you execute PHPUnit, it uses the `phpunit.xml` file to inform how it executes. It will scan all listed directories for test files and execute them accordingly, providing test feedback in the command-line window (or IDE). Every project you write tests for will require a `phpunit.xml` file like this in order to run any tests.

There's more...

If you plan on writing functional JavaScript tests, you will also need Chrome, Chrome WebDriver, and Selenium. Installing and configuring this can vary, depending on whether you are using Lando, DDEV, Docksal, Docker Compose, or other tools to run Drupal. Please consult the documentation for the best information on how to install these tools to properly execute functional JavaScript tests. Assuming you are using **Lando**, you would add this in the `services` section of your `.lando.yml` file:

```
chrome:
    type: compose
    services:
        image: drupalci/webdriver-chromedriver:production
        command: chromedriver --log-path=/tmp/
            chromedriver.log --verbose
```

chrome becomes a new wired service in the **Lando** stack (referenced in the `MINK_DRIVER_ARGS_WEBDRIVER` setting in `phpunit.xml`, which makes this all work for functional JavaScript tests). If you want to install and use Firefox as an alternative browser to test with, you can do that as well, but Chrome is the most common browser used for testing.

The way these tools are added can vary, depending on what you use. Please consult the documentation on the best approach to add Chrome and Chrome WebDriver. There are simply too many stack-specific configurations to cover in this book.

Running PHPUnit

First, we can verify that we have set up correctly by executing the `phpunit` command. There are no tests yet, but that's okay. This step just verifies that the tool is installed and our configuration file is properly read.

How to do it...

> **Consult the documentation**
>
> From here, we are going to provide bare-bones, verbose commands to use PHPUnit to execute tests. If you use Lando, DDEV, Docksal, or otherwise, please consult their documentation on how to best run PHPUnit. They usually have command wrappers that are small and convenient.

In your command line, execute the following:

```
phpunit
```

This is the main command you will run. PHPUnit will automatically detect our `phpunit.xml` configuration in the project directory.

> **Can't find phpunit?**
>
> If you get an error about the `phpunit` command not being found, you may need to instead use the full path to it from the project root with `vendor/bin/phpunit`. Composer should automatically alias commands for you, but depending on how a project is set up, this may be required.

You should see output similar to the following:

```
PHPUnit 9.5.26 by Sebastian Bergmann and contributors.

No tests executed!
```

You can also run specific `testsuites` or individual tests by adding the `--testsuite` and `--filter` arguments to phpunit:

```
phpunit --testsuite unit
```

The preceding command will run all unit tests found in the directories listed in your `unit` testsuite in `phpunit.xml`:

```
phpunit --testsuite unit --filter FooBarTest
```

The preceding command will run only the `FooBarTest` unit test. These two approaches are useful for testing certain `testsuites` only or specific tests themselves for faster feedback, when testing, debugging, and iterating your code.

How it works...

When you execute PHPUnit, it scans all listed directories in the `phpunit.xml` file and provides test feedback in the command-line window.

In this instance, PHPUnit said that no tests were found or executed, which is correct because we do not have any yet. We are now ready to write our first unit test.

Writing a unit test

Let's write our first test. As previously mentioned, a unit test is the lowest-level type of test you can write. It only executes and tests raw PHP code that has no dependencies on services such as a connected database or other integrated APIs. This means the test can execute using PHP only.

Getting ready

Let's create a scenario that will help you think about when and how to apply unit testing. Imagine you have to provide data to a frontend component. The frontend developer has requested that you provide all JSON keys in `camelCase` format in the API response. `camelCase` would turn strings such as `field_event_date` into `fieldEventDate`.

`snake_case` is used in many places in Drupal; the most common place you will see this is with machine names (such as on the preceding event date field). All machine names in Drupal are in `snake_case`.

This is a very simple example but perfect to illustrate how we can wield a unit test to test our class.

How to do it...

Go ahead and create a custom module called `chapter13`. This is where we will be writing example code and its tests for the rest of this chapter. Refer to *Chapter 4, Extending Drupal with Custom Code*, if you need a refresher on how to create a custom module in Drupal.

With the custom module created, let's add the `CamelCase` class in the `chapter13` module under the `src` directory:

```php
<?php

declare(strict_types=1);

namespace Drupal\chapter13;

/**
 * Class CamelCase
 * @package Drupal\chapter13
 */
class CamelCase {

  /**
   * Convert snake_case to camelCase.
   *
   * @param string $input
   * @return string
   */
  public static function convert(string $input): string {
    $input = strtolower($input);
    return str_replace('_', '', lcfirst(ucwords
        ($input, '_')));
  }

}
```

Looks like it works, right? Let's prove it with a test.

In your custom module, create a tests directory. Under this directory, create an src directory, and within the src directory, create a Unit directory. You should have a path now that looks like chapter13/tests/src/Unit. Note that the src directory in your tests directory is different than the src directory at the root of the chapter13 module, where the CamelCase class resides.

In the chapter13/tests/src/Unit directory, create a new file and name it CamelCaseTest. php. All test files must have Test at the end of their filenames to be discovered by PHPUnit.

Our test file needs to do two things:

- Provide test data to convert with the CamelCase class

- Assert that the convert method returns what we expect

Any method that begins with test in your test class will be evaluated by PHPUnit. With that in mind, let's go ahead and fill in our unit test in CamelCaseTest.php:

```php
<?php

namespace Drupal\Tests\chapter13\Unit;

use Drupal\Tests\UnitTestCase;
use Drupal\chapter13\CamelCase;

/**
 * Class CamelCaseTest
 * @package Drupal\Tests\chapter13\Unit
 */
class CamelCaseTest extends UnitTestCase {

  /**
   * Data provider for testToCamel().
   *
   * @return array
   *   An array containing input values and expected output
   *      values.
   */
  public function exampleStrings() {
    return [
      ['button_color', 'buttonColor'],
```

```
      ['snake_case_example', 'snakeCaseExample'],
      ['ALL_CAPS_LOCK', 'allCapsLock'],
    ];
  }


  /**
   * Tests the ::convert method.
   *
   * @param $input
   *    The input values.
   *
   * @param bool $expected
   *    The expected output.
   *
   * @param bool $separator
   *    The string separator.
   *
   * @dataProvider exampleStrings()
   */
  public function testCamelCaseConversion($input,
    $expected) {
    $output = CamelCase::convert($input);
    $this->assertEquals($expected, $output);
  }


}
```

Go ahead and run phpunit:

```
phpunit --testsuite unit --filter CamelCaseTest
```

It will result in the following:

```
Testing
...   3 / 3 (100%)
Time: 00:00.044, Memory: 10.00 MB
OK (3 tests, 3 assertions)
```

This output indicates that the test was called three times (one for each set of data in @dataProvider) and each one passed. In other words, $input equaled $expected, which is what assertEquals evaluates. If a test were to fail, this output would indicate what test failed and on what line.

How it works...

PHPUnit reports that all three tests pass. But, wait – didn't we only write the testCamelCaseConversion test method?

When the test is executed, PHPUnit detects a special annotation in our test method called @dataProvider, which tags the exampleStrings method. The exampleStrings method provides an array of data. Each array contains a value to send in and the value we expect to get back. PHPUnit will loop the data provider values, so our test method is called three times (one for each set of values) and evaluates the test. This means PHPUnit sees the test method called like this when executed:

```
testCamelCaseConversion("button_color", "buttonColor")
```

The three values test that the method works for two or more words and returns the proper case.

Within the test, we pass the input along to CamelCase::convert. From that method, we pass the value it returned to assertEquals, one of the many value assertion methods of PHPUnit.

Every item you add to a data provider will be asserted by the test method(s) that use them. dataProviders is an excellent way to test our code under a variety of scenarios. Therefore, we know that any string passed to convert will be transformed from foo_bar to fooBar and returned. The test proves that.

So, how does automated testing help here? With our setup, any developer on a team is able to run the testsuites and see their output. If they fail, they can see what code is failing and where. This provides an opportunity to fix the code before it is deployed to production.

Under continuous integration setups, you can prevent code from being merged into your main branch until all tests pass. As we mentioned, this is an excellent way to reduce bugs and errors from surfacing on production to your users.

There's more...

Over time, requirements can and often do change. Assume that after you have deployed this code, your frontend developer returns and asks that any string such as foo-bar is also converted to camel case.

With our test in place, we can add this new case to our data provider:

```
public function exampleStrings() {
  return [
    ['button_color', 'buttonColor'],
```

```
      ['snake_case_example', 'snakeCaseExample'],
      ['ALL_CAPS_LOCK', 'allCapsLock'],
      ['foo-bar', 'fooBar'],
   ];
 }
```

When we run the test now, we get the following:

```
Testing
...F     4 / 4 (100%)
Time: 00:00.046, Memory: 10.00 MB
There was 1 failure:

1) Drupal\Tests\chapter13\Unit\CamelCaseTest::
   testCamelCaseConversion with data set #3 ('foo-bar',
        'fooBar')
Failed asserting that two strings are equal.
--- Expected
+++ Actual
@@ @@
-'fooBar'
+'foo-bar'

FAILURES!
Tests: 4, Assertions: 4, Failures: 1.
```

This is fine – we have not updated our implementation yet. Adding new cases to the test first lets us iterate and improve the implementation code until the test passes. This provides a fast feedback loop because we can modify the implementation in the CamelCase class all we want. If the tests all pass, we know we have met the requirements and that our functionality works, and we can move on to other features in our module.

See also

Writing tests first before having any implementation code is referred to as **test-driven development**. This means the tests drive the specification or requirements, and the implementation code makes them pass. There are many schools of thought on whether you should write all tests first or not.

If you are new to testing, it is fine to write some initial code for a proof of concept if you need to hash out an idea in your Drupal module. You can always add tests to it at any point during development. The important point is to add tests for your code; don't worry so much about when.

The more you practice and write tests, the better you will get, and you will eventually shift to writing the tests first.

Continue experimenting with the `CamelCase` class and its `CamelCaseTest` class. See whether you can invent some new requirements, change the code, run the tests, and get them to pass.

Drupal core has hundreds of great examples of unit tests. The most-popular contributed modules are useful as well. Be sure to check them out if you are stuck or need guidance.

Now that you know the basics of unit testing in Drupal, let's look at kernel tests.

Writing a kernel test

Let's build upon the previous example. Assume now that stakeholders have asked you to output a field value on the screen in the camel case format. The good news is we have a working implementation and unit test, so we can make short work of this task in Drupal.

In this case, we need to make a field formatter class for string fields. When the formatter is used on a field to display output, we want to run the user input through our existing `CamelCase` class. If you need a refresher on field formatters and managing entity displays, refer to *Chapter 2, Content Building Experience*.

This provides an excellent example to step into a kernel test. Earlier, we mentioned that kernel tests create a minimal installation of Drupal with the setup that you specify in your test, in order to run and evaluate their test methods. There is no danger in running kernel tests, as they do not touch or interfere with your current site database in any way. When the test is done, it is *torn down*, or removed, from the database with no trace.

How to do it...

Create a new directory in your `tests/src` directory called `Kernel`. This is where your kernel tests for the `chapter13` module will live. This time around, we are going to write the test first.

Under `chapter13/tests/src/Kernel`, create the `CamelCaseFormatterTest.php` file. Next, we are going to fill it in with the following code. There is a fair amount of boilerplate in the setup, but we will review what's going on:

```php
<?php

namespace Drupal\Tests\chapter13\Kernel;
```

```php
use Drupal\Core\Entity\Entity\EntityViewDisplay;
use Drupal\field\Entity\FieldConfig;
use Drupal\field\Entity\FieldStorageConfig;
use Drupal\KernelTests\KernelTestBase;
use Drupal\Tests\node\Traits\ContentTypeCreationTrait;
use Drupal\Tests\node\Traits\NodeCreationTrait;

/**
 * Tests the formatting of string fields using the Camel
 *       Case field formatter.
 *
 * @package Drupal\Tests\chapter13\Kernel
 */
class CamelCaseFormatterTest extends KernelTestBase {

  use NodeCreationTrait,
    ContentTypeCreationTrait;

  protected $strictConfigSchema = FALSE;

  /**
   * Modules to enable.
   *
   * @var array
   */
  protected static $modules = [
    'field',
    'text',
    'node',
    'system',
    'filter',
    'user',
    'chapter13',
  ];

  /**
```

```
   * {@inheritdoc}
   */
  protected function setUp(): void {
    parent::setUp();

    // Install required module schema and configs.
    $this->installEntitySchema('node');
    $this->installEntitySchema('user');
    $this->installConfig(['field', 'node', 'filter',
        'system']);
    $this->installSchema('node', ['node_access']);

    // Create a vanilla content type for testing.
    $this->createContentType(
      [
        'type' => 'page'
      ]
    );

    // Create and store the field_chapter13_test field.
    FieldStorageConfig::create([
      'field_name' => 'field_chapter13_test',
      'entity_type' => 'node',
      'type' => 'string',
      'cardinality' => 1,
      'locked' => FALSE,
      'indexes' => [],
      'settings' => [
        'max_length' => 255,
        'case_sensitive' => FALSE,
        'is_ascii' => FALSE,
      ],
    ])->save();

    FieldConfig::create([
      'field_name' => 'field_chapter13_test',
```

```
    'field_type' => 'string',
    'entity_type' => 'node',
    'label' => 'Chapter13 Camel Case Field',
    'bundle' => 'page',
    'description' => '',
    'required' => FALSE,
    'settings' => [
      'link_to_entity' => FALSE
    ],
  ])->save();

  // Set the entity display for testing to use our
      camel_case formatter.
  $entity_display = EntityViewDisplay::load
      ('node.page.default');
  $entity_display->setComponent('field_chapter13_test',
  [
    'type' => 'camel_case',
    'region' => 'content',
    'settings' => [],
    'label' => 'hidden',
    'third_party_settings' => []
  ]);
  $entity_display->save();
}


/**
 * Tests that the field formatter camel_case formats the
      value
 * as expected.
 */
public function testFieldIsFormatted() {
  $node = $this->createNode(
    [
      'type' => 'page',
      'field_chapter13_test' => 'A user entered string'
```

```
    ]
  );
  $build = $node->field_chapter13_test->view('default');
  $this->assertSame('aUserEnteredString',
      $build[0]['#context']['value']);
  }
}
```

Don't be discouraged by the amount of code in this test. A majority of the code is setting up the conditions we need to run the test itself:

- Installing the required modules needed to provide the field and Node entity
- Installing the module configuration and entity schema
- Creating a page content type
- Creating field_chapter13_test and assigning it to the page Node type
- Modifying the Node default view mode and setting field_chapter13_test to use the camel_case field formatter

An alternative way to do this would be to create all of these items in Drupal (the content type, the field, set the formatter) and export that configuration into a module that is used only for this test. The result is more or less equivalent in the end, but you may find that creating the conditions entirely out of code is more maintainable in the long run than a few dozen YAML files.

> **Names in tests**
>
> When naming content types, entities, or fields in a kernel test, you can make them whatever you want. They don't have to match your system exactly, especially if all you need is a random content type that can hold a field. What we are testing is the output returned, not the names.

If we run the test now, it will fail; now, we can make the implementation so that the tests will pass.

To solve the ask, we need to create a FieldFormatter plugin that uses our existing CamelCase class. This exercise is easy, since the bulk of the work already exists for changing inputs to camel case format.

Add a Plugin/Field/FieldFormatter directory under the src directory of the chapter13 module. Within that directory, add a file called CamelCaseFormatter.php. Our implementation will be as follows:

```php
<?php

declare(strict_types = 1);
```

```
namespace Drupal\chapter13\Plugin\Field\FieldFormatter;

use Drupal\chapter13\CamelCase;
use Drupal\Core\Field\FieldItemInterface;
use Drupal\Core\Field\FieldItemListInterface;
use Drupal\Core\Field\Plugin\Field\FieldFormatter\
    StringFormatter;

/**
 * Plugin implementation of the 'camel_case' field
 *     formatter.
 *
 * @FieldFormatter(
 *   id = "camel_case",
 *   label = @Translation("Camel case"),
 *   field_types = {
 *     "string"
 *   }
 * )
 */
class CamelCaseFormatter extends StringFormatter {

  /**
   * {@inheritdoc}
   */
  public function viewElements(FieldItemListInterface
    $items, $langcode) : array {
    $elements = [];

    foreach ($items as $delta => $item) {
      $view_value = $this->viewValue($item);
      $elements[$delta] = $view_value;
    }
```

```
    return $elements;
  }


  /**
   * {@inheritdoc}
   */
  protected function viewValue(FieldItemInterface $item) {
    return [
      '#type' => 'inline_template',
      '#template' => '{{ value|nl2br }}',
      '#context' => ['value' => CamelCase::convert($item
          ->value)],
    ];
  }


}
```

By extending the `StringFormatter` class from core Drupal, we can make modifications that leverage our `CamelCase` class.

Now, let's run our kernel test:

```
phpunit --testsuite kernel --filter CamelCaseFormatterTest
```

This results in the following:

```
Testing
F    1 / 1 (100%)
Time: 00:01.500, Memory: 10.00 MB


There was 1 failure:
1) Drupal\Tests\chapter13\Kernel\CamelCaseFormatterTest::
   testFieldIsFormatted
Failed asserting that two strings are identical.
--- Expected
+++ Actual
@@ @@
-'aUserEnteredString'
```

```
+'a user entered string'
FAILURES!
Tests: 1, Assertions: 9, Failures: 1.
```

It failed! What happened? Remember when we mentioned before that requirements can change? Our test case passes A user entered string as test data. Our CamelCase class does not currently handle strings with spaces, dashes, or commas. Since this is a field in Drupal, users can enter just about anything. We need to account for that.

Modify the CamelCase class to account for this new requirement:

```
public static function convert(string $input): string {
  $input = strtolower($input);
  $input = preg_replace('/[, -]/', '_', $input);
  return str_replace('_', '', lcfirst(ucwords
      ($input, '_')));
}
```

The addition of replacing the comma, space, and dash character should now satisfy new use cases. Let's run the kernel test again:

```
Testing
.          1 / 1 (100%)
Time: 00:01.491, Memory: 10.00 MB
OK (1 test, 9 assertions)
```

However, let's not forget about our unit test that broke earlier – let's add our two new example strings to the exampleStrings data provider method:

```
public function exampleStrings() {
  return [
    ['button_color', 'buttonColor'],
    ['snake_case_example', 'snakeCaseExample'],
    ['ALL_CAPS_LOCK', 'allCapsLock'],
    ['foo-bar', 'fooBar'],
    ['This is a basic string', 'thisIsABasicString'],
  ];
}
```

Now, when you run PHPUnit, both the unit and the kernel test should pass:

```
Testing
......   6 / 6 (100%)


Time: 00:01.419, Memory: 10.00 MB
OK (6 tests, 14 assertions)
```

We now have another new and tested feature added to the site that we can deploy with confidence. Of course, we are free to reuse this functionality for our Drupal application when we need to.

How it works...

When running a kernel test, Drupal will install an additional copy of itself to run tests in. The kernel test will use the install profile and modules you require in the test. This way, you can ensure that you are testing your code in the cleanest possible setup, with no interference from unnecessary contributed modules or other code. When the tests finish running, Drupal will automatically clean up and remove this second installation, including any data that was created within the test itself.

So far, we have written code and tests that prove they do what we need – but they can't test that a user on the site sees the right thing. Let's dive in and add a functional test to do just that!

Writing a functional test

Now that we know our code is working, let's prove that a user can see the formatted string when they visit a node. Functional tests use an emulated browser that allows us to simulate users navigating the site. Functional tests install Drupal and test in an isolated fashion, so there is no risk of corrupting your current Drupal installation.

How to do it...

With a functional test, we can navigate the browser as if we were a real user, navigating and performing all kinds of assertions that unit and kernel tests cannot do. Like before, we do need to set some configurations in place in order to test. Within your tests/src directory, create a new directory called Functional, and then create a file inside of it called CamelCaseFormatterDisplayTest.php.

In this new test file, we are going to borrow some of the setups from the previous kernel test:

```php
<?php

namespace Drupal\Tests\chapter13\Functional;
```

```php
use Drupal\Core\Entity\Entity\EntityViewDisplay;
use Drupal\field\Entity\FieldConfig;
use Drupal\field\Entity\FieldStorageConfig;
use Drupal\Tests\BrowserTestBase;

/**
 * Class CamelCaseFormatterDisplayTest
 *
 * @package Drupal\Tests\chapter13\Functional
 */
class CamelCaseFormatterDisplayTest extends
    BrowserTestBase {

  /**
   * @var bool Disable schema checking.
   */
  protected $strictConfigSchema = FALSE;

  /**
   * @var string The theme to use during test.
   */
  protected $defaultTheme = 'stark';

  /**
   * Modules to enable.
   *
   * @var array
   */
  protected static $modules = [
    'field',
    'text',
    'node',
    'system',
    'filter',
    'user',
    'chapter13',
```

```php
];

/**
 * {@inheritdoc}
 */
protected function setUp(): void {
  parent::setUp();

  // Create a vanilla content type for testing.
  $this->createContentType(
    [
      'type' => 'page'
    ]
  );

  // Create and store the field_chapter13_test field.
  FieldStorageConfig::create([
    'field_name' => 'field_chapter13_test',
    'entity_type' => 'node',
    'type' => 'string',
    'cardinality' => 1,
    'locked' => FALSE,
    'indexes' => [],
    'settings' => [
      'max_length' => 255,
      'case_sensitive' => FALSE,
      'is_ascii' => FALSE,
    ],
  ])->save();

  FieldConfig::create([
    'field_name' => 'field_chapter13_test',
    'field_type' => 'string',
    'entity_type' => 'node',
    'label' => 'Chapter13 Camel Case Field',
    'bundle' => 'page',
```

```
      'description' => '',
      'required' => FALSE,
      'settings' => [
        'link_to_entity' => FALSE
      ],
  ])->save();


  // Set the entity display for testing to use our
      camel_case formatter.
  $entity_display = EntityViewDisplay::load
      ('node.page.default');
  $entity_display->setComponent('field_chapter13_test',
    [
      'type' => 'camel_case',
      'region' => 'content',
      'settings' => [],
      'label' => 'hidden',
      'third_party_settings' => []
    ]);
  $entity_display->save();
}


/**
 * Test that a site visitor can see a string formatted
      with our custom
 * field CamelCaseFieldFormatter.
 *
 * @return void
 */
public function testUserCanSeeFormattedString() {
  $this->drupalCreateNode(
    [
      'type' => 'page',
      'field_chapter13_test' => 'A user entered string'
    ]
  );
```

```
$this->drupalGet('/node/1');
$this->getSession()->getPage()->hasContent
    ('aUserEnteredString');
  }
}
```

There are some differences here for the functional test.

In a functional test, you can specify two properties, $profile and $defaultTheme. $profile specifies which installation profile to use for this test, and $defaultTheme specifies which theme to activate for this test. By default, the *testing* profile is used, the absolute minimum needed to install Drupal. You can also specify *minimal* or *standard*, which installs either one of those profiles to use in testing.

> **Install profiles and testing**
>
> If you use install profiles that come with configurations or extras that create content types and roles, for example, be sure to not try to create them again in your test, with methods such as createContentType. In those cases, we will receive an error, since the install profile will have already created them.

Finally, you can also create your own install profile for testing that contains Drupal configuration files that you need – this is useful if you don't want to write code in the state in the setUp method of the test.

All we need for this test to run are the defaults, so run PHPUnit:

```
phpunit --testsuite functional --filter
   CamelCaseFormatterDisplayTest
```

This results in the following:

```
Testing
  .                1 / 1 (100%)


Time: 00:07.390, Memory: 10.00 MB
OK (1 test, 3 assertions)
```

It passes, but do note that the total time to perform functional tests is far higher than unit or kernel tests. This is due to having to install a full version of Drupal to run the functional tests in. On this machine, it took 7 seconds with the core *testing* profile. If we switch to the core *standard* profile, which installs a lot more, we can see the time increase:

```
protected $profile = 'standard';
Testing
.               1 / 1 (100%)


Time: 00:18.441, Memory: 10.00 MB
OK (1 test, 2 assertions)
```

The time elapsed is double over the smaller install profile. This is not necessarily a problem, but do keep that in mind when writing tests. In the end, valuable tests and concrete feedback are worth a little extra time to make sure we get things right with custom code.

How it works...

Functional tests are more robust than kernel tests. Like a kernel test, Drupal will install another copy of itself to run tests in, but the installation is more *full* or complete than a kernel test. These tests are run with a browser emulator called Mink, and that is how it is able to navigate URLs, check for HTML elements, and perform actions as if a real user were navigating the site.

See also

There are many things you can do with functional tests (see the end of this chapter for ideas on how to expand what we covered previously). However, Mink is not an actual browser and has no capability to run or react to JavaScript interactions. For example, if we had to hide the field text on the page after 5 seconds, or display the field value with AJAX, we would need to use a functional JavaScript test to do that.

Writing a functional JavaScript test

Assume that you now have one last request. You have been asked to use AJAX to display the value from the Camel Case formatter 3 seconds after a user has visited a page.

Testing this requires using an actual browser such as Google Chrome. Checking anything that involves AJAX, cookies, user interactions, or the DOM cannot be done with a regular functional test.

Fortunately, writing a functional JavaScript test is not all that different; we just extend from a different base class for the test – `WebDriverTestBase` instead of `BrowserTestBase`.

> **Chrome and Selenium required**
>
> If you use DDEV, Lando, Docksal, or other ready made tools to run Drupal locally, check their documentation on how to best integrate Chrome and Selenium for functional JavaScript tests. They all have variations in approach to installing them.

How to do it...

In your `tests/src` directory, create a new directory named `FunctionalJavascript`. Within that new directory, create a file named `CamelCaseFormatterDisplayAjaxTest.php`. You can copy the previous functional test code into this file, with these changes:

- Update `namespace` from `Functional` to `FunctionalJavascript`
- Extend `WebDriverTestBase` instead of `BrowserTestBase`
- The class name should be changed to `CamelCaseFormatterDisplayAjaxTest`

Since we now have a requirement to add JavaScript around the display of this text on the page, you can remove the old functional test, since it will fail. Text won't be present on the page at first and the old test can't listen or wait for AJAX, so we no longer need that test.

Now, we can update the test method to account for the new requirement. Assume that JavaScript has been written already and that the field value is fetched and output by AJAX. The implementation details are not important here, but we can change our test method to *wait* until AJAX has completed before checking for text on the page:

```php
public function testUserCanSeeFormattedString() {
  $this->drupalCreateNode(
    [
      'type' => 'page',
      'field_chapter13_test' => 'A user entered string'
    ]
  );

  $this->drupalGet('/node/1');
  $this->assertSession()->assertWaitOnAjaxRequest();
  $this->assertSession()->
    pageTextContains('aUserEnteredString');
}
```

And after running our new test with PHPUnit, this is the result:

```
Testing
.                1 / 1 (100%)


Time: 00:19.721, Memory: 10.00 MB
OK (1 test, 2 assertions)
```

How it works...

Functional JavaScript tests are functional tests, with the added functionality of being run in a real browser such as Google Chrome. This is what makes it possible to assert even more tests for HTML elements, interactivity, AJAX, cookies, and other features that require using a real browser to perform actions.

Writing a NightwatchJS test

Similar to a functional JavaScript test, NightwatchJS uses Google Chrome to evaluate tests. However, instead of PHP files, the test files are written entirely in JavaScript and require NodeJS and `yarn` to run and interact with.

Getting ready

NightwatchJS is not included as part of PHPUnit, so you will need to install it using `yarn`:

1. Inside the `/core` folder, run `yarn install`.
2. Configure **NightwatchJS** settings by copying `.env.example` to `.env` and editing as necessary. These settings will mostly be the same as your local environment settings. `DRUPAL_TEST_BASE_URL` will be the value of your local site URL, for example.

How to do it...

NightwatchJS looks for tests in the following directories:

- `mymodule/tests/src/Nightwatch/Tests`
- `mymodule/tests/src/Nightwatch/Commands`
- `mymodule/tests/src/Nightwatch/Assertions`
- `mymodule/tests/src/Nightwatch/Pages`

Here, `mymodule` is your custom module name, like `chapter13`, which we have been using for all the code in this chapter.

You can run NightwatchJS tests using `yarn`:

```
yarn test:nightwatch (args)
```

Alternatively, you can run a single test – for example, a test in your custom module:

```
yarn test:nightwatch mymodule/tests/src/Nightwatch/Tests/
  exampleTest.js
```

Let's convert the `CamelCase` PHP class to a JavaScript function and test it with `nightwatch`.

Create a directory called `js` at `chapter13/js`. Inside, create a file called `camelCase.js`. The file will contain the following code:

```
module.exports = (inputText) => {
  let text = inputText.toLowerCase();
  text = text.replace(/[, -]/g, '_');

  let extractedText = text.split('_').map(function(word,
    index) {
    if (index !== 0) {
      return word.charAt(0).toUpperCase() +
          word.slice(1).toLowerCase();
    } else {
      text = word;
    }
  }).join('');

  text = text.toLowerCase() + extractedText;
  return text.replace('_', '');
}
```

We can unit-test this JavaScript function just like we did with the PHP class at the start of the chapter. To do that, create a new directory under `chapter13/tests/src/Nightwatch`, and within that directory, create another directory called `Tests`.

Create a file in the `Tests` directory called `CamelCaseTest.js`. It will look like this, getting the same result that we got from the previous functional JavaScript test:

```
const assert = require('assert');
const camelCase = require('../../../js/camelCase');
```

```
const dataProvider = [
  {input: 'button_color', expected: 'buttonColor'},
  {input: 'snake_case_example', expected:
    'snakeCaseExample'},
  {input: 'ALL_CAPS_LOCK', expected: 'allCapsLock'},
  {input: 'foo-bar', expected: 'fooBar'},
];

module.exports = {
  '@tags': ['chapter13'],
  '@unitTest' : true,
  'Strings are converted to camelCase' : function (done) {
    dataProvider.forEach(function (values) {
      assert.strictEqual(camelCase(values.input),
          values.expected);
    });
    setTimeout(function() {
      done();
    }, 10);
  }
};
```

Now execute the test with:

```
yarn test:nightwatch chapter13/tests/src/Nightwatch/Tests/
  CamelCaseTest.js
```

Nightwatch will execute the JavaScript function, loop over the `dataProvider` values, and assert that the function returns what we expect it to:

```
yarn test:nightwatch ../modules/custom/chapter13/tests/src/
  Nightwatch/CamelCaseTest.js
yarn run v1.22.19
[Nightwatch/CamelCaseTest]
✔ Strings are converted to camelCase


Done in 3.77s.
```

This is useful for testing JavaScript functions you have written for your custom modules or themes. Testing JavaScript functions or behaviors can be a time-intensive task to do manually. NightwatchJS is handy for automating that task.

How it works...

NightwatchJS is also capable of doing browser-based test assertions such as the functional JavaScript tests we discussed earlier in the chapter. There are caveats though, as the scope of JavaScript is more limited than a language such as PHP – depending on what you are trying to test, the test setup may take way longer than it would in PHP. You can certainly script your way there by using JavaScript in the test to log in as an admin and navigate Drupal to create fields, nodes, and elements, but this would take a *lot* of JavaScript to do, and it is more suitable to make your own install profile in this case.

Having said that, there are various tests in Drupal core that use NightwatchJS, so be sure to refer to them for pointers, examples, and ideas.

See also

You are not strictly limited to writing tests using PHPUnit or NightwatchJS for Drupal. There are many third-party test harnesses you can use to write and run tests for different use cases in Drupal. Be sure to check out the following:

- Behat Drupal Extension
- Drupal Test Traits
- Cypress.io

14

Migrating External Data into Drupal

Whether you have been developing for a while or just getting started in your career, one very common situation you will encounter is the need to bring in data from an external source. This can include migrating from older versions of Drupal, migrating from sites not based on Drupal, different database engines, static HTML files, or incorporating data from CSV or HTTP APIs with JSON or XML.

No matter the scenario, Drupal contains several powerful tools to solve these needs with the core Migrate module. Under the hood, it also contains a powerful plugin system that allows you to extend and define your own data source or process plugin, as well as a healthy ecosystem of contributed modules to enhance the migration experience in Drupal.

In this chapter, we will look at the Migrate module in Drupal 10, and you will learn how to achieve the following:

- Migrating from a previous version of Drupal
- Migrating data from a **comma-separated value** (CSV) file
- Migrating data from a remote HTTP API
- Writing a custom migration source plugin
- Writing a custom process plugin for migrations

Technical requirements

You can find the full code used in this chapter on GitHub: `https://github.com/PacktPublishing/Drupal-10-Development-Cookbook/tree/main/chp14`

Migrating from a previous version of Drupal

Drupal ships with a couple of core modules that assist you in updating your site from Drupal 6 or 7 to Drupal 10. The architecture between previous versions of Drupal before version 8 was radically different in design, and you cannot upgrade from 6 or 7 the same way you can from 8 or 9.

To mitigate the challenges of upgrading from Drupal 6 or 7, the Migrate Drupal module helps prepare a new environment for your older Drupal database to migrate to and is included in the core release of Drupal 10.

> **Custom modules, custom themes, and custom Drush commands**
>
> An important thing to note about upgrading from versions of Drupal prior to version 8 is that you will need to *manually* port custom modules, custom theme(s), and custom Drush commands you may have created. There are no tools to automate this, and they *will not work* until you have ported them to be compatible with Drupal 10. This must be done prior to upgrading, or you may encounter several errors while attempting to migrate or review your progress.

Getting ready

Before you perform any migration from an older version of Drupal, it is important to have prepared the following:

- A working environment running Drupal 10
- A copy of the Drupal 6/7 database to use in the upgrade
- An inventory of modules and theme(s) used on the site you are migrating from
- A database server that has both the Drupal 10 database and the old Drupal 6/7 database
- The database credentials needed to connect to the Drupal 6/7 database in your server
- A copy of all public and private files from the old site in a place accessible by the new site
- Enabling the Migrate Drupal and Migrate Drupal UI module in your Drupal 10 site
- A *database backup* of your current Drupal 10 installation

We will walk through these steps in the next section.

It is likely that you will need to iterate on the migration before it is complete, especially with old, complex sites. So, before you proceed, make sure you take a *database backup* of your Drupal 10 site. That way, if something goes wrong during the migration, you can restore the database, make changes, and try again. This is much faster than having to completely reinstall Drupal 10 to start the migration over. Always keep a clean database backup available. Let's begin!

How to do it...

With your new Drupal 10 site installed and ready, the first step you need to take is to review the modules you were using in your Drupal 6/7 site. You should log in to the site you are migrating from and go to the module list section of the admin. You can also get this list using the Drush command-line tool if you prefer.

Write down the list of contributed modules and themes that are in use in the old Drupal site. You are going to have to evaluate the following questions per module:

- Do I still need this module on Drupal 10?

- Has the contributed module moved to the core?

- Does the contributed module have a Drupal 10 version available? If not, do I still need it? Is there an alternative module with similar functionality?

- Does this module provide an upgrade path and migration integration to move data from a previous version of Drupal?

Keeping an inventory like this is required when upgrading from versions of Drupal prior to version 8.

As you go down the list and answer each question, you can update your Drupal 10 site by selecting the module you need with Composer. The idea is that you get the Drupal 10 environment ready first by making the modules and themes available that were being used in the previous Drupal site.

Some modules, such as views, have been moved into Drupal core and do not have a contributed version available. Others, such as Pathauto, have newer versions available for Drupal and also include migration plugins. These migration plugins are used automatically by the Migrate Drupal module when migrating your old site.

Not all modules have compatible versions for Drupal 10, unfortunately. This can happen when they are replaced by a competing module (Field Collections versus Paragraphs, for example) or the maintainer(s) decided not to port the module beyond Drupal 7. If you find that there is a module in your Drupal 6/7 site you absolutely need for your Drupal 10 site, you have limited options in this case. You can do the following:

- Check the module issue queue to see whether a newer version has been worked on

- Check the module yourself and with your development team to assess how hard porting it would be

- See whether an alternative module exists for Drupal 10 that is similar and make the configuration changes you need (it may be possible to provide a migration path as well)

- Use a tool such as Drupal Module Upgrader (`https://www.drupal.org/project/drupalmoduleupgrader`) to help you figure out how to port the module

- Consult the official Drupal Slack channel, Drupal Stack Exchange website, and/or a development agency to help you port the functionality to Drupal 10 if you or your team are unable to

---

Choosing to port the module?

If you do wind up porting the module to Drupal 10, be sure to contribute the work back to the community on `Drupal.org`. Not only is it a good learning experience on how to develop a module and learn the new APIs of Drupal 10, but paying it forward also helps other people who may be stuck too. You can request to be a maintainer of the module and ensure bug fixes and feature enhancements are published.

Now that you have gone through the list of modules, begin adding the ones you need to your Drupal 10 site with Composer:

```
composer require drupal/(module_name):^VERSION
```

Once you have all the required modules and theme(s), be sure to enable them. Don't worry about configuring all of the added modules; the migration will take care of that for you. If they are not enabled, the migration process won't see or use any migration plugins they may have, and you may not get all of your data migrated across.

If these modules contain migration plugins for Drupal 6/7, these will be incorporated when running a migration into your Drupal 10 site automatically.

Running the Drupal migration

Now that our environment is ready and we have all the modules we need, let's proceed with the migration.

Navigate to /upgrade. You will be greeted with this screen:

Upgrade ☆

Upgrade a site by importing its files and the data from its database into a clean and empty new install of Drupal 10. See the Drupal site upgrades handbook for more information.

Definitions

Old site
   The site you want to upgrade.

New site
   This empty Drupal 10 installation you will import the old site to.

Preparation steps

1. Make sure that **access to the database** for the old site is available from this new site.
2. **If the old site has private files**, a copy of its files directory must also be accessible on the host of this new site.
3. **Enable all modules on this new site** that are enabled on the old site. For example, if the old site uses the Book module, then enable the Book module on this new site so that the existing data can be imported to it.
4. **Do not add any content to the new site** before upgrading. Any existing content is likely to be overwritten by the upgrade process. See the upgrade preparation guide.
5. Put this site into maintenance mode.

The upgrade can take a long time. It is better to upgrade from a local copy of your site instead of directly from your live site.

Figure 14.1 – The Upgrade screen provides a wizard for upgrading from older versions

The Migrate Drupal UI module provides this interface to help you perform the migration from within the administrative section. Review the preparation steps one last time, and then click **Continue**.

On the next screen, we need to set which version of Drupal we are migrating from, as well as the database credentials required to connect to the old database. If you are unsure of what to enter for the database host or credentials, check the platform documentation of what to use (Lando, DDEV, Docksal, etc.) to connect to a second database.

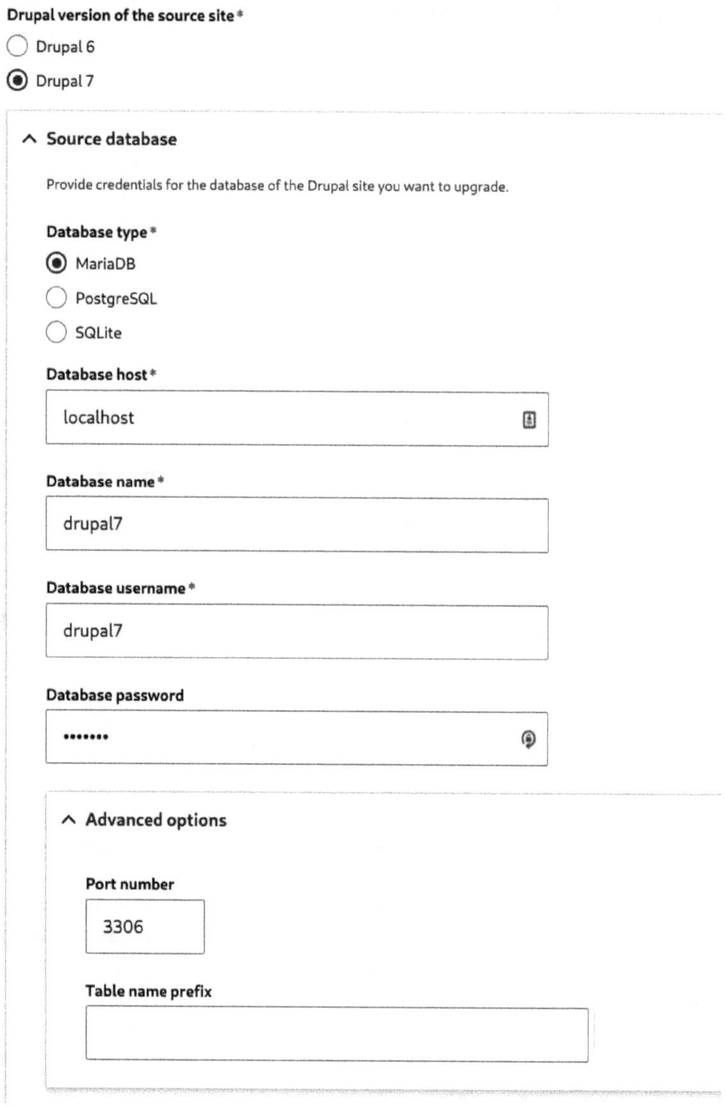

Drupal version of the source site *

○ Drupal 6

◉ Drupal 7

⌃ **Source database**

Provide credentials for the database of the Drupal site you want to upgrade.

Database type *

◉ MariaDB

○ PostgreSQL

○ SQLite

Database host *

| localhost | ▣ |

Database name *

| drupal7 |

Database username *

| drupal7 |

Database password

| •••••••• | ◉ |

⌃ **Advanced options**

Port number

| 3306 |

Table name prefix

| |

Figure 14.2 – The migrate wizard will prompt for the database credentials of the previous version of Drupal

> **Where is the option for Drupal 8 or 9?**
>
> If you are updating from Drupal 8 or 9, you do not need to leverage Migrate Drupal or this interface. Instead, you should proceed with the regular update process for Drupal to go from Drupal 8 or 9 to Drupal 10. If you are migrating partial data from a Drupal 8 or 9 site and starting over in Drupal 10, you will need to write your own migration script(s). See the later sections in this chapter for examples.

Setting the public/private files source

On the bottom of the previous screen, you can set the source for any public and private files that were uploaded to the old site.

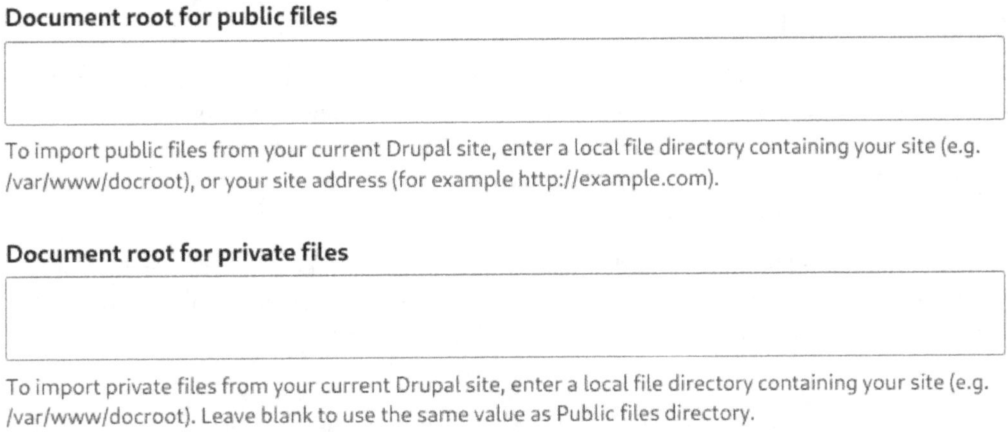

Document root for public files

To import public files from your current Drupal site, enter a local file directory containing your site (e.g. /var/www/docroot), or your site address (for example http://example.com).

Document root for private files

To import private files from your current Drupal site, enter a local file directory containing your site (e.g. /var/www/docroot). Leave blank to use the same value as Public files directory.

Figure 14.3 – You can specify where the uploaded files are located
on the old site so that the migration can locate them

You have the option of either setting a local path to the files or adding a URL to a public website.

The migration will source the files from their old paths, so if your files were previously uploaded to sites/default/files, you need to supply them in the same location. For the value of the public files, you then enter /var/www/web, the location of the web root for your site.

> **Document root**
>
> Note that, in some cases, the webroot can be named docroot instead of web. This can vary depending on your setup of Lando, DDEV, Docksal, and so on, and/or vary if you use a managed hosting provider such as Acquia, Pantheon, or **Platform.sh**. If unsure, check the documentation that applies in your case.

You can do the same for private files.

If you choose to use a web address instead, this will also work. However, running a migration that pulls files across the internet may result in a migration taking a lot longer than you expect. Also, you risk knocking your live website offline with several file requests. While you can opt for this route, it is generally not advised for larger migrations.

When you have added all the applicable settings, click **Review Upgrade**. This screen will display a list of items that will be upgraded and is the final step before executing the migration.

Running the migration

At this point, the system is now performing the migration from the old version of Drupal to Drupal 10. The batch process will run until it completes (or encounters an error). Depending on the size and build of your old site, this can take a while. You may leave the computer and take a break; just be sure to leave the browser window open.

If the migration has an error, the process won't complete. While unfortunate, this can happen, depending on how complex your previous site was. At this point, you should review the site logs to see what the errors were. These can be addressed and the migration can be performed again. You may need to adjust some migration settings, you may need a patch for a module (to support the migration), or it may be some other kind of error altogether.

Remember the database backup we made of the Drupal 10 site in preparation? After addressing what you found in the site logs, go ahead and restore the database. You should be able to go back to the first upgrade screen and start the migration over, which is faster than setting up Drupal 10 again from scratch.

If everything went fine, the migration will finish and you will have migrated your old Drupal site to Drupal 10!

Migration complete!

When it has completed, take a look around your admin. You should see familiar items, such as content types, taxonomy, media types, user roles, uploaded files, redirects, and other items from your previous site, as well as all of your content and user accounts restored.

Do note that certain items such as view configurations cannot be automatically migrated. This is due to the complex nature of views themselves. Fortunately, views are very easy to build out in the admin, and you can always tackle that once you verify the migration was successful.

How it works...

Drupal core contains dozens of plugins and migration paths to migrate from older Drupal 6 or 7 installations. These help explain to newer versions of Drupal how to access, transform, and save data into the new system during migration.

For example, the core Filter module has existed in several versions of Drupal. However, its schema, configuration, and data structure have changed over the years. It does not map 1:1 with Drupal 10. If you look in the module directory at `core/modules/filter`, you will notice a directory called `migrations`. There are a handful of files in here that help Drupal understand how to map old filters from Drupal 6 and 7 into your new Drupal 10 installation. You can see an example of this in `d7_filter_format.yml`:

```yaml
id: d7_filter_format
label: Filter format configuration
migration_tags:
  - Drupal 7
  - Configuration
source:
  plugin: d7_filter_format
process:
  format: format
  status: status
  name: name
  cache: cache
  weight: weight
  filters:
    plugin: sub_process
    source: filters
    key: '@id'
    process:
      id:
        plugin: filter_id
        bypass: true
        source: name
        map:
          editor_caption: filter_caption
          editor_align: filter_align
      settings:
        plugin: filter_settings
        source: settings
      status:
        plugin: default_value
```

```
            default_value: true
        weight: weight
  destination:
    plugin: entity:filter_format
```

Without getting too deep into the details just yet, this definition helps the migration process understand how to transform and move the filter and filter settings coming into Drupal 10. Files like these are loaded and used automatically when using the Migrate Drupal module, and you can see several examples of them spread around Drupal core.

Contributed modules can provide these as well. This is how we are able to migrate from older versions of Drupal without losing data. Most popular contributed modules will migrate fine with no problems, but some modules do not include files. You can check the issue queue(s) for help, but it is also possible to write your own in a custom module too.

We will look at custom migration source and migration process plugins in later sections.

Migrating data from CSV file(s)

From time to time, you will encounter the need to migrate data into Drupal, which comes in various formats. One such popular format is **CSV**, or a **comma-separated value**. CSV files can be exported from various database clients and spreadsheet software and make an excellent data source candidate for migrations.

Getting ready

From here, we are going to need to add two modules to migrate from CSV files. Using Composer, download the following modules:

- Migrate Plus (https://www.drupal.org/project/migrate_plus)
- Migrate Tools (https://www.drupal.org/project/migrate_tools)
- Migrate Source CSV (https://www.drupal.org/project/migrate_source_csv)

You will also need to create a custom module where we will place our migration definitions, source plugins, and process plugin classes. At this point, you should be familiar with creating a custom module. Consult the previous chapters if you need to refresh.

How to do it...

When you have to perform migrations in Drupal that cannot use Migrate Drupal, you have to write your own migration YAML configuration files in a custom module. This is because the Migrate Drupal module is specifically for migrating in from older versions of Drupal, treating that old version of Drupal as the *source*.

In this case, the CSV file(s) will be the *source* of the migration. Every migration consists of three main parts:

- The **source**: This is the provider of data consumed by the migration.

- The **destination**: This is where each record will be migrated into and stored – typically, an entity (node, user, media, taxonomy, etc.).

- The **process**: This pipeline defines how source data is transformed and saved for a migration item. Here, you can define various fields and properties on the *destination* and use a number of *process* plugins to make the *source* data fit into the field(s) the way you want (or the way Drupal may require it to be).

Before we proceed, let's look at a quick example of a migration definition for migrating from a CSV file:

```
id: redirects
migration_tags: {}
migration_dependencies: {}
migration_group: default
label: Old website redirects.
source:
  plugin: csv
  path: data/redirects.csv
  ids: [id]
  constants:
    uid: 1
    status: 301
destination:
  plugin: 'entity:redirect'
process:
  redirect_source: old_path
  redirect_redirect: new_path
  uid: constants/uid
  status_code: constants/status
```

Let's assume we need to use a CSV file to migrate in URLs from an old website and store them in Drupal as redirects, using the Redirect contributed module (https://www.drupal.org/project/redirect). By doing so, we can ensure URLs that existed on the old site can successfully redirect to their new URLs in Drupal so that we don't lose visitors.

In order to do this, we've defined a migration definition file named `migrate_plus.migration.redirects.yml` in the `config/install` directory of our custom module. This is for migrations that need the Migrate Plus contributed module to execute (as Migrate Source CSV does).

Here, you can clearly see the `source`, `destination`, and `process` sections.

The `source` section tells the migration that we are going to use the CSV plugin (provided by the Migrate Source CSV module), a path to the CSV file itself, the ID keys (what Migrate will use to track unique row values), and some constant values to use in the process pipeline.

The `destination` section tells the migration we want to save data using the `entity:redirect` plugin. This plugin ensures migrated values are saved as Redirect entities.

The `process` section maps fields and properties on the entity to data values in the migration source. In this case, `redirect_source`, `redirect_redirect`, `uid`, and `status_code` are being mapped to `old_url` and `new_url` in our CSV file, and constant values are used for `uid` and `status_code` (defined in the preceding source section).

The CSV file under `/data/redirects.csv` of the module contains all of the data for the migration. The file contains the following:

ID	old_path	new_path
1	`/foo`	`/node/1`
2	`/foo/bar`	`/node/2`
3	`/foo/bar/baz`	`/node/3`

Table 14.1 – The CSV file under /data/redirects.csv

The CSV file contains a few hundred records like the preceding one.

> **What about the alias?**
>
> When migrating redirects the URLs into Drupal, the destination (in this case, `new_path`) needs to be the Drupal entity path (`/node/1`, for example). Drupal will save the redirect correctly. If you have Pathauto auto-alias patterns in place, they will be generated when the migration saves each row of data. With the redirect contributed module installed, a 301 redirect will be created and related to the node we are redirecting to automatically.

When we enable our custom module, the migration appears in the list of migrations in the admin section under **Structure | Migrations**. Any migration that you define will appear in this section. You can run migrations from this interface, or you can do it from the command line using Drush, courtesy of the **Migrate Tools** contributed module.

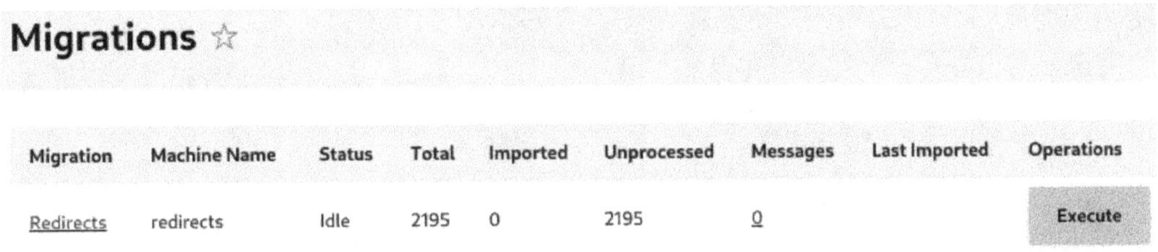

Migrations ☆

Migration	Machine Name	Status	Total	Imported	Unprocessed	Messages	Last Imported	Operations
Redirects	redirects	Idle	2195	0	2195	0		Execute

Figure 14.4 – The Migrations screen lists all registered migrations in Drupal and the tasks you can perform with them

Then, we can execute the migration:

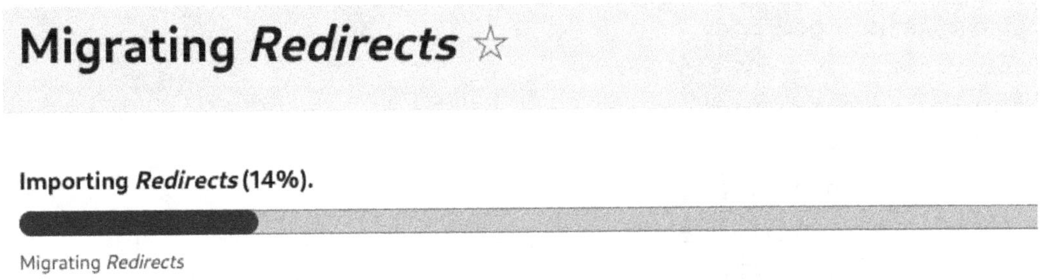

Migrating *Redirects* ☆

Importing *Redirects* (14%).

Migrating *Redirects*

Figure 14.5 – A migration running in the admin, displaying a progress meter

We can see that redirects are now showing up in Drupal that were migrated from the CSV file:

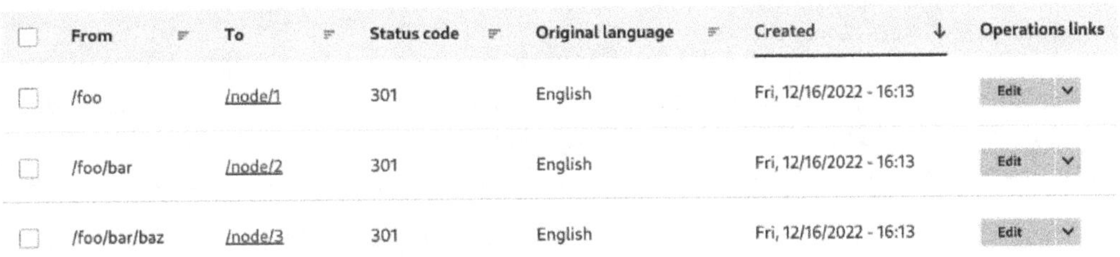

	From		To		Status code		Original language		Created	↓	Operations links
☐	/foo		/node/1		301		English		Fri, 12/16/2022 - 16:13		Edit ⌄
☐	/foo/bar		/node/2		301		English		Fri, 12/16/2022 - 16:13		Edit ⌄
☐	/foo/bar/baz		/node/3		301		English		Fri, 12/16/2022 - 16:13		Edit ⌄

Figure 14.6 – The migration created all the URL redirects we expect from our CSV file

Migrating into nodes from CSV

Suppose for a second that we have another CSV file that contains data we want to migrate into a node type in Drupal. What might the migration definition look like? Not all that different actually!

```
id: chapter14csvnodes
label: Old website articles.
```

```
source:
  plugin: csv
  path: /data/articles.csv
  ids: [id]
  constants:
    uid: 1
destination:
  plugin: 'entity:node'
  default_bundle: article
process:
  title: old_title
  body/value: old_body
  body/format:
    plugin: default_value
    default_value: full_html
  uid: constants/uid
  field_one: old_field_one
  field_two: old_field_two
  created:
    plugin: format_date
    from_format: 'Y-m-d\TH:i:sP'
    to_format: 'U'
    source: created_date
```

Using the CSV source plugin again, we made a few modifications, and now we have another migration defined that is ready to use. In the destination section, we swapped entity:redirect for entity:node, and also provided the node type (bundle) that we want to save the migrated data to.

Under the process section, we've added specific node properties and fields from the Article node type that we want to map migrated data to. There are also examples here of process plugins that have configurations attached about how we want to handle the data.

You will see a mapping like this in a migration file:

```
field_one: old_field_one
```

This is a shorthand for the `get` plugin provided by the Migrate module. The `get` plugin uses the provided value as-is from the source to store in Drupal. The longer way to write out using the `get` plugin would be as follows:

```
field_one:
  plugin: get
  source: old_field_one
```

The created property shows off another process plugin, `format_date`. The `format_date` process plugin allows you to take a date and format it before saving it to Drupal. In the preceding example, it is converting a date-time value to a timestamp, which is how Drupal stores create and change dates on nodes.

How it works...

The *Migrate Source CSV* module provides a CSV source plugin that takes care of parsing and reading provided CSV files for you, parsing out headers and records. This makes it possible to create a migration definition and quickly map records to destinations in Drupal.

There are dozens of migrate process plugins just like these that you can use in your migrations to make the process easier. For a full list of plugins that you can use, consult the online documentation:

- Migrate process plugins (`https://www.drupal.org/docs/8/api/migrate-api/migrate-process-plugins/list-of-core-migrate-process-plugins`)

- Migrate Plus process plugins (`https://www.drupal.org/docs/8/api/migrate-api/migrate-process-plugins/list-of-core-migrate-process-plugins`)

There are other contributed modules that add more process plugins, but between them, the core Migrate and contributed Migrate Plus modules cover nearly all that you will need to do migrations. When there is no process plugin that meets the needs of converting data during a migration, you can make your own. See the section on creating process plugins later in the chapter.

Migrating data from an HTTP API

CSV files and SQL databases are not the only data source you can use for migrations. The **Migrate Plus** contributed module comes with a URL source plugin. By using the URL plugin as a migration source, the migration can fetch and parse data over HTTP in the following formats:

- JSON
- XML
- SOAP

This means that you can migrate data from any API over the internet, making Migrate Plus an indispensable tool when you need to migrate data over the wire.

Let's take a look at how this could be used to migrate data from an HTTP API.

How to do it...

At this point, we have given two examples of migration definitions in this chapter. Even though we are migrating from a different kind of source, the format of the migration definition itself is not going to change all that much. We still have our source, destination, and process section.

Imagine that we want to grab data from a public API that returns a JSON response and save it as nodes in Drupal. The JSON response in this example looks like this:

```json
{
    "data":[
        {
            "id": 1,
            "title": "Item One",
            "body": "Lorem ipsum dolor sit amet",
            "archived": false
        },
        {
            "id": 2,
            "title": "Item Two",
            "body": "Lorem ipsum dolor sit amet",
            "archived": true
        },
        {
            "id": 3,
            "title": "Item Three",
            "body": "Lorem ipsum dolor sit amet",
            "archived": false
        }
    ]
}
```

We need to consume that response and insert nodes for every item under `data`. Our migration definition would look like the following:

```
id: chapter14httpjson
label: Migrates external API data.
migration_tags: {}
migration_dependencies: {}
source:
  plugin: url
  urls:
    - 'http://example.com/api/v1/content'
  data_fetcher_plugin: http
  data_parser_plugin: json
  item_selector: data
  fields:
    -
      name: id
      label: 'ID'
      selector: id
    -
      name:  title
      label: 'Title'
      selector: title
    -
      name: body
      label: 'Body content'
      selector: body
    -
      name: archived
      label: 'Archived status'
      selector: archived
  ids:
    id:
      type: integer
destination:
  plugin: entity:node
  default_bundle: article
```

```
process:
  title: title
  body/value: body
  body/format:
    plugin: default_value
    default_value: basic_html
  status: archived
  uid:
    plugin: default_value
    default_value: 1
```

The destination and process sections look the same as the other migrations at the beginning of the chapter. By now, you should see a pattern – migration definitions always look similar regardless of the source or destination. Each source plugin has different configuration values. Let's break down what the `Url` plugin is doing.

How it works...

The `Url` plugin has a few configuration properties that can be set. The most important ones are `urls`, `data_fetcher_plugin`, and `data_parser_plugin`. These must always be set when using the `Url` plugin.

The `urls` property accepts one or more URLs for the migration. Each URL will have its contents migrated in one by one. This is useful if you have a scenario where you have multiple locations and need to migrate the data into the same place (assuming the response format is the same).

The `data_fetcher_plugin` and `data_parser_plugin` properties are unique to the Migrate Plus module. Migrate Plus introduces the `DataFetcher` and `DataParser` plugin types as well as plugin managers for them. It also includes the `File` and `Http` data fetcher plugins, and the `Json`, `Xml`, and `Soap` data parser plugins.

When the migration is executed, the configuration is read. This loads the `Url` plugin, which contains the following:

```
/**
 * Returns the initialized data parser plugin.
 *
 * @return \Drupal\migrate_plus\DataParserPluginInterface
 *   The data parser plugin.
 */
public function getDataParserPlugin() {
```

```
  if (!isset($this->dataParserPlugin)) {
    $this->dataParserPlugin = \Drupal::service
      ('plugin.manager.migrate_plus.data_parser')->
        createInstance($this->configuration[
          'data_parser_plugin'], $this->configuration);
  }
  return $this->dataParserPlugin;
}


/**
 * Creates and returns a filtered Iterator over the
     documents.
 *
 * @return \Iterator
 *   An iterator over the documents providing source rows
         that match the
 *   configured item_selector.
 */
protected function initializeIterator() {
  return $this->getDataParserPlugin();
}
```

The `initializeIterator` method is required to be provided by any migration source plugin. This tells the migration how to parse the data, which hands it off to the `Json` plugin. The `Json` plugin then gets the `data_fetcher_plugin` value from the migration definition, which we have set as `http`. The `Xml` and `Soap` data parsers have a similar implementation. When you combine those, this is how the migration knows to make a call over the internet to get data and how to parse that data to prepare it for migration.

Once the data has been retrieved and parsed, it needs to know how to *access* items within the response. Sometimes, you get API responses where the results you want are deeply nested.

The `item_selector` property in our source definition informs the parser how to read and extract items from the response. Since the example JSON structure is simple, all we have to do is give it `data` for the item selector. If the items we wanted were nested in some way, we would enter the path to the results as `foo/bar/data`, for example.

The fields portion under `source` describes to the migration the fields that we want to map, and how we want to refer to those fields in the process section. This was not necessary for the CSV migrations because the header records automatically become reference fields to use in the process pipeline mapping. In this case, we need to map them:

```
Name:  title
label: 'Title'
selector: title
```

The `name` property is how we want to refer to this in the migration in the process section. The `label` property is what it is called (visible in the migration source area within Drupal), and the `selector` property is the actual name of it in our JSON result. You can make `name` and `label` whatever you want, but `selector` has to match what's in the response fields returned from the API.

Again, we can navigate to **Structure | Migrations** in the Drupal admin to see this new migration and execute it.

There's more...

Here's one final note on using the `Url` plugin. Earlier, we mentioned that Migrate Plus comes with two data fetcher plugins. We covered `Http`; the other is `File`. If you want to migrate data in from JSON or XML files on disk, you can. If you change your `data_fetcher_plugin` from `http` to `file`, the `Url` plugin will locate it and use it as a migration source.

Writing a custom migration source plugin

At this point, you have seen a few powerful ways that Drupal can migrate in data using available source plugins. What happens when one does not exist to meet your needs? You can write a migration source plugin, of course!

Consider this scenario. You need to migrate data in from a MySQL database as nodes into Drupal. While the migration system in Drupal can understand how to connect to databases, it does not understand how to query for the data you are trying to obtain. In these instances, you can write a source plugin.

How to do it...

Let's assume that the database has a table named `articles` that we want to pull data from in the migration, and it has `id`, `title`, `body`, `is_published`, and `published_on` as fields. Before we can write our source plugin, the first thing we need to do is establish a connection that will access this database.

In your `settings.php` file, add the following MySQL database connection:

```
$databases['migrate']['default'] = array (
  'database' => 'DATABASE_NAME',
  'username' => 'DATABASE_USERNAME',
  'password' => 'DATABASE_PASSWORD',
  'prefix' => '',
  'host' => 'DATABASE_HOSTNAME',
  'port' => '',
  'namespace' => 'Drupal\\Core\\Database\\Driver\\mysql',
  'driver' => 'mysql',
);
```

Note the `migrate` key name in the `$databases` array. This entry will be used in our source plugin to make the connection. This key can be any name you want, other than `default`, which is used by Drupal for its default database connection. If you choose to use a key name other than `migrate`, be sure to remember it, as it will be referenced in your migration definition.

Back in your custom module, create a new directory at `src/Plugin/migrate/source`. Next, create a file in this directory named `ArticlesSource.php`. This will be the source plugin that powers the data retrieval for the migration.

There are three methods that we need to fulfill for our source plugin – a `query` method, a `fields` method, and an `id` method. For every SQL source plugin you create, these three methods are required:

- The `query` method will contain our actual SQL query to retrieve the data
- The `fields` method will return an array of available fields on the source, keyed by their machine names and a description
- The `id` method defines the source field(s) for uniquely identifying a source row

In our new `ArticlesSource.php` file, we can start defining our source plugin:

```php
<?php

namespace Drupal\chapter14\Plugin\migrate\source;

use Drupal\migrate\Plugin\migrate\source\SqlBase;

/**
 * Get the article records from the legacy database.
```

```
 *
 * @MigrateSource(
 *   id = "legacy_articles",
 *   source_module = "chapter14",
 * )
 */
class ArticlesSource extends SqlBase {
```

Our plugin class extends `SqlBase`, a core migrate plugin that deals with database source connections. It will do most of the heavy lifting after we provide the three aforementioned methods.

Our plugin class also has the `@MigrateSource` annotation. This is **required**. Without this annotation, Drupal will not discover this class as a usable source plugin, and the migration will fail to do anything.

The `id` property of the annotation defines the plugin ID. The `source_module` property identifies the system providing the data the source plugin will read from. For contributed sources, this is almost always the module they are defined in.

Next, we provide the `query` method. If you have ever used the database API in Drupal before, this will be familiar. It uses the same APIs. It looks like any other Drupal SQL query; the only difference is it will be executed in the other database – the one we defined in our `settings.php` file earlier.

Filling that in is straightforward:

```
/**
 * {@inheritdoc}
 */
public function query() {
  $query = $this->select('articles', 'art');
  $query->fields('art', [
      'id',
      'title',
      'body',
      'is_published',
      'published_on',
    ]);

  $query->orderBy('art.id');
  $query->orderBy('art.published_on');
  return $query;
}
```

How it works...

The database API in Drupal is fairly easy to use. The query method here selects all articles and their fields, ordering them by their ID and published dates. The results of this query are what will power our migration later in this section.

For the fields method, we need to list out the fields we are using within the migration:

```
/**
 * {@inheritdoc}
 */
public function fields() {
  return [
    'id' => $this->->t('The article id.'),
    'title' => $this->->t('The article title.'),
    'body' => $this->->t('The article body content.'),
    'is_published' => $this->->t('The published state.'),
    'published_on' => $this->->t('The published date.'),
  ];
}
```

Finally, for the id method, we need to specify which field is the unique identifier for the migration:

```
/**
 * {@inheritdoc}
 */
public function getIds() {
  return [
    'id' => [
      'type' => 'integer',
      'alias' => 'art',
    ],
  ];
}
```

In this case, it is simply id, the unique field from the legacy database articles table.

Using a custom source plugin in the migration

With our source plugin in place, we can now focus on the migration itself.

Like in our other examples, we need to define a migration definition YAML file:

```yaml
id: articles
label: Migrates articles from the legacy database.
Migration_tags: {}
migration_dependencies: {}
source:
  plugin: legacy_articles
  key: migrate
destination:
  plugin: entity:node
  default_bundle: article
process:
  title: title
  body/value: body
  body/format:
    plugin: default_value
    default_value: basic_html
  status: is_published
  created: published_on
  uid:
    plugin: default_value
    default_value: 1
```

One of the best parts about migrations in Drupal is that the API is well defined, so regardless of how you may be obtaining data or processing data, the definitions always follow the same patterns.

In this migration, we have specified our new source plugin, `legacy_articles`, which is the plugin ID we provided in our `ArticlesSource` class. The `key` property in the source section is the same name as the database key we added in `settings.php`. Since we extended `SqlBase`, the key property is used when establishing a database connection to execute the query against. If you're curious, you can review the `getDatabase` method of `SqlBase` to see how it uses the `key` property.

Since we defined our fields in the `fields` method of our source plugin, we can skip the fields section in the migration definition entirely and use them as provided. In this case, the migration will already know what the fields are. The same is true of the `ids` property; the source plugin already defines it, so we do not need to list it here like the other migrations in this chapter.

From here, the rest of the migration looks the same as what you have seen in other examples in this chapter. The `destination` section informs the migration to create `article` nodes, and the `process` section defines how to map our source fields to node fields.

Once again, you can view this migration at **Structure | Migrations** in the admin and run it. Feel free to create a database alongside your Drupal database to experiment with the source plugin – once you know how to do it, you will be able to pull anything into Drupal and be a true migration wizard.

Writing a custom process plugin for migrations

At this point, we've covered migrating data from CSV, JSON, and database sources, but what about cases where the data from these sources don't quite align with the way they need to be stored in Drupal?

Migrations can be a tricky thing. While Drupal provides several avenues to source data to migrate in, there will be many cases where you need to manipulate that incoming data to get it to a satisfactory state, either for storage or cleanup purposes. Fortunately, creating process plugins is easy, and you will be manipulating data in a migration in no time.

How to do it...

Let's take a look at an example of writing a process plugin. Using the previous example, a custom source plugin that fetches data from a database table, assume we now have to pull an additional field for the migration, `no_index`. While querying the data is easy, the data itself is not suitable for storage in the metatag field (https://www.drupal.org/project/metatag), as its value is either a 0 or 1. When the value is 1 (`true`), the author has indicated they do not want this page crawled by search engines. In the previous system, the presence of this value would add additional metatags to the head of the page.

The contributed Metatag module is able to replicate this functionality. However, the metatag field stores this data in a serialized fashion in the database. We cannot use the value as-is from the source, but we can add a process plugin to *convert* the data to the way we need it.

Assuming you added a Metatag field to the Article content type in Drupal, you can migrate the data by doing the following.

First, let's update our source plugin to account for a new field:

```
$query->fields('art', [
    'id',
    'title',
    'body',
    'is_published',
    'published_on',
```

```
        'no_index',
    ]);
```

Then, we add it to our `fields` list:

```
public function fields() {
  return [
    'id' => $this->t('The article id.'),
    'title' => $this->t('The article title.'),
    'body' => $this->t('The article body content.'),
    'is_published' => $this->t('The published state.'),
    'published_on' => $this->t('The published date.'),
    'no_index' => $this->t('Indicates this article should
        not be crawled.'),
  ];
}
```

Now that it has been added to the source plugin, the migration is receiving the value for each record.

Back in our migration definition, let's map the metatags field and get set up to write the custom process plugin:

```
field_metatags:
  - plugin: set_no_index
    _source: no_index
```

Here, we are piping the value of the no_index field to a plugin whose ID is set_no_index. Now, we can start to manipulate the data during the migration so that it can be stored properly.

In the custom module, we create a directory at `src/Plugin/migrate/process`. Within this directory, we are going to create a file called `SetNoIndex.php`. This is our new custom process plugin.

Custom process plugins at a minimum need to implement the `transform` method. This method is responsible for handling and returning data for this step in the pipeline.

The process plugin code would look like the following:

```
<?php

namespace Drupal\chapter14\Plugin\migrate\process;

use Drupal\migrate\ProcessPluginBase;
```

```
use Drupal\migrate\MigrateExecutableInterface;
use Drupal\migrate\Row;

/**
 * @MigrateProcessPlugin(
 *    id = "set_no_index",
 * )
 */
class SetNoIndex extends ProcessPluginBase {

  /**
   * {@inheritdoc}
   */
  public function transform($value, MigrateExecutableInter
      face $migrate_executable, Row $row, $destination
          _property) {
    return (bool) $value ? ['robots' => 'noindex, nofollow,
        noarchive, nosnippet'] : [];
  }

}
```

Like the custom source plugin, note the annotation at the top of the class. This is required so that the plugin can be discovered by Drupal. The `id` value is the same one we used in the migration definition.

How it works...

When the migration runs, if the value passed in is 1, we get an array of values back. This is exactly what we need! However, we need to do one more thing before this will be successfully saved into Drupal.

Remember how we mentioned earlier that data is stored as a serialized array? Passing a plain PHP array along from our custom process plugin is not enough. In a migration, you can use several process plugins in a field mapping. They are run in the order they are listed, and this offers a composable way to transform the source data.

Fortunately, the core Migrate module provides a process plugin that will help us out, the `callback` process plugin. The `callback` process plugin calls a PHP function using the value from the previous process plugin (our result from `set_no_index`) and returns the value from the callback provided.

Combining the two in the pipeline would look like this:

```
field_metatags:
  - plugin: set_no_index
    _source: no_index
  - plugin: callback
    _callable: serialize
```

After updating the migration definition, we need to bring those changes into Drupal. This can be done using Drush:

```
php vendor/bin/drush config-import --partial --source=/var/www/
html/web/modules/custom/chapter14/config/install -y
```

This command will re-import the configuration files in the `config/install` directory of the `chapter14` module. This command is a good way to continually bring in changes to a definition as you work on a migration definition bit by bit.

> **Migration definitions are configuration**
>
> Migration YAML files are configured just like any other Drupal configuration file. When you make updates to a migration YAML file and import the changes with the command above, be sure to `config-export` when ready to deploy or commit the work to a repository.

When we run the migration, we have the new data in our metatags field. In this example, you could validate that it worked in two ways:

- First, you can look at the migrated content on your site in the admin, edit one of the migrated nodes, and see that the metatags field has the correct data on the node form:

Used to define this page's language code. May be the two letter language code, e.g. "de" for German, or the ISO country code, e.g. "de-AT" for German in Austria. Still used by Bing.

Robots

☐ index - Allow search engines to index this page (assumed).

☐ follow - Allow search engines to follow links on this page (assumed).

☑ noindex - Prevents search engines from indexing this page.

☑ nofollow - Prevents search engines from following links on this page.

☑ noarchive - Prevents cached copies of this page from appearing in search results.

☑ nosnippet - Prevents descriptions from appearing in search results, and prevents page caching.

☐ noodp - Blocks the Open Directory Project description from appearing in search results.

☐ noydir - Prevents Yahoo! from listing this page in the Yahoo! Directory.

☐ noimageindex - Prevent search engines from indexing images on this page.

☐ notranslate - Prevent search engines from offering to translate this page in search results.

Provides search engines with specific directions for what to do when this page is indexed.

Shortlink URL

Figure 14.7 – The metatags fields on the node form

- Secondly, you can check the metatags field in the database and see the raw data is there:

ABC field_metatags_value
a:1:{s:6:"robots";s:39:"noindex, nofollow, noarchive, nosnippet";}
a:1:{s:6:"robots";s:39:"noindex, nofollow, noarchive, nosnippet";}
a:1:{s:6:"robots";s:39:"noindex, nofollow, noarchive, nosnippet";}

Figure 14.8 – The metatags table in the database reflects the values we want to migrate

If you remember from the previous chapter, we discussed the importance of *knowing* that code we wrote actually works using unit tests. Process plugins are pretty easy to write tests for. We may be viewing data in Drupal from the migration, but let's be 100% certain that our process plugin is doing the right thing.

Our unit test for the `set_no_index` plugin would look like this:

```php
<?php

namespace Drupal\Tests\chapter14\Unit\Plugin\migrate\
    process;

use Drupal\chapter14\Plugin\migrate\process\SetNoIndex;
```

```
use Drupal\Tests\migrate\Unit\process\
    MigrateProcessTestCase;

/**
 * Tests the set_no_index process plugin.
 */
class SetNoIndexTest extends MigrateProcessTestCase {

  /**
   * {@inheritdoc}
   */
  protected function setUp(): void {
    $this->plugin = new SetNoIndex([], 'set_no_index', []);
    parent::setUp();
  }

  /**
   * Data provider for testPluginValue().
   *
   * @return array
   *    An array containing input values and expected output
   *       values.
   */
  public function valueProvider() {
    return [
      [1, ['robots' => 'noindex, nofollow, noarchive,
        nosnippet']],
      [0, []],
      [NULL, []],
    ];
  }

  /**
   * Test set_no_index plugin.
   *
   * @param $input
```

```
 *     The input values.
 *
 * @param $expected
 *     The expected output.
 *
 * @dataProvider valueProvider
 */
public function testPluginValue($input, $expected) {
  $output = $this->plugin->transform($input, $this->
      migrateExecutable, $this->row,
          'destinationproperty');
  $this->assertSame($output, $expected);
  }
}
```

The `valueProvider` method feeds our test method values and the result we expect our `set_no_index` plugin to return when evaluated. Now we know for certain that our migration will always provide the right data and that no migrated articles will be incorrectly crawled by search engines. For more on unit testing in Drupal, be sure to refer to *Chapter 13, Running and Writing Tests with Drupal.*

See also

In this chapter, we have demonstrated the power and flexibility of the Migrate and Migrate Plus modules of Drupal. Wielding both of these will empower you to migrate data from just about any source and process it accordingly. We also demonstrated how you can write custom source and custom process plugins to achieve this goal as well.

Be sure to check the contributed module ecosystem of Migrate on `Drupal.org`. There are several modules that provide countless source and process plugins, covering various data sources, such as CSV, JSON, XML, XLS, HTML, and HTTP APIs.

Index

Packtpub.com

Subscribe to our online digital library for full access to over 7,000 books and videos, as well as industry leading tools to help you plan your personal development and advance your career. For more information, please visit our website.

Why subscribe?

- Spend less time learning and more time coding with practical eBooks and Videos from over 4,000 industry professionals

- Improve your learning with Skill Plans built especially for you

- Get a free eBook or video every month

- Fully searchable for easy access to vital information

- Copy and paste, print, and bookmark content

Did you know that Packt offers eBook versions of every book published, with PDF and ePub files available? You can upgrade to the eBook version at packtpub.com and as a print book customer, you are entitled to a discount on the eBook copy. Get in touch with us at customercare@packtpub.com for more details.

At www.packtpub.com, you can also read a collection of free technical articles, sign up for a range of free newsletters, and receive exclusive discounts and offers on Packt books and eBooks.

Other Books You May Enjoy

If you enjoyed this book, you may be interested in these other books by Packt:

Digital Marketing with Drupal

José Fernandes

ISBN: 978-1-80107-189-5

- Explore the most successful digital marketing techniques
- Create your digital marketing plan with the help of Drupal's digital marketing checklist
- Set up, manage, and administer all the marketing components of a Drupal website
- Discover how to increase the traffic to your Drupal website
- Develop and implement an e-commerce marketing strategy for your Drupal Commerce store
- Manage your daily marketing activities using Drupal
- Get started with customizing your consumers' digital experience
- Find out what's next for Drupal and digital marketing

Drupal 9 Module Development

Daniel Sipos

ISBN: 978-1-80020-462-1

- Develop custom Drupal 9 modules for your applications
- Master different Drupal 9 subsystems and APIs
- Model, store, manipulate, and process data for effective data management
- Display data and content in a clean and secure way using the theme system
- Test your business logic to prevent regression
- Stay ahead of the curve and write PHP code by implementing best practices

Packt is searching for authors like you

If you're interested in becoming an author for Packt, please visit authors.packtpub.com and apply today. We have worked with thousands of developers and tech professionals, just like you, to help them share their insight with the global tech community. You can make a general application, apply for a specific hot topic that we are recruiting an author for, or submit your own idea.

Share Your Thoughts

Now you've finished *Drupal 10 Development Cookbook*, we'd love to hear your thoughts! Scan the QR code below to go straight to the Amazon review page for this book and share your feedback or leave a review on the site that you purchased it from.

https://packt.link/r/1-803-23496-2

Your review is important to us and the tech community and will help us make sure we're delivering excellent quality content.

Download a free PDF copy of this book

Thanks for purchasing this book!

Do you like to read on the go but are unable to carry your print books everywhere? Is your eBook purchase not compatible with the device of your choice?

Don't worry, now with every Packt book you get a DRM-free PDF version of that book at no cost.

Read anywhere, any place, on any device. Search, copy, and paste code from your favorite technical books directly into your application.

The perks don't stop there, you can get exclusive access to discounts, newsletters, and great free content in your inbox daily

Follow these simple steps to get the benefits:

1. Scan the QR code or visit the link below

https://packt.link/free-ebook/9781803234960

2. Submit your proof of purchase
3. That's it! We'll send your free PDF and other benefits to your email directly

Printed in the USA
CPSIA information can be obtained
at www.ICGtesting.com
LVHW071454301123
765370LV00037BA/548

9 781803 234960